*Selected Plays of
James Purdy*

T0159496

JAMES PURDY

Selected Plays

BRICE
THE PARADISE CIRCUS
WHERE QUENTIN GOES
RUTHANNA ELDER

Ivan R. Dee
CHICAGO

SELECTED PLAYS OF JAMES PURDY. Copyright © 2009 by James Purdy. All rights reserved, including the right to reproduce this book or portions thereof in any form. For information, address: Ivan R. Dee, Publisher, 1332 North Halsted Street, Chicago 60642, a member of the Rowman & Littlefield Publishing Group. Manufactured in the United States of America and printed on acid-free paper.

The plays were developed, assembled, and edited by John Uecker in close association with James Purdy. Ian McGrady, J. W. McCormack, and Susan Aston provided additional editorial assistance.

CAUTION: Professionals and amateurs are hereby warned that this edition of SELECTED PLAYS OF JAMES PURDY is subject to a royalty. It is fully protected under the copyright laws of the United States of America and of all countries covered by the International Copyright Union (including the British Commonwealth and Canada), and of all countries covered by the Pan-American Copyright Convention, and of all countries with which the United States has reciprocal copyright relations. All rights, including professional, amateur, motion pictures, recitation, public reading, radio broadcasting, television, video or sound taping, all other forms of mechanical or electronic reproduction, and the rights of translation into foreign languages are strictly reserved.

All inquiries concerning performance rights should be addressed to Samuel French, Inc., 45 West 25th Street, New York, NY 10010, in advance of anticipated production.

Copying from this book in whole or in part is strictly forbidden by law, and right of performance is not transferable.

Library of Congress Cataloging-in-Publication Data:
Purdy, James.
  [Plays. Selections]
  Selected plays / James Purdy.
      p. cm.
  Title on t.p. verso: Selected plays of James Purdy
  ISBN 978-1-56663-798-5 (pbk. : alk. paper)
  I. Title. II. Title: Selected plays of James Purdy.
PS3531.U426A6 2009
812'.54—dc22   2009003596

For the two who stood behind me,
Tennessee Williams
John Uecker

Two Visionaries

JOHN UECKER

While it is well known that James Purdy's work has been met with "vehement condemnation as well as lavish praise"—even Purdy himself stated that it "is like an underground river flowing often undetected through the American landscape"—the fact that he began as a dramatist is unknown.

Writing plays for his brother from the age of ten, Purdy performed these dramatic works on his own stage and with representational figures, playing all the parts himself and writing all the dialogue. This production of dramatic works continued through his twenties when he began writing short stories. He had to learn to write exposition.

Dame Edith Sitwell, in her review of *Children Is All*, surprisingly compared Purdy to Federico García Lorca as "an abstractor of the quintessence." She had not known that Purdy had begun writing plays as a child in the same way Lorca had. Nor did she know that the "marrow of form" and the "highly muscled technique" she had attributed to his stories had come directly from these early dramatic works. Toward the end of her life, Dame Edith lamented the fact that the theater never took up Purdy's *Children Is All*, which she had hailed "as a sublime work of pity and tenderness."

Gordon Lish had also discovered this "marrow of form." His editing of the Raymond Carver stories was based on the form of the early stories of Purdy (which had in turn been derived from Purdy's early work in drama).

When a dialogue-driven short story for Lee Strasberg's master class was presented, Strasberg said, "Who wrote this? It is the best modern dialogue I ever heard!" It was "Don't Call Me by My Right Name" by James Purdy. Strasberg was not alone in this assessment of Purdy's dialogue and his theatrical viability—both Herbert Berghof and Sanford Meisner had already become fascinated by the possibilities of Purdy's tightly distilled dramatic dialogue.

I had done some adaptations of Purdy's short stories along with one of his short plays in a workshop that Tennessee Williams had come to see. Williams hired me as his assistant the next day. Tennessee immediately wrote the *Chalky White Substance*, which he dedicated to Purdy. After Williams's death, Lady Maria St. Just determined the apocalyptic work to have major vision and depth, despite being only nine pages long.

Tennessee Williams had long been an admirer of Purdy's "mighty fine dialogue." It was thought that Williams's novel, *Moise and the World of Reason*, was inspired by Purdy's *I Am Elijah Thrush*. While in Key West I had found three copies of this book in Williams's workroom. I told Tennessee that Kim Stanley thought *Children Is All* was a great work. I also told him that Sanford Meisner had thought it was great (but he also said, "No known director can direct it.") Williams only listened but didn't respond.

But when Tennessee heard that Dame Edith Sitwell had praised the work so highly, calling it "a masterpiece in every aspect" and a "sublime work," he asked to see *Children Is All* as soon as possible. Dame Edith, as Tennessee observed, was "the champion of the lost cause." She had given *Camino Real* a rave review and appeared to be the only critic who valued and understood the work.

By this time Tennessee had already been to see the adaptations of his short stories and Purdy's newer short plays Off Off Broadway. He had done readings in small gatherings of friends of some of Purdy's short plays. He took James to dinner and practically begged him to consider writing larger works for the stage. He said all Purdy had "to do to write a play is to want to write one."

Purdy was nervous about writing plays because he felt a play had always to be on the subject or the audience would become restless. He admired—as did I, and as did Tennessee—the hypnotic structures of Christopher Marlowe's plays, where the play rests on a singular driving force throughout. Purdy considered the structure of the novel looser: "one can breathe a little while writing them."

Tennessee became fascinated by Purdy's tight dialogue. He had begun in his later one-act plays to work from this model. He had already noted in his introduction to his distilled adaptation of *The Seagull (The Notebook of Trigorin*—probably the best adaptation of a Chekhov work ever done in our language) that our theater, the modern theater, "had to scream to be heard."

At one point Tennessee turned to me and said, "I think I'm in my James Purdy period."

Tennessee carried *Children Is All* (the New Directions edition with the short stories and two plays) around with him in his manuscript case for four years. It was the only thing in there that wasn't Tennessee's own work. He studied both the plays, reading them over and over. And then he began to explore a "final" work, *In Masks Outrageous and Austere.*

Tennessee asked to see James Purdy's short story "Some of These Days" in the days before his demise. Purdy had inscribed the words of Thomas Chatterton on the title page, which had some years earlier been the inspiration for the story:

> "Water witches crowned with reeds,
> Bear me to your lethal tides."

Williams, whose body and health had been "breaking down," was discovered on the floor as if he had expired from sheer exhaustion. His head was resting right next to those words.

Years after Williams died, Purdy said, "I would like to write a play, but I don't know what it would be." I recommended a story that had fascinated him, but it was too complicated. Then I remembered how Tennessee had taken short stories and turned them into plays. I suggested "The Story of Ruthanna Elder," a parallel story from Purdy's novel *Narrow Rooms.* To my great surprise, he agreed. I had never known him to work like this. But in twelve days the play was completed. Purdy felt he had written it for Tennessee.

Encouraged by the outcome of *Ruthanna Elder,* I pulled out other plays in various stages of completion from Purdy's filing cabinets. *The*

Paradise Circus and *Brice* both had been begun but then dropped less than halfway through, and now Purdy finished them. After it was completed, I gave *Brice* to a psychotherapist, a member of the Actors Studio, who commented, "Oh, it's his family play." I had worked on it with Purdy for months and did not realize that this is exactly what it is.

Purdy had always been fascinated that Brahms as a young composer played piano in brothels. I had introduced Purdy to Terence Sellers, who was in awe of his work, and also to Angel Stern, a writer who for years in the great city ran what he called the "Asphodel Parlours." This all revolved in his mind when he wrote *Where Quentin Goes*.

Several days after I put this down, Purdy succumbed to complications in the hospital. His body was cremated, and his ashes are to be scattered over Dame Edith Sitwell's grave as was his wish.

*Selected Plays of
James Purdy*

BRICE

CHARACTERS and their ages

WILLIAM HAWKINS, 41
BRICE HAWKINS, 15
MELISSA, 75
HARRIET, 74
DEREK JOHNS, 39
EDGARS, 20
BARNEY COMSTOCK, 42
DELLA HAWKINS, 39
ELMO, 42
SIMEON, 80
LILA REECE, 39

A small town in the farm country of the Midwest, 1927.

ACT I

Scene 1

WILLIAM *and* BRICE *are seated in the living room.* WILLIAM, BRICE'S *father, is 41,* BRICE 15.

WILLIAM: I feel she will eventually come to her senses.

BRICE: (*looking up from his studies shakes his head*) Once she makes up her mind . . . I don't think so.

WILLIAM: She can't just walk out on us like this. . . . What have I done? (*said to himself*) I haven't done anything that bad.

BRICE: Well, she's fierce about it all.

WILLIAM: Fierce? Do you see that in her?

BRICE: She don't even act like my mother when I plead your case for you in front of her.

WILLIAM: (*offended*) Plead my case. You don't do that. She must know you don't do that when you visit her.

BRICE: Well what am I doing then when I go there.

WILLIAM: You're her son ain't you? And until there is a reconciliation the judge said you must visit her.

BRICE: But, Dad, you know as well as I that when I go there I only go for one reason. To plead your case!

WILLIAM: (*said with humor*) Then you're a damned poor attorney.

BRICE: He's turning you against me, she always says.

5

WILLIAM: (*in a wild high voice*) Does she have another man? Tell me, Brice.

BRICE: She keeps roomers. . . . That is a big house now we've moved out . . .

WILLIAM: That don't answer my question. I don't know how to put it to you since she's your mother. . . . Does she have . . . fellows? (*BRICE stares at him*) You know . . . lovers. . . . Do men make love to her?

BRICE: I don't watch . . . her.

WILLIAM: (*anger coming*) What!

BRICE: I'm sorry. I only meant I try not to think what she might do . . . when it's nightfall.

WILLIAM: She wouldn't have to wait for nightfall, Brice.

BRICE: (*getting beside himself*) Oh Dad. Stop it. I want to forget her. . . . Why can't you forget her. We could go on without her.

WILLIAM: I am going to see Melissa. Your grandmother has always liked me. . . . She still calls me her boy.

BRICE: Yes, Grandma likes you.

WILLIAM: She knows the separation is not good for us.

BRICE: But she listens to her daughter. To my mother . . . to your . . . wife.

WILLIAM: I will go to see Melissa one more time. . . . Maybe this time she can bring all the threads together.

BRICE: I tried to explain how you feel, Dad, but it only makes Mama scream and rave. She seems to want to be . . . all alone.

WILLIAM: In a house full of roomers!

BRICE: Oh but that's all they are to her . . . She must get awful lonesome.

WILLIAM: Yes, I would think she would need a man in the house. (*goes toward the hall-tree to get his hat*)

BRICE: She told me once she was sick and tired of the whole human race.

WILLIAM: Well I could say that with more justice than her! But I go on. I don't give up.

BRICE: (*imploring*) If you could forget about her, Dad.

WILLIAM: (*puts on his hat, and begins to leave*) One can't forget injustice, Brice. (*exits*)

BRICE: (*rising and looking after his father*) But why can't you get it through your head she don't love you. She don't want you! You're poison to her. . . . Why can't you accept facts, huh. You never could, you never would. You want the impossible. (*begins to sob, then angrily hits his fist in his palm*) We've had enough boo-hooin' in this family. I won't be like either of them. I won't . . .

Scene 2

HARRIET *and* MELISSA *are seated in a large parlor. They are both sewing.* MELISSA *is sewing a woman's dress,* HARRIET *a large expensive tablecloth.*

MELISSA: Yes, it's true. . . . They all come to me with their troubles! But did you ever think, Harriet, if nobody came to me at all, if nobody wanted me to sew! What would I do? I would turn to dust.

HARRIET: But, Melissa, they come too often. They burden you with their sorrows, with their piteous pleas for help!

MELISSA: Oh, Harriet. . . . If I couldn't help my family . . . (*bites a thread*) . . . True they have more than their share of trouble. . . . I don't like a broken home! I wish Della had somehow made her peace with William! Why couldn't they have made a go of their marriage? Other people have. You did. . . . You were with your husband until the end, a happy happy pair if there ever was.

HARRIET: Oh that was so long ago. . . . Yes, I suppose I was happy.

MELISSA: Suppose. You know you were. Marriage should last till death, as the Good Book says.

HARRIET: (*in a kind of reverie*) But if one is not happy with the spouse one is married to Melissa . . . Must we suffer until death because we cannot be happy.

MELISSA: Now you sound like my daughter. She wanted freedom. Look at what she has. She runs a rooming house. Some of her roomers are the offscourings of humanity, yet she puts up with them. She was a lady, brought up as a lady. Now see how she lives. Runs a house where anybody can demand admittance. She smokes one cigarette after another. *You look like the terrible woman Carmen, I once said to her, a cigarette always hanging from your mouth. If you must smoke, sit down and do so, don't go about your work with the thing hanging from your lower lip.* She won't listen to me, but she always comes to me for advice, and . . . (*sadly*) money. As if money grew on trees. And there is William, wanting his wife to come home. . . .

HARRIET: But you yourself, dear, have always said what a poor provider he was. . . . How he was always traveling, never at home. How he failed in all his undertakings. . . . How money ran through his fingers like water. You called him once a ne'er-do-well!

MELISSA: That was Della's word for him. I must have picked it up.

HARRIET: I've heard you critical of him.

MELISSA: True, but she put most of those ideas into my head. . . . I've been thinking about William lately. He wasn't as bad as Della said. And he is the father of her son! Della won't keep him because she says he takes his father's part! But a boy that young needs both mother and father. And together, not separately. Parents cannot be parents if they live away from one another. They fight for the loyalty of the child, as they have done in Brice's case.

HARRIET: Brice will come through all right.

MELISSA: Let's hope he will. . . . I'm sure his dad loves him. But I don't know what Brice thinks of his dad. One day in the garden in summer I was walking with Brice between the peony beds and the apple orchard, and I said, *Do you respect your dad, Brice?* . . . He looked at me dumbfounded. I repeated my question. *Do you respect your dad, dear? Is that the right word, Grandma,* he said. *But you love him, don't you,* I exclaimed. *Don't tell me now you don't love him. . . . I'm coming to that,* he replied. *. . . Coming to it, oh Brice,* I cried. . . . I was so terribly upset by his answers. . . . And I felt suddenly he had nobody. I pressed him to my breast, and we both wept bitterly.

HARRIET: Isn't he too young to know whether he loves anybody, Melissa?

MELISSA: Oh, Harriet, how can you speak so. One is never too young to acknowledge one's love. Never! (*the front doorbell rings*) Good heavens. Who can that be at this hour? (HARRIET *rises to go to the front entrance.*) Just stay, a moment. . . . Let us be quiet. . . . Maybe whoever it is will go away.

(*Enter* WILLIAM, *holding his straw hat in his hand.*)

WILLIAM: Mother! (*in a kind of prayerful way*) Mother! You're always at work. Don't your busy fingers ever stop. (*He moves over to* ME-LISSA *and kisses her, takes up her hand and kisses it.*)

MELISSA: (*moved*) William. You will always be my boy, Will. Sit down. Take that comfortable chair over there.

WILLIAM: (*turning to* HARRIET) Evening, Miss Harriet.

HARRIET: Good evening, William. . . . Supposin' I leave now, Melissa.

MELISSA: William and I are not going to say anything you can't share, Harriet. Are we, William.

WILLIAM: Indeed not. We're old friends, and old friends have had their say out.

HARRIET: Just the same, I believe I will turn in. I'm a bit tired, to tell the truth.

MELISSA: Tired! Hear her, Will. She can outwork me, and she's even older than I am. No, Harriet, you are never tired. But go upstairs if you wish. A person has to have time to their own thoughts. We can't be talking and working twenty-four hours a day.

HARRIET: Goodnight, William. . . . Goodnight, my dearest. (*She bends down and kisses* MELISSA, *then exits stage left.*)

MELISSA: I awoke the other afternoon, I was stealing a nap, never took naps a few years ago but I felt the need of slumber. . . . And I awoke suddenly with a start. I thought, *In four or five or at the most six years, I will be no more! I will cease to exist! I will be like that dust that is supposed to move aimlessly about the stars. . . . I will be no more.* (*comes out of her reverie*)

WILLIAM: Nonsense, Mother. . . . You will live a long time yet. (*holds his hat tightly*) You have an indomitable will. . . . And everything to live for.

MELISSA: True, I have many loved ones . . . who depend on me . . .

WILLIAM: Mother, must you work so hard . . . I mean . . .

MELISSA: To me, truly, it's not work. If my fingers can't move, Will, I am at a great loss . . . I hope I die sewing. What would pass the long hours without my needlework. No, take away my sewing, I wouldn't last the winter.

WILLIAM: You are the best woman I ever knew.

MELISSA: Oh, Will . . . I do love you so much. . . . And my heart is broken that you and Della have parted. . . . It is my . . . great disappointment.

WILLIAM: And mine! I can think of nothing else.

MELISSA: You still love her, dear boy.

WILLIAM: Yes. Yes. Yes. (*Each yes is said with deeper despair.*)

MELISSA: I have talked to her till I'm black in the face. . . . She is so changed. She is so . . . heedless of anything but her own . . . desires.

WILLIAM: (*bitterly*) What are her . . . desires do you suppose?

MELISSA: Freedom . . . Freedom. I said to her, *Perhaps you want to be the wind and not a woman, to go wherever and whenever you list. . . . What good is freedom, if when you are old, you are alone,* I said to her. *Your boy will leave you, and go about his life, and what will you have then but freedom. . . . You will find out it is only a word, only the wind. . . .* And oh how she retorted. *You have always been easily satisfied,* she said. *Easily made happy.* No, no, I responded. . . . *But there is only true happiness doing for others.* Oh she laughed me then to scorn. *And what do others do for you. Here you sit, ignored by all your rich sons, and must sew for a living . . . like a gypsy.*

WILLIAM: (*shocked*) Gypsy! She said gypsy.

MELISSA: (*sews a little*) Said in anger, you know. . . . She feels my sons, her brothers, should keep me in a palace. Doing nothing. . . . Taking tea with other wealthy women. I would not last the winter living like that! (*sews on*)

WILLIAM: (*in admiration*) Mother, mother.

MELISSA: I have done all I can do to make her see the right path. (*She touches* WILLIAM.) I can do no more. Her heart . . . is hardened against you.

WILLIAM: Sometimes I wonder why I cannot give her up, why I hold on so, like a man grasping at a rope from a high cliff he knows he must fall from. . . . I cannot let go my grasp.

MELISSA: I will see her one more time. . . . I will plead for you.

WILLIAM: (*suddenly taking out something from his pocket*) I have something here of great price. . . . It was my mother's. I know you keep a strongbox, Mother . . . In case something happened to me, I want you to have it. . . . If my boy should need help sometime . . . perhaps it could be sold. (*He gives her the diamond.*)

MELISSA: Oh, Will . . . What a dazzling stone it is . . . It must be worth . . . a fortune. . . . But shouldn't you keep it in the bank vault.

WILLIAM: (*energetically*) No! No. If something should happen to me . . .

MELISSA: (*frightened*) But it won't, Will.

WILLIAM: If it should . . . it is yours. . . . You have my perfect trust . . .

MELISSA: I will put it in my strongbox . . . with a notarized statement that it is yours, Will . . . and how is Brice?

WILLIAM: Brice, yes . . . He has such a wild streak in him, Mother. . . . I wonder if he will ever grow up. . . . He seems like a wild young deer of some kind, or sometimes like a young lynx that one knows will never be anything but wild, no matter what is done for him. . . . Had he a mother, I daresay he would be different. . . . (*seeing her look of pain*) I mean a mother who lived under the same roof . . .

MELISSA: Yes, a boy needs both parents to grow right. . . . (*then, said as if to herself*) A wild lynx.

WILLIAM: (*almost kneeling down before her*) You will plead with her one more time. For Brice's sake, Mother. . . . For his sake.

MELISSA: Is anything wrong . . . I mean has Brice done anything he shouldn't?

WILLIAM: Oh no. Nothing. . . . Only he is so wild. And he's always outdoors.

MELISSA: Like the lynxes and the deer.

WILLIAM: (*rising*) Thank you, Mother. You will never know how I appreciate your many kindnesses. Don't you see, I could not go on without your encouragement and kindheartedness.

MELISSA: (*rising*) I have done nothing. . . . Nothing for anybody. . . .

WILLIAM: You do not even know what you are worth! That is a true sign of your greatness. (*He goes out.*)

Scene 3

WILLIAM *stands disconsolate, almost paralyzed under the street lamp of the town, as if he had lost his direction.* DEREK *comes on stage left, stares at him.*

DEREK: Will, you look like you'd received bad news. (*He is obviously a bit drunk.*) Put her there. (*tries to shake hands, but* WILLIAM *is still in a haze and barely notices him*) Will! Remember me.

WILLIAM: Derek, how are you? (*shakes hands*)

DEREK: You haven't changed much since we went to country high school together.

WILLIAM: Well, things have changed, Derek.

DEREK: (*pulling out a bottle*) Have a nip for old time's sake.

WILLIAM: No, no. I don't touch it, Derek, you know that.

DEREK: You need a swig to judge by your face, Will. Come on now. And what's your bad news?

WILLIAM: I thought everybody knew my bad news, Derek.

DEREK: I travel you know a lot. . . . Often gone months at a time.

WILLIAM: You're still selling farm machinery.

DEREK: And anything else I can make a dollar on. (*drinks*)

WILLIAM: (*annoyed by* DEREK'*s drunkenness*) You've said I look like the recipient of bad news. What's yours?

DEREK: What's what?

WILLIAM: What's your bad news?

DEREK: Bein' alive, Will. That's the bad news for everybody.

WILLIAM: Oh come now.

DEREK: I hear Della has left you.

WILLIAM: That's stale news, Derek. . . . Yes, she left over a year ago.

DEREK: Come on now, Will, don't be a sourpuss just cause you know how. Have a drink.

WILLIAM: I've never liked the stuff, Derek. You know that. . . . I'm sorry. (*seeing he has offended him*) I don't like what it does to you.

DEREK: She's not worth it, Will.

WILLIAM: Who are you talking about now?

DEREK: *Who*, he asks. Your one and only. Della. She's not worth pinin' over, cryin' over, achin' for like you've been doing this past year and more! Della! (*makes sound of disgust and drinks*)

WILLIAM: Mind your speech now. (*offers to go off*)

DEREK: Come back here, you. . . . What do you mean mind my speech! (*He pulls* WILLIAM *toward him.*)

WILLIAM: You're too drunk to talk to. (*pulls away from him*)

DEREK: You've got somethin' worse than my habit, Will, oh yes you have. Think you're better than me, don't you. Better than anybody, don't you. That's why Della left you.

WILLIAM: I'm warning you. You watch that lip of yours. It's got you into plenty of trouble before.

DEREK: But my wife never left me, trouble or no trouble.

WILLIAM: Derek! You—

DEREK: Because I'm human, that's why. Like Della is. . . . You were too sober for her.

WILLIAM: A lot you know.

DEREK: She was starved for the love of a real man. . . . Now she's getting what you didn't give her. In that place she calls a rooming house!

WILLIAM: Derek Johns!

DEREK: That's what they call me, true enough. (*drinks*) I answer to that name.

WILLIAM: Oh. (*goes off but* DEREK *follows him*)

DEREK: I'm glad for her, though sorry for you.

WILLIAM: I don't need anybody to be sorry for me.

DEREK: Then why are you so sorry for yourself!

WILLIAM: Goodnight, Derek.

DEREK: And when your head hits the pillow tonight, you can think that Della is in bed with a different man each night to make up for all the nights she spent with an icicle like you! Think of that.

WILLIAM: (WILLIAM *returns, hits* DEREK. DEREK *half falls, then comes up to his full posture, spits in* WILLIAM's *face.* WILLIAM *hits him, knocks him down.* DEREK *feels his face and jaw.*) Derek! Let me help you up.

DEREK: Leave me alone. I'll get up by and by.

WILLIAM: You're not hurt, are you.

DEREK: I deserved it, Will. . . . I deserved it.

WILLIAM: When a man hears such a thing, he's not himself.

DEREK: (*getting up slowly*) I'm drunk, Will. Forget what I may have said.

WILLIAM: Forget! I'm not likely to forget what you said if I live to be a hundred.

DEREK: Incompatibility is no man's fault.

WILLIAM: No? (DEREK *throws away the bottle, goes off stage left.*) If you'd let me drink a whole gallon of that and every drop was poison I'd be better off than having heard what you said. . . . I could have killed you when I hit you. . . . I should have. (*He shakes his fist in the direction of where* DEREK *has exited.*)

Scene 4

WILLIAM's *house.* BRICE *and* EDGARS *are seated at a small card table playing two-handed hearts. A phonograph is playing not too loudly near them.* EDGARS *is a handsome but rough appearing youth of about 20.*

EDGARS: (*throwing down a card*) All mine! (*laughs gleefully*)

BRICE: You always win. Well, they say your grandpa was a river gambler.

EDGARS: They say! They know! He was lucky he wasn't sent to be hanged. . . . I don't pretend my folks was born with a gold spoon in their mouth.

BRICE: (*cautiously*) Meaning?

EDGARS: (*relents of causing unpleasantness and dealing*) Meanin' nothin'. But I ain't ashamed of my folks anyhow.

BRICE: I didn't say that to make you.

EDGARS: At least my folks stayed together. They may have missed jail by an inch, but they stayed close-knit, kept their vows.

BRICE: (*almost horrified*) Vows?

EDGARS: They may have been nothing to look up to, but they stayed together my Mom and Dad and their Mom and Dad before them. . . . They kept their marriage vow and their duty to us kids.

BRICE: All right, all right. So your folks stuck together. So what.

EDGARS: (*after a long, ominous silence*) You know I wandered off past the Ketsley estate the other day.

BRICE: (*trying to get over the hurt* EDGARS' *words have caused*) Yes.

EDGARS: Brice, you don't have to act that interested in what I'm goin' to tell you.

BRICE: But Edgars, I am interested. You're my best friend.

EDGARS: (*looks at him searchingly*) As a matter of fact I got lost.

BRICE: (*looks up from his cards*) Yeah.

EDGARS: I could have been in China. I come after a while to the ruins of the old Star-Lite Stables. Remember them?

BRICE: I sure do. Remember the owner too.

EDGARS: Cliff Derringer, yes, he died in the fire too. . . . But, Brice, listen. . . . Not all of them horses perished in the fire.

BRICE: (*very intent on every word*) God.

EDGARS: They run wild in the pasture and the woods around there.

BRICE: You saw them?

EDGARS: You're darn tootin'. They are as wild as the wind. Snortin' and rushin' around like they had fire in their bellies.

BRICE: (*dreamily*) Did you go up to them?

EDGARS: Do you think I want them to kill me.

BRICE: They're that wild.

EDGARS: And vicious.

BRICE: Why don't the sheriff do something about them if they're dangerous.

EDGARS: Who cares what happens there. It might as well be on the mountains of the moon. Who'd pay for them being caught and hobbled and took into custody. (*puts down a card and yells at another victory*)

BRICE: Edgars, I can't win with you.

EDGARS: Would you like to go there some time with me?

BRICE: Would I like to! You know what my answer is.

EDGARS: We'll go then when your old man is out of town or laid up with a fever.

BRICE: He's never laid up with anything. Do you know my Dad has never been sick in his whole life. Never had a cold or a headache or nothin'.

EDGARS: (*said sarcastically*) You mean he's perfect.

BRICE: (*moonily*) I sometimes wonder all right. . . . He's too . . .

(*Enter WILLIAM, stage right. He holds his straw hat over his injured right hand.*)

WILLIAM: The sound of that damned phonograph music turns my stomach. (BRICE *jumps up and begins to make a motion to turn off the phonograph.*) No, let it go. Evenin', Edgars.

EDGARS: (*sheepish, afraid*) Evenin' Mr. Hawkins.

(BRICE *looks at his father's hat covering his hand.* WILLIAM *shifts in the seat he has just taken.*)

WILLIAM: Why don't you go on with your card playin'.

EDGARS: Matter of fact Mr. Hawkins, I was just plannin' to shove off.

WILLIAM: Sorry if I broke up you boys' card game. (*rises and turns his back to them, as he pretends to fiddle with an account ledger but actually is looking at his injured hand*)

EDGARS: (*to* BRICE) I'll be sayin' goodnight now. . . . See you later. . . . If you want to go to the old Star-Lite Stables sometime . . .

BRICE: Sure, Edgars, I would. . . . You know that.

WILLIAM: (*turning around*) Did you mention the Star-Lite Stables?

EDGARS: Yes sir.

WILLIAM: I was about to help the owner sell that, when lo and behold the whole place burned down mysteriously. We presume Cliff Derringer died in the blaze, but they never really identified his body.

EDGARS: The horses that escaped, I was tellin' Brice here, are runnin' wild in the old pasture and woods.

WILLIAM: (*musing*) You don't say! (*comes close to the boys, his hat is allowed to fall from his injured hand, so both young men see he has hurt his hand, for it is bleeding*)

EDGARS: (*shocked at the sight*) Mr. Hawkins!

WILLIAM: Yes.

EDGARS: I must be goin'. My dad will give me . . . (*he goes out hurriedly*)

WILLIAM: (*after a long pause*) I wonder if he is the right company for you, Brice.

BRICE: (*nettled*) Not everybody wants to come see me, Dad.

WILLIAM: (*in a kind of expressionless sleepy voice*) What is that supposed to mean?

BRICE: (*also as if talking in his sleep*) They feel, the others . . .

WILLIAM: The others?

BRICE: My schoolmates.

WILLIAM: Yes.

BRICE: Without a woman at the head of the house here, (*frightened by his father's terrible appearance*) with our family not united. . . . Dad, what is wrong with your hand! (*He is frightened for it is bleeding and drops of blood are falling to the floor.*)

WILLIAM: I hit it against something.

BRICE: (*goes over to* WILLIAM *and carefully takes hold of his hand*) It ain't broke is it?

WILLIAM: I can move it.

BRICE: Shouldn't you see the Doc?

WILLIAM: Oh no.

BRICE: You say you hit it against . . .

WILLIAM: Against a man . . . It hit a man and knocked him down.

BRICE: Oh.

WILLIAM: I suppose that makes you ashamed of me too. Maybe even the Edgars snot won't visit you now when people find out I have knocked down Derek Johns.

BRICE: Dad, I ain't ashamed of you. I ain't . . .

WILLIAM: Shut up. . . . Go to bed!

BRICE: If you hit him I'm sure he needed it.

WILLIAM: Thank you. (*sits down*)

BRICE: Dad, let me bathe your hand in warm water.

WILLIAM: Oh well, suit yourself.

BRICE: Why don't you take off your jacket Dad? (*He hurries out stage left.* WILLIAM *removes his jacket and looks disgustedly at his hand then looks away.*)

WILLIAM: (*to himself*) I never liked the looks of that Edgars. (BRICE *brings back a basin of warm water and some cloths. He rolls up his father's sleeve and washes his hurt hand.*) So your friends don't come here because we are a broken family.

BRICE: That's not exactly the whole reason . . .

WILLIAM: Well what is the whole reason?

BRICE: I don't think my classmates look up to me too much . . . on my own. . . . With Edgars . . .

WILLIAM: (*said with anger*) Edgars!

BRICE: Edgars accepts me. . . . I mean . . .

WILLIAM: Don't say any more . . . You've said enough for one evening.

BRICE: (*dries WILLIAM's hand with a towel*) I'm glad you hit him, Dad . . .

WILLIAM: All right, all right, go to bed.

BRICE: (*picks up the basin and begins to go out stage left*) You didn't . . . kill him did you, Dad?

WILLIAM: (*laughing*) I'm afraid not, Brice. Goodnight. . . . I'll be up in a little while.

BRICE: You don't need anything?

WILLIAM: Just time, I guess. . . . They say it cures all things . . .

BRICE: You know where I am if you need me, Dad.

WILLIAM: (*as if asleep himself*) Pleasant dreams. . . . And thanks for the . . . ministrations, Brice. . . . You're a good boy, say what they will.

(BRICE *studies his Dad, then sighs, and leaves the room.*)

Scene 5

DELLA's *house. A phonograph is playing an old-fashioned waltz.* DELLA *dances with* ELMO, *a middle-aged man who fancies himself a ladykiller and general roustabout. Stage right* BARNEY *is seated. He is obviously a man who has done lots of hard manual labor but has in his middle age come into some money and effects expensive clothes, rings, and watch chain, etc. He smokes a cigar as he watches* DELLA *and* ELMO.

BARNEY: (*rises and goes over to the pair, pulls* ELMO *away from* DELLA) Let me have my turn now! (*makes a threatening gesture to* ELMO)

DELLA: Lower your voice, if you please.

BARNEY: (*mimicking her angrily*) *If you please!* I've been sitting in that corner for a good half hour.

DELLA: If you're going to treat me to one of your bawlings out you can leave. I won't be bawled out anymore. I've had my fill of that.

BARNEY: Then supposin' you dance with me. After all, I'm the one who brings you the gifts.

DELLA: Are you going to throw that up to me also! I declare.

ELMO: Oh go on dance with him, Della. I don't mind.

BARNEY: I don't need permission to dance with her from you. Get that straight.

ELMO: The trouble with you, Barney, is all you know is to shout orders. You weren't sergeant in the army for nothing were you.

BARNEY: (*takes* DELLA *roughly in his arms*) You have poor taste in men, Della.

DELLA: Then why am I dancing with you, will you tell me.

BARNEY: You've been teasing me all evening. You're a tease. Like every other woman. You don't like to dance with Elmo and you know it.

DELLA: I'd advise you to learn to keep your place.

BARNEY: I know my place. And I know my girl. (*He kisses her.*)

DELLA: Your kind of freshness turns me off. (BARNEY *kisses her again. She tries to break away.*) Will you behave!

BARNEY: Della, you know you go for me! Why do you have someone else here on the one evening I am free. What's your game?

DELLA: I don't ever want to belong to one man again. I had that once.

BARNEY: You call William then a man? (*laughs*)

DELLA: I wish you would learn to keep your mouth shut. Your mouth and your fists. You ought to learn to control them.

BARNEY: There's something else I suppose I should learn to control. (*He attempts to kiss her again; then they begin to dance rather furiously.*)

DELLA: (*stopping but obviously pleased at the whirl he has given her*) I'm quite out of breath. Help me to the chair, Barney. (*She laughs. ELMO stares at the pair with ill-concealed jealousy.*)

DELLA: You are a wonderful dancer for such a heavy brute!

BARNEY: (*seats himself beside her and holds her hand*) Why don't you get wise to yourself. Why don't you take the one man that was meant for you, huh?

DELLA: (*said with coquetry*) One man is too many! I had my fill of one man, let me tell you.

BARNEY: You've never had a real man, that's your trouble. You're untouched. . . . That's why . . . I want you to be . . .

ELMO: (*picking up his hat*) I think I'll leave you sweethearts to yourself.

DELLA: (*rising*) Don't go, Elmo, on account of Barney. Please! We'll dance some more.

ELMO: (*noticing the phonograph has stopped*) Shall I put on another record?

DELLA: Yes, Elmo, dear, do. . . . (*turns distracted to* BARNEY *who scowls at her*) I thought we were having a wonderful time, the three of us. (*The doorbell rings but nobody appears to hear it. It rings again. She lights a cigarette.*) I would never have believed though that Barney was such a divine dancer. Who taught you? (BRICE *has entered at stage left and stares balefully at the party going on; she is startled at the sight of her son.*) Brice, what on earth? Is anything wrong? What do you want?

BRICE: (*staring with real hatred at the two men*) I came to . . . talk with you.

DELLA: At this hour?

BRICE: What hour should a son come to talk with his mother . . . I've never known . . .

DELLA: Don't be impertinent.

BARNEY: Good evening, sonny.

ELMO: Nice to see you Brice. (*He and* BARNEY *go over to* BRICE *then move away from him, as* BRICE *remains silent and pays no attention to them.*)

BRICE: I would think I was in a dance hall all right.

DELLA: I said you are not to be impertinent. This is my home. I'll do what I please.

BRICE: That's all I've ever heard you talk about. Doing what you please! And so this is what it is! (*stares at the two men again*)

BARNEY: That's no way to talk to your mother, son.

BRICE: (*bitterly*) Son!

DELLA: Here we were having an innocent evening of dancing and you come in acting just like your father. Lecturing me! Criticizing, condemning without even knowing what is going on!

BARNEY: Brice, go home, for your own sake! It's not the right time for a talk. Your mother is having herself a little relaxation.

BRICE: Why don't you and that other jake get out of here so I can talk with my mother.

DELLA: Brice, I will not have this. I will not be interfered with.

BRICE: (*suddenly picks up a chair and threatens* BARNEY) Will you get out of here, and leave me to talk with this woman . . .

BARNEY: (*menacingly*) Now see here, sonny. Nobody talks to Barney Comstock like that. Boy or no boy.

BRICE: I'll break your head! I'm warning you.

ELMO: Brice, don't do anything rash. . . . Come on, Barney, let's get out of here and go somewhere less exciting.

BARNEY: If you were a boy of mine I'd pound some sense into you.

BRICE: (*offering to strike him with the chair*) I'd like to see you try, you cheap whoremaster!

DELLA: See here! See here. (*weeping*) Barney, Elmo, do as he says. . . . Go, I mean it. Leave the premises. . . . Do you hear me, go both of you.

BARNEY: So you prefer to be alone with your snot, do you. . . . You make me tired. You're nothing but a tease if you ask me.

DELLA: Nobody asked you. Go out, both of you. Go, or I'll make real trouble for you.

BARNEY: (*addressed to* ELMO) Did you ever hear such a bitch.

BRICE: (*threatens* BARNEY *again with the chair*) You watch your lip now.

DELLA: (*putting herself between* BARNEY *and* BRICE) If you would do as he says, Barney, and leave! For God's sake! Will you get out of here. (*She sits down, as* BARNEY *and* ELMO *leave stage left.* BRICE *slowly puts the chair down, she is weeping.*) Now see what you've done.

BRICE: See what I've done. . . . How could you . . . how could you know such men when you were married to my father. When you were married to William.

DELLA: A lot you know about being married, don't you. A boy with the peach fuzz still on his cheeks. (*weeps on*)

BRICE: When you had a decent man, when you'd come to the time of life you should settle down quietly. . . . You opened a house like this to run wild in . . .

DELLA: Well, what of it? All my years with your father, from long before you were born were like living in a plot in a cemetery!

BRICE: (*horrified*) Mother!

DELLA: Yes, mother. You can say that. It was all . . . a life sentence.

BRICE: You were never happy . . . ever.

DELLA: A little till after you were born. . . . But he always took you away from me. . . . You were his, not mine. . . . He saw to that. . . . What was I in the house, but a prisoner. There was no happiness, no fun, no . . . dancing.

BRICE: (*warning but beginning to feel less sure of his judgment of* DELLA) Mother.

DELLA: I was in bondage to him. He was incapable of love. Incapable. No tenderness, no . . . letting go. . . . All duty, dignity, respectability, righteousness. . . . I was suffocating.

BRICE: So you never loved me.

DELLA: (*as if aware of his existence for the first time*) What?

BRICE: (*rising to go*) You heard me.

DELLA: Don't go now. You have ruined the whole evening.

BRICE: (*bitterly*) You'll have other evenings for the rest of your life.

DELLA: So you don't think I ever loved you.

BRICE: I know it!

DELLA: How could I love you when he always stood between us. . . . He corrected every loving look or touch or expression I offered you. He was always between me and my love for you. . . . Even now when I want to hold you to me, it is as if he prohibited it. (*approaches him and holds him to her*)

BRICE: No, no, it is too late. . . . Especially after what I saw tonight.

DELLA: Kiss me. . . . Kiss your mother, Brice. It's not too late. (*they kiss, then he pushes her away from him*)

BRICE: It's too late, Mother. . . . Yes, I see you belong here.

DELLA: And even if I were to come back which is what you always plead for on these visits of yours. What would I come back to. Your father has even less substance than he had when he was young. . . . The dead would be revisiting the dead!

BRICE: Come back for me . . .

DELLA: Oh, Brice, Brice . . . Yes, if you were alone maybe I would come back.

BRICE: And give up your dance hall.

DELLA: My dance hall. I give one little dance a month and he calls it my dance hall. You are your father's son.

BRICE: If he were to die, and I was alone there. . . . Would you come back to me . . .

DELLA: (*puzzled by such a strange offer*) I suppose, Brice, I suppose.

BRICE: You suppose. Don't you know?

DELLA: You have confused me so terribly. . . . I don't know what I would do. . . . He won't die in any case for years. I'm so . . . heart-broken tonight.

BRICE: You're what he said of you. All emotion, all feeling, all passion and yearning and desiring the impossible.

DELLA: Yes, that is what I am. . . . I could never get enough love, I admit it.

BRICE: Never?

DELLA: Never never. I could never get enough. . . . I'm starved. I'm a starving woman. . . . I could never go back to his rectitude, his justice, his perfection, his level masculine rightness. . . . I'm starved.

BRICE: (*taking her in his arms*) Oh, Mother, Mother. (*They hold one another as the curtain comes down.*)

Scene 6

MELISSA's *house. She is seated alone, sewing. It is a different evening, but it might as well be the same evening on which we have first met her. All her evenings are alike. A bell rings from outside.* MELISSA *does not even stop sewing.*

DELLA: (*calls from outside*) Mother! Can't you hear me?

MELISSA: What can she want now! All right, all right. (*She puts away the dress she has been working on, and goes toward the exit at stage left.* DELLA *enters with her and comes in and flings herself down.*) I can't imagine what you are doing out at this hour.

DELLA: I can't imagine what you are doing working through the night.

MELISSA: (*sits down and takes up the dress she is working on*) I don't need reasons to do what I do.

DELLA: (*angry*) Then why do I need reasons for being out at this hour. . . . (MELISSA *gives her a terrible look.*) I couldn't sleep, so I thought I would take a walk through the pastureland.

MELISSA: The pastureland of all places! Why didn't you go sailing on the lake!

DELLA: (*remembering her terror*) Suddenly out of nowhere these wild horses appeared, and ran straight toward me!

MELISSA: (*shocked*) Della!

DELLA: But on the last of the horses as they ran past me, I thought I saw my boy and that terrible friend of his, Edgars. I know it was just my imagination. But it was so terribly real just the same.

MELISSA: Your boy! He's not your boy anymore. You deserted him.

DELLA: Don't take their part! (*They exchange looks.*) You don't love me either.

MELISSA: I loved you too well, that's why you are the way you are. I gave you everything. Stood by you in your darkest hour. Helped you raise your child. . . . Then you disappointed me. . . . But I still stand with you. Still love you.

DELLA: No, Mother, you do not love me.

MELISSA: (*stung*) Whom do you love, Della? Tell me who?

DELLA: I will never get over my fright. I will never dare go to the pastureland again, certainly.

MELISSA: I should hope not.

DELLA: Who are you making that dress for, Mother?

MELISSA: (*pauses a moment, bites a thread, looks at her daughter*) Mrs. Van Nuys.

DELLA: But it's so out of fashion, so ornate, so . . .

MELISSA: She wants it for some historical ball they are giving.

DELLA: Mother, let me try it on.

MELISSA: Try it on. . . . But you're different sizes.

DELLA: It's too good for me, you mean.

MELISSA: Della! The very idea. You are just as you were when you were eighteen. I should never have allowed you to marry, Della. It was my fault. You knew nothing . . . (*stops*) you weren't ready for marriage.

DELLA: That was certainly true. But I don't blame you. You and Papa were so eager to get me out of the house.

MELISSA: Your father may have been.

DELLA: You know he was. He hounded me to get married from the time I was fifteen.

MELISSA: Well he's dead and gone now and we can't keep blaming him.

DELLA: I wasn't ready! I wasn't.

MELISSA: Come on, dear, you can try on the dress. And we have the finest mirror in the entire county for seeing yourself in.

DELLA: Oh, Mother. . . . All I ever wanted I think was to remain your little girl.

MELISSA: (*laughs in spite of herself*) Della.

DELLA: (*kneels down at* MELISSA's *side and clasps her knees*) I wanted to stay with you forever.

MELISSA: Take off your own dress, dear, and put this one on. Go on. (DELLA *takes off her dress slowly and lays it on a chair.*) You look still like a young woman, Della. Such beautiful untouched complexion. And your stomach is so firm after having your boy. You do sometimes look like my little girl before you went and got married.

DELLA: (*trying on the dress*) Why it nearly fits! Oh, Mother, dare I ask you . . .

MELISSA: Go ahead, Della.

DELLA: Make me one just like it!

MELISSA: (*pretends to be vexed, but very much pleased at the request*) But where would you wear it?

DELLA: (*as if not having heard her*) You made my graduation ball gown, and you made my wedding dress. . . . Yes, where would I wear this? (*bursts into sobs*) For my shroud I guess.

MELISSA: (*rising*) Oh my precious dear. You should not have said such a thing! There are plenty of places you could wear such a dress to. Plenty!

DELLA: Where, Mother. Tell me where. . . . I am invited nowhere . . .

MELISSA: I will give a party for you and you can wear the dress then.

DELLA: But who will come, Mother . . .

MELISSA: I will make the dress for you just the same.

DELLA: Let me come back here and live with you.

MELISSA: And what about the big house where you are. Your father left that to you, though you never lived in it until after Will and you . . .

DELLA: I'm afraid I'll hear those wild horses again every night. . . . Even if I never go out in the pastureland again.

MELISSA: (*suspicious of her story*) Have you planned to call the sheriff?

DELLA: The sheriff? No, I haven't.

MELISSA: Then you should do so. They should shoot them.

DELLA: Shoot them? For running wild.

MELISSA: Didn't you complain how they frightened you. And where are their owners.

DELLA: (*hysterical*) They have no owners. . . . But Mother how could you want to shoot them. . . . They mean no harm . . .

MELISSA: Then they should be rounded up and sent somewhere.

DELLA: I suppose. . . . Put behind terrible barbed wire fences or hobbled.

MELISSA: How beautiful you look! Della Della! You are such a child. (DELLA *kneels before her mother and* MELISSA *strokes her head.*) I know my little girl enough to say you didn't come here just to tell me how frightened the wild horses in the pastureland made you.

DELLA: (*rises then slowly even reluctantly*) I was frightened a long time before the horses.

MELISSA: I asked you a question, Della. Whom do you . . . whom did you love?

DELLA: I thought I loved Will. Yes, indeed I believe I did.

MELISSA: After you were married you seemed to be very happy.

DELLA: Seemed, that's the right word. . . . I persuaded myself, Mother. And I wanted to persuade you and Father.

MELISSA: You mean to sit there and tell me you were never happy then.

DELLA: I think the wild horses have given me the courage to answer your question. I was never happy from . . . the first hours of our marriage. What songwriters and storybooks call the wedding night. Mine was the first of many bitter awakenings.

MELISSA: Then how were you able to persuade all of us, the whole world in fact, that you were so happy.

DELLA: Will was what every other woman wanted for her husband. My eyes followed him as he came and went as dreamily as the other lovesick girls who envied me. They called him Prince Charming, thought he should be in the movies. His outer semblance kept me quiet, I was married to a vision of a man. Then there was the child of course, and Will receded further and further from me.

MELISSA: And then his business failures.

DELLA: I could have endured a hundred of failures like that if only . . .

MELISSA: You can say it all now, Della, if that is what you want.

DELLA: I shrank even from his touch finally. I didn't want him near me. His least embrace froze me. His sweet breath, for me, came from the grave.

MELISSA: Della, come over here. (*DELLA goes to MELISSA.*) Take my hand. I knew it all, but like you I let myself be fooled.

DELLA: You could not have known it all.

MELISSA: You stayed with him though over the long years. You endured that. And you say you cannot live with him now—for Brice's sake. Don't interrupt me, Della. It's Brice that needs you both. And you swear you can't take Will back for the boy's sake.

DELLA: I knew you would bring him up. So I am to blame too for his running wild. And running wild he is, God knows. I've had the lash of his rage only tonight.

MELISSA: And yet your own freedom is more important to you than the lives of your husband and boy. Is that what you're saying?

DELLA: Mother, I am leaving. (*rises*)

MELISSA: No, you are not leaving. Take your seat again. I could have said the same thing years ago when your Father and I had our differences. Oh yes we had them—differences much greater than you and Will ever knew. But I stayed. I swallowed my pride, I discarded my own hankering after what you call freedom. And I raised my sons and my daughter. You didn't think did you Della that when you gained your freedom, you bestowed on your boy another kind of freedom. The whole town is aware of Brice's wildness. And where will that end do you suppose.

DELLA: Pour it on, Mother. Pour it on. As if I didn't know of his wildness. One reason I am here tonight is he attacked two of my guests and threatened, yes more than threatened to brain both of them. I never saw such a look in that boy's eyes.

MELISSA: And yet you want to go your own way. And what about the look in your eyes, Della.

DELLA: (*almost savagely*) What about it, Mother.

MELISSA: You have a wilder and more anguished look than either your husband or your boy. You are the living embodiment of sorrow and rage. Because you have done the wrong thing. (*DELLA bows her head.*) And I think in your heart of hearts you know you are wrong. But if you lived with Will again and established that kind of order . . .

DELLA: You would call that order, Mother . . .

MELISSA: Let me finish. If you and Will stayed together if it were only a formality, all the wildness in Brice would vanish in an hour.

DELLA: Oh, Mother, Mother. You would have me be the most miserable woman on earth.

MELISSA: You are the most miserable woman on earth, Della.

DELLA: I'm glad someone said it so I don't have to tell it again to myself. Yes, I am the most miserable.

MELISSA: You don't have to love Will. You don't have to touch him. He wouldn't demand that of you now. But you would provide both Will and your boy some peace.

DELLA: And what about my peace.

MELISSA: You would not be then the most miserable woman on earth.

DELLA: Why is it Mother, the woman is the one who is always asked to make the greatest sacrifice, and receive the sharpest pain.

MELISSA: You will never find happiness or even one hour of peace a year with your freedom.

DELLA: How can I go back to a man as proud and unyielding, as cold and as silent. And as dull. Duller than an old judge. Why not sentence me to prison walls.

MELISSA: Della, what can I offer you to persuade you to go back to him. Do you think my marriage to your father was constant joy and bliss, and that he brought me the kind of amusement and frivolity your men callers evidently bring you.

DELLA: I never dreamed you were miserable with Papa.

MELISSA: You never dreamed because you have always thought first of yourself. I spoiled you. Your father spoiled you. Everybody spoiled you.

DELLA: What are you ordering me to do?

MELISSA: I don't need to tell you, do I. Think of Brice at least.

DELLA: I will give up the rooming house, Mother, for I loathe and detest it. Yes I will close it.

MELISSA: And will you take Will back?

DELLA: Never, as I live and breathe I will never return to Will's bed and board as the lawyers put it. I will try to save Brice. But to return to Mr. High and Mighty, never.

MELISSA: (*rises in great agitation then after a long pause*) Very well. Now let me help you off with the dress.

Scene 7

MELISSA *meets* WILLIAM.

WILLIAM: (*advancing to meet* MELISSA) Mother, you're a sight for sore eyes. I was sitting here a bit down in the dumps and then you come, like the sun breaking out on a dark cloudy day. Sit over here, Mother, where I can see the light fall on you. I want to have a good look at my best friend.

MELISSA: You talk about a sight for sore eyes. Will, that is a better description I think of you. (*takes something from her purse*) I found this old photograph, Will, it's of you and me I think from the time you were first coming to the house. My husband George was still alive then, and of course you were not . . . married then. (*gives him the photo*)

WILLIAM: What a splendid likeness of you, Mother. Who took the photo?

MELISSA: Remember my nephew, Keith.

WILLIAM: I do of course. A fine young man. But he died in the war, didn't he?

MELISSA: Yes, he was one of our first casualties from the town.

WILLIAM: Everything is so transitory, Mother, after all. Poor Keith. May I keep his photo?

MELISSA: I brought it, Will, for you.

WILLIAM: Can't I fetch you something to drink, Mother.

MELISSA: Oh, I don't think so, Will. Unless you have some of that apple cider you and Brice used to make.

WILLIAM: I do as a matter of fact. Just you sit here, and relax and I'll be back with a glass in no time. (*exits*)

MELISSA: (*picks up the photo he has left behind on a small table*) How little Will has changed in all those years, except a few lines of care. It's a face that has withstood a lot, but who knows, it may have more and graver things to withstand. (*puts down photo*) I shouldn't have come. How can I tell him what Della expects me to say. I'm not an attorney. I don't have the gift of gab.

(WILLIAM *enters bearing a tray, a bottle, and two glasses.*)

WILLIAM: Here we are, Mother. (*gives her a glass*) Shall we drink a toast.

MELISSA: Oh, I can catch the smell of the apples. (*tastes*) A delicate wonderful flavor isn't it? (*tastes again*)

WILLIAM: What's that old song they used to sing about Apple Blossom Time or something like that. (MELISSA *smiles and goes on tasting the cider.*) Mother, I wish we saw one another more often. You haven't any idea how just the sight of you gives me a life. I feel lighter, and younger. Perhaps the photo does something too. (*picks it up and stares at it, then puts it down*)

MELISSA: The wonderful thing about photos Will, they don't change. Except every time one looks at them, they seem slightly different or . . .

WILLIAM: Or we see more in them each time we look.

MELISSA: That's more like it, isn't it.

WILLIAM: (*after a silence between them*) Do you have a special reason for coming today. Not that you need one, of course.

MELISSA: (*uneasy*) I'm afraid I don't have anything too pressing, Will. But perhaps I am keeping you from something.

WILLIAM: Even if you were, Mother, it would have to wait. No, I have nothing demanding my attention.

MELISSA: Will, I have spoken with Della. I believe you asked me to speak with her.

WILLIAM: (*becoming downcast*) Yes, indeed I did. You've spoken with her, then.

MELISSA: She has spoken certainly. I'm afraid I had trouble getting a word in edgeways.

WILLIAM: When you came in a little while ago, Mother, you looked like someone bearing good tidings.

MELISSA: (*almost turning away*) Della was my most difficult child, Will. I sometimes think your Brice takes after her. Headstrong, stubborn, indomitable, both of them.

WILLIAM: What is it, Mother. Let's not drag it out if we can help it.

MELISSA: Oh, Will, my greatest happiness would be if you two could be together again. If you could patch up all difference. If you could be as you were when you were going together.

WILLIAM: Yes, Mother, and if everything were not so changeable or, as the word we used a while ago, if everything were not transitory.

MELISSA: Will, I have spoken with her, I have poured myself out. Yes, I have pleaded to the point of, oh, I don't know to the point of what. She has closed herself off to me. Like a deaf woman.

WILLIAM: I knew it.

MELISSA: I would part with nearly everything I have to bring you two together. For your separation has brought a chill to my life, and early heavy bitter winter that will not go away. What has changed her, what is the terrible thing between you?

WILLIAM: If I knew, Mother, I would tell you.

MELISSA: I believe you. Yes, if you knew you would tell me.

WILLIAM: Then there is no hope at all?

MELISSA: Not according to her. She will not even reconsider asking you back. I have played my last card.

WILLIAM: Oh, Mother. Thank you anyhow. Your love I believe is all that sustains me. No, I mean it. You alone somehow keep me going.

MELISSA: Will, I stand ready and able to do all I can for you at any time, from here to the end. But I cannot move her, my own daughter from where she stands now.

WILLIAM: Mother, don't try. You've done your best. I can't ask more of you. But let me come to you from time to time. Let me partake of some of your goodness and love.

(WILLIAM *and* MELISSA *rise, and begin by taking hands, then they embrace at length.*)

MELISSA: You are like my own son, Will. Let me go on calling you Son. Don't cry, Will. Please please don't cry. You will break my heart. (*She turns to go.*)

WILLIAM: Just so I can see you, Mother, from time to time. I love your house and to see you sewing. I can't tell you what it does for me. I feel when I see you at work I have no cares or sorrow, I can go on and on.

MELISSA: Goodbye, Will. I think of you every hour. (*She goes out.*)

WILLIAM: (*picks up the photo*) Oh but Mother I have changed. You did not look at my face close enough. (*He buries his face in his hands.*) I have failed everyone but chiefly myself. I have not traveled one straight mile since my wedding day.

Scene 8

WILLIAM *has come to a near collapse after* MELISSA's *departure. For a while he walks aimlessly about the room muttering to himself, then exhausted from his torment, he slumps down in a chair and buries his face in his hand. He is unaware that* BRICE *has entered the room and is watching him.*

WILLIAM: (*taking his hands away from his face*) I could smell it on you, Brice.

BRICE: (*rudely impertinent*) What, Dad?

WILLIAM: You're chewing tobacco ain't you?

BRICE: I suppose. You object so to my smoking cigarettes. And thanks for bringing in your granddad's spittoon. (*He goes over to the cold shining spittoon and spits into it.*)

WILLIAM: He was your great grandfather too, don't forget.

BRICE: I'm surprised to see a grown man crying. . . . I can tell you.

WILLIAM: Well, be surprised then to hell and back. Tears are just as manly as tobacco juice in my book.

BRICE: (*sorry he has spoken so angrily*) I'm sure you're right . . . what is wrong Dad?

WILLIAM: Oh you've already heard me out a hundred times. Your grandmother was here.

BRICE: Down the street I ran into what's his name, that old guy at the sheriff's office.

WILLIAM: (*coming to attention*) You mean old Simeon.

BRICE: Yes. He said he had to see you about something. Had a sheaf of papers in both hands. He's on his way over.

WILLIAM: It never rains but it pours. *Simeon!* What in hell does he want out of me now.

BRICE: What did Grandma want, Dad?

WILLIAM: Grandma as always, Brice, wanted nothing. It's what I want I guess. Oh you must know the story by heart now. Grandma asked your mother if she would come back . . . to us.

BRICE: To you, you mean, Dad.

WILLIAM: All right, to me. Though if she came back or I went back or whoever went to whoever . . . she would come back to you.

BRICE: When I no longer need her.

WILLIAM: Brice, please wipe your mouth. (*He takes a handkerchief out of his breast pocket.*) You look a fright if old man Simeon is coming.

BRICE: You should use the handkerchief to dry your tears, Dad.

WILLIAM: Thanks again.

BRICE: (*takes the handkerchief and wipes his mouth indifferently*) There, is that good enough. Well, and are you and Mama going back together again then?

WILLIAM: You know the answer to that. She's not coming back to me. Or to you. To nobody. And besides they say she is closing down the rooming house.

BRICE: Can you believe it?

WILLIAM: I'm too troubled to believe anything. Why in hell does old man Simeon want to see me. What have I done now, damn it to hell. (*He rises and walks about aimlessly, there is a heavy rap at the door.*) You'd better leave, Brice. I don't know what it's about. (*He goes to the door and admits* SIMEON, *a man of advanced years, but who carries himself straight as an arrow.*)

SIMEON: I think that was a wise decision on your part, Will. (*He takes out a sheaf of papers from an inside coat pocket.*) Confidentiality is the ticket.

WILLIAM: (*nervously*) Mr. Simeon, is this a serious matter you have come on?

SIMEON: It's more than serious, Will, I'm afraid. And it's as great a surprise to me as I'm sure it must be to you. But Will, I hope you will forgive me for being the messenger of what's written down here. (*takes out the papers*)

WILLIAM: Let me see those papers. (*He takes the papers from* SIMEON.)

SIMEON: Everybody in the sheriff's office takes your part, Will.

WILLIAM: (*not having heard, reads the sheaf of papers angrily turning the pages and showing great turbulence, then looking up*) She's suing me for non-support, and gross negligence! For God's sake, who has put Della up to this, Simeon? Non-support! I've spent a fortune trying to keep her in the style her mother provided her. And as to gross negligence! (*swears under his breath*)

SIMEON: Will, you'll forgive an old man if I offer you something. I know you don't drink, Will (*pulls out a bottle*) but a sip or two of rye might help.

WILLIAM: No thank you, Simeon. (SIMEON *puts the bottle down on a table near where* WILLIAM *is sitting.*) I know you mean well. I've known you since I was a boy. You need not worry about our local superstition that the messenger is to be blamed for the bad news he brings. No, siree.

SIMEON: Will, take an old man's advice. Take a swig.

WILLIAM: (*stares at the bottle absentmindedly*) Simeon, tell me. How does a man proceed in a divorce case. Do you know, you must, since you've worked as a deputy since before the sheriff was even sheriff.

SIMEON: You can refuse to reply to Della's suit, Will. (*He picks up the papers and silently reads them.*) Or you can fight her and there will be a trial. You will probably lose and besides pay a lot of money to lawyers. (WILLIAM, *again absentminded as if he was not listening and with his eye on the bottle of liquor*) Do you want my advice, Will, since I have knowed you for so long a time, as you say, since you was a boy.

WILLIAM: (*bitter*) Yes, advice is what I need.

SIMEON: Then don't contest her suit.

WILLIAM: (*getting riled*) And let the whole world believe her charges are true!

SIMEON: Why care about the world, Will, since Della has already left you, and gone her own way.

WILLIAM: And what if I told the world of her own . . .

SIMEON: Her own what, Will. Be careful.

WILLIAM: That she keeps . . . a roadhouse.

SIMEON: But then wouldn't the judge think *you* should divorce *her* and not try to remain her husband.

WILLIAM: I don't know what in hell the judge will think. But I know what you think Simeon. You think I'm licked. (*He stares at the bottle of rye.*)

SIMEON: I don't think no such thing. I think you're the best young man I ever knew. But Will, listen here, you can't win a divorce case like this, and even if you won and cleared yourself of the charges do you think Della would want to live with you after the scandal of a trial in this small community, after which both your reputations will be black as the lowest ring of hell.

WILLIAM: And so, you mean to tell me, if I sit here stock still, she will have her divorce granted. And I will be known as a man who never supported her and (*looking at the papers*) grossly neglected her. (*rises*) She's a damn liar. A damned dirty liar. And she has disgraced her own name and mine by running a . . . She's disgraced her boy, disgrace . . . Brice.

SIMEON: Will, simmer down. (*He goes over to* WILLIAM *and takes his arm.*) Sit down, sir. (WILLIAM *sits down.*) And think before you speak. I believe I said that to you one day when you was having a fistfight with the older Starrett boy. Gabe Starrett, who died a hero after that in the war.

WILLIAM: I remember that fight yes, Simeon. I remember Gabe too. But I *won* the fistfight against him.

SIMEON: So you did. But your fistfightin' days should be over.

WILLIAM: Should they now, Simeon. (*laughs bitterly*) And my days with the fair sex should be over too. . . . I was looking in the mirror just the other day. My hair is getting on to being gray. I can tell you.

SIMEON: Aw, you've got more black in your hair than gray, Will.

WILLIAM: These damned papers (*touches them*) will turn me into a white-headed old . . .

SIMEON: (*picking up the bottle of rye*) Take a swig, for by Christ, if anybody ever needed it, you do. Go ahead. Take an old man's advice. (*He unseals the bottle and hands it to* WILLIAM.)

WILLIAM: (*tasting the rye*) God, it's worse than medicine. (*gives the bottle back to* SIMEON) Remember, Sim, I drank it only to please you.

SIMEON: Listen to what I say to you, Will. I'm old enough to be your dad, even your granddad. Drop it all, drop her, forget Della. Look after your boy. Listen here.

WILLIAM: Wait a minute now, Sim, wait a minute.

SIMEON: He's the one needs your help and your love, not Della. . . . Will, your boy is . . .

WILLIAM: I know all about Brice.

SIMEON: You think you do, Will. That boy is headed for bad trouble.

WILLIAM: (*absentmindedly, not listening*) No, Sim, you're looking at bad trouble when you look at me. These god damned papers. Do you know what they remind me of. A death warrant, that's right. A writ of execution for my death! God damn lawyers and judges.

SIMEON: You always loved her too much, Will, more than she loved you. Can't you give her up and tend to your son for a change. She don't need you, can't you get that through your head. Della don't need you!

WILLIAM: Quit it, Sim, keep your mouth closed for the flies are buzzing to let you swallow them. (*He picks up the bottle of rye, then slams it down on the table.*) I'm glad though Sim, you was the messenger. I can still feel gratitude, and I thank you for being the one who come here today with the bad news.

SIMEON: And what shall I tell the sheriff, then, Will?

WILLIAM: You tell him anything you like Sim.

SIMEON: You know the sheriff better than that. (*He picks up the papers as if to have his own question answered.*)

WILLIAM: You can tell the sheriff anything you please.

SIMEON: Will, let go of the past. Look after Brice. He's the needful one!

WILLIAM: (*speaking gravely, slowly*) Goodbye, Sim . . . go on now, I mean it. I am giving you goodbye. You can tell the sheriff Will Hawkins is through with everything and everybody. . . . So go please, and thank you, thank you, Sim, for being the only messenger I could stomach. But go—leave me! and take your bottle with you. Go ahead. (*offers him the bottle which* SIMEON *does not take*)

SIMEON: (*going toward the door, his back to* WILLIAM) I will tell the sheriff you don't know yet if you'll contest or not. And that you will be looking after your boy.

WILLIAM: I've already said goodbye and thanked you. (*He takes the bottle of rye in his hand as* SIMEON *exits.*)

Scene 9

MELISSA's *house.* MELISSA *and* WILLIAM *are in animated conversation.*

MELISSA: Don't talk nonsense, Will. I wouldn't mind if you came here to see me every day. And do you know something, I wouldn't mind at all if you moved in here with me! There! I've said it. The whole upstairs is vacant. But I know what you are going to say: what would Della think, what would they think in town, and so on, if you were to move in with me!

WILLIAM: Let me say it again, though the last time I said it you told me never to . . .

MELISSA: *Never to say it again*. Well, say it. Or I'll say it for you. What would you do without me. What would I do without you, though. Why don't you think of that.

WILLIAM: You really mean that, I believe, Mother.

MELISSA: Of course Della and I are close. Have always been. Too close. But the minute I see you, Will, I feel I have the strength to go on for a while longer. I know, *I know*. You're going to say all the trouble you've caused me. But the trouble was spent in a good cause.

WILLIAM: I can't agree with you there, Mother. I've given you nothing but sorrow. And again, yes again that's why I'm here. To give you new worries. I have no one else to turn to.

MELISSA: And do you know, Will, I'm glad I don't have to share you with anybody.

WILLIAM: What a strange thing to say. And when you said it I felt a wonderful warm feeling (*touches his heart*) that I guess I feel only with you. The rest of the world blows ice and freezing cold clouds.

MELISSA: Sit here, Will, so the light can fall on your face. And I'll sit close by. Then we can talk to our hearts content. I often think that in the life to come all we will have to do is talk with loved ones. There'll be no time or pain or tears, we will remember everything that has passed and we will speak of it all with our dear ones.

WILLIAM: (*sitting down and listening to* MELISSA) Go on, go on. Don't stop. And while you speak I'll try to collect my thoughts. (*to himself*) How to tell her, how to get the damned words out! Without their choking me to death.

MELISSA: There you go again, Will, mumbling like an old man, when you're the picture of a strong young man in his prime. Oh, Della used to complain you were always mumbling and muttering and talking to yourself.

WILLIAM: It's a habit I could never break myself of, Mother.

MELISSA: I think I know why you're muttering. Shall I tell you?

WILLIAM: I'll tell you, Mother. They've served the papers on me. The divorce settlement papers! She's not content now with our being separated. She wants the knot severed for once and all. That word *freedom*! It's like wildfire in her veins. She talked about freedom the first night we were married. I stared at her openmouthed.

MELISSA: Yes, since a girl, she's had that word on her lips. And where will you find freedom, I used to scold her when she would threaten to run away as a girl of only fourteen. Do you think you'll find it by leaving those who love you most, I would yell at her. It's her religion. Freedom, being free, running away.

WILLIAM: (*after a struggle*) Shall I contest it, Mother? That's why I've come to you. Shall I put up a fight?

MELISSA: (*suddenly old, hard of hearing*) Shall you what?

WILLIAM: (*almost angry*) Contest the divorce settlement! Go to court against her. Don't you understand. Mother! (*fearing she has had a sudden mental collapse*)

MELISSA: You needn't shout, Will. I hear you perfectly. It suddenly takes its toll. (*this last to herself*) Will, listen. Of course I knew she was filing divorce proceedings. I tried to blot it out of mind. I told her not to. Let separation be enough, Della, I said. Don't waste more grief and money on lawyers and judges and make your name and your person something folks can look down on. (*pauses*) So she *has* filed proceedings.

WILLIAM: (*rises*) And what am I to do. You tell me. And whatever you tell me, Mother, I'll follow your advice.

MELISSA: Look at him, would you! You're nothing but an overgrown boy, aren't you. (*laughs*) My husband George was the same. In the end, when something serious would come along, something worrisome, he turned like you into a big overgrown frightened boy. . . . (*a long pause*) And what do you want me to say, Will? I'm to act the Sibyl for you again.

WILLIAM: (*almost incoherent in his pain*) Act anything you like, just give me the word. It will satisfy me.

MELISSA: No, it won't. You are after all like Della. Self-willed, stubborn, bullheaded. You always wanted to bend her to your own way of seeing things.

WILLIAM: Bend Della? As soon try to tame those damned wild horses Brice is always talking about.

MELISSA: Don't contest the suit.

WILLIAM: What! Mother? Am I hearing you right. Or are you talking in your sleep.

MELISSA: I'll say it again. Don't contest the suit.

WILLIAM: You mean admit I'm licked.

MELISSA: Not licked, no! But a prudent and a strong man doesn't fight when there is no chance of winning. Only a fool does that.

WILLIAM: Do you remember Mother when you lent me the seventy-five thousand dollars.

MELISSA: For God's sake never mention that again. It's the only secret I've ever kept from Della.

WILLIAM: Then you remember it, Mother, to my shame and your folly. For I know it was your lending me that money that brought us all to this . . .

MELISSA: (*sourly*) To genteel poverty the lawyers call it.

WILLIAM: Threadbare is more like it. I ruined you, Mother, and my ruin spoiled my marriage to Della.

MELISSA: But you've come back. Will. You've not gone down.

WILLIAM: I've lost everything but your love, Mother.

45

MELISSA: I didn't hear that. Instead I heard your son's name, Brice.

WILLIAM: Brice judges me. Hard, hard.

MELISSA: But he judges you because you're all he has.

WILLIAM: And he has? And what about . . . Della.

MELISSA: I said what I said.

WILLIAM: Then I'm not to contest it?

MELISSA: I didn't say that, exactly. She wants you to fight it. Della always has loved a fight. If you contest it, the lawsuit could last in Judge Duncan's gloomy old high-ceilinged courtroom for days on end. And you will lose of course. She has kept all the records of your not supporting her while you roamed the country looking for a fortune. She will . . .

WILLIAM: All right, she will tar and feather me, why not say it.

MELISSA: Certainly disgrace all of us. And then, Will, it will come out . . .

WILLIAM: Can there be more?

MELISSA: With Della there is always more. She doesn't know the word stop or yield. She wants to break you.

WILLIAM: (*again muttering*) Break the broken! All right, I won't do it then. I'll be a quitter. For you.

MELISSA: Don't put it on me. Don't you say what you're going to say either. I'm not commanding you. Go ahead and contest . . . and lose Brice.

WILLIAM: Let me tell you, I've lost Brice.

MELISSA: But you can get him back.

WILLIAM: How in . . . hell can that be. Have you watched his face when he hears my name? Have you?

MELISSA: He has only one father. All you have to do is claim him.

WILLIAM: I've tried.

MELISSA: Not hard enough. Where are those divorce papers?

WILLIAM: Here against my rib cage where they're chewing the flesh out of me. (*pulls the papers out and hands them to* MELISSA)

MELISSA: You can choose, Will. See the grate over there, and the long Blue Devil box of matches by the side of it. Do you? (WILLIAM *takes the divorce proceedings papers from her.*) It's up to you, not me. I've said my say.

WILLIAM: And you think if I fight I'll lose my boy.

MELISSA: Yes, him and you'll lose yourself in the bargain.

WILLIAM: And I won't get her back after all.

MELISSA: Oh, supposing you won, and in your victory she came back to you. Would you have Della then for your wife. No, not Della. You would have a dead woman by your side. Oh you men! God in heaven. Was there ever a breed so deaf and dumb. Go ahead fight her.

(WILLIAM *walks like a sleepwalker toward the grate. He picks up the box of Blue Devil matches, and strikes one, then slowly sets fire to the divorce proceedings papers.*)

WILLIAM: (*slowly coming back to* MELISSA *but still watching the papers burn*) It's true, Mother. I feel a load off my shoulders already. If I've done the wrong thing, it feels like the right thing. I feel what Della is always talking about, Mother, her word. I feel *free*. (*He kneels down and puts his head in* MELISSA's *lap.*)

MELISSA: It's strange, Will, but those papers are giving off a kind of sweet pleasant smell, like pine cones, or forest dry leaves. And don't come tomorrow and tell me you regret it, either. My how they burn. All those words and highfalutin' phrases, all that lawyer talk, and threats and jargon. To think it can give off such a pleasant smell from its ashes.

ACT II

Scene 1

WILLIAM's *house.* LILA *and* WILLIAM *in animated conversation.* WILLIAM *is in his undershirt while putting on a shirt.*

LILA: I had no idea. I know it's too late for visitors, Will. . . . Please don't look so terribly amazed. You'll drive me out with a look like that!

WILLIAM: I'm not amazed. I feel I'm dreaming. I've often in fact dreamed, Lila, you paid me a visit. When you came in just now I felt . . .

LILA: The dream had come true. May I sit down for a moment. Then I'll be gone.

WILLIAM: A moment! Then I'll be sure I dreamed it all.

LILA: (*seeing the bottle*) Will, don't tell me you are drinking. I don't think anybody in town has been spared your lectures against whiskey.

WILLIAM: I daresay. This happens to be a gift of old Simeon. Yes, I taste it now and then. It's the rottenest taste in the world if you ask me. But I've had such bad news, Lila, and even our friend, the great Upton Sinclair—he wrote *The Jungle* you know—Upton Sinclair who is as much opposed to strong drink as the ladies of the W.C.T.U.—says in case of exposure or sudden shock, a taste of whiskey will do no harm. As medicine, he means. As medicine.

LILA: (*laughs*) I'll tell no one, Will. But let me tell you why I've come and at such a late hour. I've learned the news. Will you forgive me for mentioning it, I see my doing so has upset you.

WILLIAM: You haven't upset me, now. I'm glad you mentioned it, or who knows, without your visit, I might have gone through the whole bottle of rye. . . . Lila, I once heard or read somewhere, maybe it was in the pages of Mr. Upton Sinclair, small communities are full of more pitfalls than a jungle of wild carnivores. Your coming here tonight so late, dear girl, may set tongues a-wagging.

LILA: Well, let them.

WILLIAM: Why not let them, Lila. (*pushes the bottle of rye away and rises, walking about the room*)

LILA: I hope and pray, that Della will . . . change her mind.

WILLIAM: (*turning to face her*) Della, change her mind? Della doesn't need to even if she wanted to. Change! (*pauses in turmoil*) She can't change her mind anyhow Lila. Shall I tell you why. I've burned the divorce settlement papers old Simeon fetched me from the court. Burned them at Melissa's house. So for all practical purposes Della is already a free woman, don't you see. For I won't contest her suit.

LILA: You don't mean you agree to . . . a divorce.

WILLIAM: I don't know that is the way to put it, Lila. Does a man agree to be hanged? Let's say I've thrown up the sponge. I'm licked good and proper where my dear Della is concerned.

LILA: I hoped somehow you *would* . . . contest it, Will. Here I am speaking about matters I have no right to speak of. But now I've said what I've said.

WILLIAM: Finish your statement, Lila. Don't mind me.

LILA: I hoped you'd contest it, and win, and then . . . I hoped that Della would reconsider and come back to you.

WILLIAM: You not only seemed like a dream tonight coming in, Lila, you are talking dream talk. Moonshine . . . Tommyrot!

LILA: I'm sorry, Will. Forgive me. I see I'm talking foolishly. After all an old maid like me, what can I know of what married folks go through.

WILLIAM: An old maid, Lila? I never saw you as such. A maid possibly, and a beautiful one at that. I think you could make some man very happy if there was one good enough in this town for you.

LILA: Oh, Will, I'm afraid I have no rejoinder to your compliments. Thank you just the same. I must be going now. (*rises*)

WILLIAM: Please, Lila. Stay just a while longer. You don't know how much your coming means to me. Stay, please. Don't you run out on me. (*LILA sits down hesitantly.*) I think the world of you. Perhaps that sounds silly.

LILA: Nothing you ever say sounds silly. I wish I could do something for you . . . and for Della.

WILLIAM: Oh leave Della out of it, Lila. She wouldn't want anybody to do good for her. She wants to do all the good there is for herself. She rules, and the rest of the world must kneel.

LILA: Then let me do anything I can for you, Will.

WILLIAM: Lila, would you give me . . . excuse me for asking . . . would you give me one kiss before you go. Not the kind of kiss you're maybe thinking but it would do me the world of good you mentioned. But if you don't feel it's proper, don't. Forgive me for asking. Forget it. I can see I've said the wrong thing.

LILA: (*greatly upset*) I will be going, Will, now. Call me if you ever should need anything.

(*They have both risen and LILA is turning away. WILLIAM suddenly takes LILA in his arms and kisses her, then carried away he holds her to him and covers her face with kisses.*)

LILA: (*freeing herself*) Will, please, don't spoil everything.

WILLIAM: Why can't you love me, when Della no longer does. Lila, why can't you make this evening something for both of us. Why should everybody else know happiness but us. Answer me, for God's sake!

LILA: I would never forgive myself, Will, if I did. After all I am Della's friend.

WILLIAM: Della's friend! Merciful Christ! And what has she ever done for you, Lila. Or for anybody but herself. Don't you understand I'm not hers anymore, I'm death itself where she is concerned. Lila, give me your love.

LILA: Will, let's not go on! (*rushes from him*) We will meet again when things are quieter.

WILLIAM: Things will never be quiet when I see you Lila. Don't you understand what you have brought me to tonight. (*He takes her in his arms.*)

LILA: You're hurting me, Will. (*He suddenly seizes her and tears her dress; they struggle.*) You've got to stop this. I can't allow you to do this. Don't you understand! (*He exposes her breasts and begins to kiss them like one famished. She pummels him with her fists as one who beats against a door. He seizes her.*)

WILLIAM: I know you want me Lila. (*He holds her as she struggles, making weeping and sobbing sounds.*) God you're beautiful. I might have known you'd be beautiful. Let me. Let me. You must let me. Now I've seen you I can't let you leave me. (*LILA strikes him; he grasps her more tightly.*) No, Lila. You've gone this far, I can't give you up now. (*He pushes her down on the davenport.*) You can make us both very happy. (*She kicks him and when he still will not let go of her; she claws him with both hands near his eyes bringing blood. She breaks away and grabs the bottle and threatens him with it.*)

LILA: Don't you dare touch me again. (*WILLIAM retreats, takes out a large white handkerchief from his hip pocket and begins wiping off the copious streams of blood. LILA puts down the bottle.*) I hope you realize you've spoiled everything now. I don't think I can ever set eyes on you again.

WILLIAM: Don't leave in anger. After all, why in hell did you have to come here at such an hour. And when you must have seen I was in such a state.

LILA: That's right, blame me. That's the man for you. Blame me all you want.

WILLIAM: Oh Lila, for God's sake, look at me.

LILA: All right. All right, I'm looking. But for God's sake let me go.

WILLIAM: And you'll pardon me.

LILA: Pardon you! (*pause*) I suppose I will whoever is to blame. You let me go home, I've got to get some calm and rest. (*She gives him one last look, then goes out.* WILLIAM *goes on wiping the blood from his face.*)

WILLIAM: What a damn streak of luck on top of all the other rotten turns. (*He picks up the bottle.*) Mr. Sinclair, this is a time for medicine. (*He takes a swig out of the bottle.*)

Scene 2

DELLA's *house.* BARNEY *is attempting to kiss* DELLA *and is rebuffed.*

BARNEY: No kiss for your best boyfriend, tonight. Look here. (*He is suddenly angry.*)

DELLA: I'm not in the mood, Barney. (BARNEY *takes hold of her and kisses her; she breaks away.*) I said I was not in the mood. I should slap you for that.

BARNEY: (*said half jokingly*) Don't you try it sweetheart.

DELLA: Barney, forgive me, I am overwrought tonight.

BARNEY: I'd hate to be around you then when you really go to pieces. Did you give Will this kind of welcome when he tried to steal a kiss?

DELLA: I suppose you've heard the news, for you were grinning all over when you came in.

BARNEY: Yes, I've heard the news. The whole town has heard the news. Even Will must have heard it, though I guess he's going steady with the music teacher.

DELLA: What do you mean by that?

BARNEY: What do I mean by it? Just what I said. He's going steady with the music teacher.

DELLA: You must be mistaken. He couldn't care for a woman . . . that plain . . . and old.

BARNEY: Old? Why she can't be more than our age.

DELLA: Your age you mean. (*moved*) He's doing it for spite of course. He couldn't care for anyone like her.

BARNEY: Tell me something, Della, and then I'll be leaving you for I can see you're not yourself tonight.

DELLA: (*almost to herself*) I haven't been myself maybe for some time.

BARNEY: Since you left Will don't you mean.

DELLA: Don't put words in my mouth. I warn you.

BARNEY: (*takes hold of her hand roughly*) Don't yell at me. Nobody yells at Barney Comstock, man woman or child for your information.

DELLA: Maybe you have too high an opinion of yourself. That is one reason we don't get along.

BARNEY: Well now that the divorce papers are signed and in Will's hands let me say something. Maybe Will wasn't the only cold fish in your marriage. And another thing, no don't interrupt me. I think I know what's eating you tonight along with your customary coldness, or I believe the word is frigidity.

DELLA: You be careful.

BARNEY: I'm tired of being careful around you. Knowing you is about as comfortable as walking on eggs. Now you listen to me.

DELLA: I won't listen and don't you say any more on this subject, do you hear.

BARNEY: Do you know what I think. I think you're scared and sorry as hell you instituted divorce proceedings. And another thing—

DELLA: (*almost hysterical*) Barney! Please stop.

BARNEY: And the other thing is this, you're still in love with your Will. And next to your Will is your Brice, whom you've spoiled and petted and turned into . . .

DELLA: (*strikes him*) Stop this talk or leave.

BARNEY: Not till I'm finished speaking my piece.

DELLA: You have the nerve to stand there and tell me I'm in love with a man who brought me more sorrow than a hundred husbands.

BARNEY: And the reason you felt the sorrow was because you would rather have sorrow from Will than all the caresses of a real man. Of course you love him. Of course you care. And of course you miss him every hour of the day. . . . Now go to the courthouse why don't you and stop the proceedings. (*DELLA sits down heavily and begins to weep; BARNEY goes over to her.*) Della, I'm sorry. I mean it.

DELLA: Just leave. Just go. For pity's sake.

BARNEY: I shouldn't have spoken the way I did. I apologize.

DELLA: Just go please. You've done enough damage for one evening. Leave me be in peace.

BARNEY: I love you, Della. I want to make up for all . . . your sorrow.

DELLA: By giving me more you mean. That's all men are good for in the long run.

BARNEY: You've never let me really have you. And you don't know what that has done to me. I'm starved for your love and you know that. Come away with me. We don't even have to be married if you like. Let's go away together. Forget this town and everybody in it. (*He kneels down and takes her hand in his and kisses it in a fervent manner.*)

DELLA: I'm too upset to know what to say or do.

BARNEY: Then give me your sorrow and your confidence. Be the way we were at the beginning of our love. Why are you so cold to the one man who would give his all for you, Della.

DELLA: I don't know, Barney, I don't know. I feel I have taken the wrong path.

BARNEY: No, no. You've taken the right one if you'll let me be your . . .

DELLA: Don't say anymore, Barney. Please leave me. I'm broken. Can't you see. I'm broken. (BARNEY *takes her in his arms.*)

Scene 3

MELISSA *and* LILA REECE *are in agitated conversation.*

MELISSA: I knew you would come. I wanted you to come. So don't say my dear, you are imposing. It's too late for such talk between us.

LILA: But I don't think you understand, Melissa. I did not come for myself. After all, think how you helped me so long ago! You rescued me.

MELISSA: I told you, Lila, we would never mention that again. You owe me nothing.

LILA: But I want to mention it. Why can't you let someone thank you. You give to everyone and you should be thanked.

MELISSA: Just to see you here is thanks enough. (*She goes over to* LILA *and kisses her tenderly.*)

LILA: Oh thank you, thank you. (*a pause*) So it's all over town then.

MELISSA: Of course. What did you expect.

LILA: (*almost to herself*) But how did they find out?

MELISSA: Thoughts themselves are wings in this town. Just a look, a certain expression, a certain kind of laugh or shy glance sets the tongues to wagging. Yes, everybody knows or pretends to know all about you and William.

LILA: Then if I'm not to thank you for how you saved me so many years ago, let me tell you what happened. Not just for my sake. I don't seem to care about *my sake*. I'm troubled over William.

MELISSA: *You're* troubled! We're all troubled.

LILA: Oh how I wish though you would let me thank you for what happened so many years ago. My . . . encounter with William brought it all back. Then another handsome man ruined me. And it was only your stepping in that prevented me from going down to total ruin . . .

MELISSA: I have often thought that maybe I was wrong, Lila. Maybe you should have had the baby and faced the town. And I would have faced the town with you.

LILA: You would have gone down then with me.

MELISSA: No, perhaps not. You would have had your baby and you and I would have outlived their tongues, and their hate. Instead with my assistance you went to New York and had the abortion.

LILA: Yes, maybe I should have had the baby. But I have learned to accept it as my only way out now. I am not as strong as you Melissa, remember that.

MELISSA: That is how you see things. You should know how I see myself. I am a walking, confused, even a hypocritical old woman. And I meddle. I meddle in other people's lives.

LILA: But you save them too.

(A *long pause.*)

MELISSA: Yes. Tell me what happened. For there's one thing I don't share with the town. My tongue is a silent one.

LILA: Well to go back to what happened between Will and me. I was so confounded by the change in him that I was unaware I had walked into real danger. He looked like a man who had fallen headlong into a pitch-black gulf. Then in our struggle I kept staring at him as if a stranger had come into view. I felt almost as if a wild horse had rushed into the room. . . . He was utterly unlike the Will I knew. I will never forget it. And I will never forgive myself for having called on him at such a late hour.

MELISSA: Ah, well, we can argue about blame to the end of our days, Lila. I sometimes think in my own case every important action I have taken was the wrong one. How are we always to know right from wrong in the turmoil of living, I ask you.

LILA: Unbelievable as it may sound, I am sorriest for Will. He has fallen from such a height! Yes, (*as if not having heard anything they have been saying*) the late hour, the coming divorce, his own worry over his son and that fool of a Simeon having left whiskey in his hands. Or who knows, maybe it is all destiny that is the culprit.

MELISSA: (*almost inaudible*) So then he forced himself on you.

LILA: Oh it was worse than that.

MELISSA: Worse?

LILA: (*passing her hand over her eyes momentarily*) We were fighting one another as if for our lives. I hated him so desperately at that moment, but I hated myself more. I hated I think the whole human race. Certainly my own life I held in abhorrence. (*begins to break*)

MELISSA: You may stop, Lila, if you wish. I think I understand what you are feeling.

LILA: No one understands who has not been there. Forgive me for saying so. No one! (*She stands up and paces about the room.*)

MELISSA: Come over here, Lila. Sit closer to me. Listen. I am so glad you have come here today. I know how heavy a burden has fallen on you. . . . But listen. It is not the end of the world. It seems so now, perhaps most of all to you. You cannot even understand your own pain. But it will pass.

LILA: Oh, if I could only believe that, Melissa. When the pain of it weighs heavier than time itself. Everything else seems obliterated by this conflict. I can barely breathe for thinking of it all. I blame myself constantly, yet what could I have done.

MELISSA: You don't need to say any more, Lila. But you've done right to come here. You spoke of your concern for Will but I am deeply concerned for you.

LILA: I don't know how I would get through this if I couldn't depend on you.

(*They embrace as the lights go down.*)

Scene 4

MELISSA's *house a short while later.* LILA REECE *and* MELISSA *are seated as the lights come up as* DELLA *enters.*

DELLA: I knew I'd find you here, Lila. . . . (*trying to compose herself*) Everyone comes to Mother when there is trouble, don't they Mother.

MELISSA: Sit down, Della. (*spoken rather sharply*) Lila and I have had a very good talk. (*then, more sharply*) Sit down. You look terribly troubled, dear. (*rises*) Let me put a comb through your hair, it's looking so unlike you. (*puts the comb to her hair*)

DELLA: Oh leave my hair alone, Mother. What difference does it make how I look.

MELISSA: (*going on combing*) It makes a lot of difference to me how my little girl looks . . . and to Lila here, I'm sure.

DELLA: (*angry*) Oh leave her out of it, Mother. I came to see you after all. If Lila has had her say, she can leave.

LILA: (*rising*) Della is right, Melissa. I have burdened you enough already with my problem.

DELLA: (*almost pushing* MELISSA *away*) And what is your problem this time, Lila, if I may ask.

MELISSA: Oh, Della, for heaven's sake, let's not have anymore unpleasantness than there has been. Lila has gone through a great deal, let me tell you. We've had a real talk today.

DELLA: But I haven't had my talk with her, Mother, have I, Lila.

LILA: I think you know we have not.

DELLA: And why should I not be brought into the secret of it all since it concerns Will Hawkins, my husband. Who is there more concerned in it all than me, I ask both of you. For I know what Lila's problem is. It's all over town as if carried by banners and sound trucks. (*breaks momentarily*)

MELISSA: Della, think before you speak.

DELLA: Yes, you two can be calm and collected, because as a matter of fact, what has Will Hawkins ever done to you two compared to what he has done to me. You will find no calm and collected answer to that question. . . . So speak up, Lila, speak up. Sit down, for after all we may have quite a lot to say to one another.

LILA: Della, I am as sorry for you as I can be.

DELLA: I don't need your being sorry for me, Lila . . . what have you done to my husband, that is what I think you owe me an explanation for. . . . Is all the talk in the town, the saloons and pool parlors and the streets true?

LILA: Oh, Della, perhaps Melissa could best answer you. I have told her everything.

DELLA: But you have not told me, Will's wife, have you. Why should my long-suffering Mother hear it from you and not his more than long-suffering wife, will you tell me? (*rises*) Answer me. . . . If rumor is true, you have never been the spotless maiden you have led the town to consider you. . . . You are not now and never were pure as the fresh fallen snow, Lila Reece.

LILA: Oh, Melissa, perhaps I had best be going.

DELLA: You shall not leave until you have answered my questions. . . . What were you doing at Will Hawkins' house in the dead of night? Will you tell me?

LILA: Della, it was hardly the dead of night. (*a long pause*) Very well, I will tell you. I went because I had caught sight of him on the street several times. The change in his appearance was shocking.

DELLA: Not as shocking as the change in appearance of his wife and boy, perhaps.

LILA: After all I have known Will as long as you have, Della. I felt as a friend—

DELLA: Shouldn't you say as a lover, Lila. For I know you have always loved Will Hawkins. Even perhaps before I was fool enough to love him.

LILA: (*suddenly stung to anger*) And so what if I did love him . . . once. But the love I may have born him was a silent one, and a pure one.

DELLA: But silent pure love can be more passionate than married love I am told.

LILA: (*angry*) And where did you find that out?

DELLA: By watching for years and years a certain music teacher.

LILA: You are being most unfair to me. You are condemning me and branding me guilty before you have heard or found out what happened between Will and me.

DELLA: You went to a married man's rooms at a late hour, a woman whose one time moral dereliction is known to Mother and me!

MELISSA: Della, stop right there. I will have no more of this!

DELLA: (*going forward with even greater anger*) I say everyone who knows Lila Reece, knows why you went away fifteen years ago. And you dare talk of silent, pure love, when you had an abortion in New York and then reappeared here as a spotless pure virgin. Which of your characters did you take on when you visited Will Hawkins at midnight, will you tell me . . . You went there not as a good Samaritan, but as a woman who wanted to offer herself to him!

MELISSA: Will you be silent, Della! Or I will ask you to leave. This is my house, and Lila is my guest.

DELLA: As for you, Mother, you have always taken Will Hawkins' part, haven't you. Always stood up for him. Always loved him more than you loved me. For you never truly loved me. And now you poured out more sympathy on this slut, Lila Reece, than you ever gave me. . . . She went to Will the other night for only one reason . . . sympathy, condolence, be damned. She went for love. And then when she had aroused him with her condolence and pity, and he took her in his arms, she got cold feet. And resumed her old role as the spotless virgin! You make me sick, both of you, Lila for her hypocrisy and you Mother, for pouring out the love and tenderness you never had for your own daughter. Very well, you two. Continue your little game of heartthrob and tears. See if I care.

MELISSA: Della, I beg you. Try to get hold of yourself for God's sake, try to understand for once. I feel Lila is telling the truth. . . . And where are you rushing to now in this terrible rage you are in. Sit down and collect yourself.

DELLA: Don't touch me, Mother. Don't ever touch me again. I am going to Will and have it out with him for once and all. . . . And I am taking Brice away from him. Do you hear. Will is not fit to be with my son after this final disgrace perpetrated by our pious butter-won't-melt-in-her-mouth maiden, Lila Reece. Let her pull the wool over your eyes, Mother, but I have always seen through her role playing. (*She rushes out.*)

MELISSA: (*walks over to where* LILA *has nearly collapsed in her chair*) See here, I believe you, and I love you. Of course I love Della too . . . But she has always been incorrigible since a young child. Today you have seen what I have always had to put up with. Della doesn't want love from other human beings. She wants enslavement and servitude from those she loves, acquiescence, compliance, no naysaying, only surrender, surrender! And then when the man has given her all she is bored and tired of him and sends him away. (*seeing* LILA's *condition*) My dear girl, wait here a moment. Don't get up. I will bring you something. (*She goes to a nearby cabinet and pours some brandy.*) Drink this, Lila, drink all of it. (LILA *drinks.*) You must not leave when you are so overwrought, my dear. Come with me in the next room and lie down for a while. . . . Please. (*leads* LILA *into the next room*)

Scene 5

EDGARS *and* BRICE.

EDGARS: I'm not in a bad temper, Brice. Not at all. I'm only saying again what I've said before.

BRICE: Then don't say it again, damn it all to hell!

EDGARS: I've never seen you in such a mood. And where have you been the last few days? Your dad says you're never home now.

BRICE: I'm practicing maybe never to be home. Did you ever think of that! Christ!

EDGARS: Are you goin' to start that line about you runnin' off again?

BRICE: Okay, I'll tell you where I went after what happened here. Or maybe I won't tell you.

EDGARS: I'm not goin' to coax it out of you. I think I know anyhow.

BRICE: Supposin' you tell me then since you're so smart.

EDGARS: All right. (*laughs angrily*) You went up north to the place where the hoboes keep camp.

BRICE: (*surprised by the truth*) And?

EDGARS: And? Don't I get a reward for guessin' where you were.

BRICE: Maybe, maybe not. It wasn't though, Edgars, the hoboes that absorbed up all my attention.

EDGARS: You've been runnin' up there to their camp so long no wonder.

BRICE: I saw all of the wild horses there.

EDGARS: (*surprised*) Oh go on. Pullin' my leg. Brice, quit it.

BRICE: I saw them! As close as you—even up where they have their bonfires—the horses were at their camp, the hoboes' camp! And listen . . . the wild horses—they don't act wild around those men. It's as though the hoboes are kith and kin to them. And even I could touch one of the smaller horses and he didn't snort or kick or run.

EDGARS: Now you're tellin' me one aren't you?

BRICE: Believe it or not.

EDGARS: (*alarmed*) Brice, you wouldn't be . . .

BRICE: Yes, maybe I would be lighting out! Yes! I think the day will come and soon . . . (*aroused*) Why shouldn't I go with the . . . tramps. How could it be worse than being around my dad and my mother. Time out of mind.

EDGARS: You'd never last with them for God's sake. And even if you lasted, how do you know they wouldn't kill you. After all you ain't one of them. They would never accept you as one of them anymore than the gypsies around here would accept you as one of them. Maybe the wild horses might be tame around the hoboes, but I don't think that's a good sign either.

BRICE: Look here, don't you go tellin' my dad or anybody else around here what I've told you. Don't you give anybody even an inkling of what we've said today. Not a word!

EDGARS: You know me better than that, Brice. What do you take me for?

BRICE: All right, I believe you. I can't stay here, that's all I know.

EDGARS: Well, okay. . . . You can't stand it here, but don't be a bigger damned fool and start hopping freight cars with . . . (WILLIAM *enters,* EDGARS *is alarmed at* WILLIAM's *appearance, for his face is showing the cuts and gashes inflicted on him by* LILA REECE.) Good evenin' Mr. Hawkins.

WILLIAM: (*in a muffled voice*) Hello, Edgars. What have you two fellows been up to?

BRICE: Hello, Dad. Oh, we've been chewing the rag, to use one of your expressions, haven't we, Edgars.

EDGARS: I've got to be going, Mr. Hawkins. I'm already late for supper.

WILLIAM: You always leave it seems to me, Edgars, the minute our paths cross.

EDGARS: I'm afraid that's so, Mr. Hawkins. But it's not intentional. Brice can vouch for me on that.

WILLIAM: All right, then, run along. Don't miss one of your mother's suppers. Everybody is always saying she sets the best table in town. Goodbye, son. (*He shakes hands with* EDGARS; EDGARS *exits.*)

WILLIAM: That boy always acts as if he couldn't wait to light out every time he sees me. I suppose like everybody else Edgars has heard all the news.

BRICE: (*deeply troubled*) Oh, Dad. Why talk about it.

WILLIAM: (*getting riled*) I suppose he discussed it all with you.

BRICE: (*acidly*) No, we had other things to talk about.

WILLIAM: (*sarcastic*) More important things of course . . . (*almost raging*) Well, what are they saying, Brice. And where have you been keeping yourself? Your mother keeps sending messages through your grandmother—where on earth is Brice at this juncture?

BRICE: Juncture? What a funny word to describe it with.

WILLIAM: Your mother is threatening to take you away from me. She's on her way over here now.

BRICE: And if she took me away from you, where would she put me do you suppose. In that fun house of hers.

WILLIAM: Is it that bad, you mean?

BRICE: (*regretting he has spoken against his mother*) Oh, who knows what kind of a house it was. I wish I could run a thousand miles to nowhere.

WILLIAM: You said once living here was nowhere.

BRICE: (*almost near tears*) I did, did I. Well I'm sorry.

WILLIAM: Don't be sorry if that's how you feel. . . . I know I've disappointed the start. And now this ruckus over Miss Reece. God damn it. Will bad luck never run out on me. Why in hell did she have to show up when I was in the shape I was in.

BRICE: What really went on here Dad? I think I have a right to know.

WILLIAM: What have you heard? What has she told everyone? God damn the whole female race. The minute they open their mouths the lies come forth. We had a misunderstanding.

BRICE: A misunderstanding?

WILLIAM: I offered her my love and she tried to claw my eyes out. She was afraid of letting someone care for her, give himself to her. So we quarreled. I don't remember exactly what happened. She clawed me I think after I had kissed her with too much feeling. Don't turn away from me Brice, I'm telling you the truth.

BRICE: Were you drinking that liquor you always told me you never drank and that I should never drink?

WILLIAM: Well I still hold to that. But Brice that was then and this is now.

BRICE: Please don't drink that stuff. Let me throw it out.

WILLIAM: By and by you can. Right now it's medicine for what is wrong with me. Besides I could never make a habit of anything that tastes like that.

BRICE: And you won't . . . contest the suit, as the lawyers phrase it?

WILLIAM: Contest the suit now, after all they've tarred and feathered me with. And what would I contest with, will you tell me. Next to dying and being buried a lawsuit can cost all a man has to his name. So your mother will soon be free.

BRICE: I'll stay with you, Dad, if you want me to. I won't run off . . . on you.

WILLIAM: I don't like the way you say that, Brice. . . . You scare me. Why would you want to run off, and *where*, will you tell me . . . You've never been anywhere but here. Do you have an inkling of what the world is beyond this little burg you were born and raised in? (*a long pause*) All right, don't reply.

(DELLA *enters.*)

DELLA: (*in a rage*) Brice, where in creation have you been all this time? Your grandmother and I have been frantic looking for you everywhere.

BRICE: Oh you couldn't have looked very hard then. I've been right here.

DELLA: Don't you give me any of your lip, young man. You've not been here. (*pauses*) But I came here to have a word with your father. You had better go on to your grandmother's while Will and I talk.

WILLIAM: He can stay so far as I am concerned, Della.

DELLA: Brice is where *I* am concerned, from now on.

WILLIAM: Oh, is that so. Well why don't you ask him then, or don't you know a boy's place is with his father as even your lawyers may get around to tell you. What do you say to that, Brice?

BRICE: What can I say, Dad . . . (*hangs his head*) If you'll both excuse me, I think I will go for a breath of air. . . . Goodbye, Mother . . . (*DELLA turns away from him.*) Goodbye Dad.

WILLIAM: Well don't make it sound like you're joining the army, Brice. Come back in an hour and we'll straighten things out.

(*BRICE exits.*)

DELLA: Do you know where your son has been these past days.

WILLIAM: No, I do not know where *your* son has been these past days.

DELLA: Don't you sass me after what you have done.

WILLIAM: And your own reputation I suppose is white as the falling snow.

DELLA: You shall not keep Brice under your roof from this time forward, do you understand?

WILLIAM: We'll leave that up to Brice, for your information. . . . And as to your divorce proceedings and papers old Simeon has brought me, I'm not contesting. Get it. I've finished with you. Now you can go home and sleep on that.

DELLA: (*surprised and then angry*) So you're too cowardly to fight.

WILLIAM: Who cares what you call me. You've called me everything in the book from the Year One. No one ever lived according to you who had as many faults as I did, while you of course shimmered in perpetual perfection above me, the woman who could do no wrong.

DELLA: Ha, so you do have some fight left in you.

WILLIAM: I don't think you ever gave me an encouraging word from the wedding day on to now. And do you know why. Keep your mouth quiet for a minute and I'll tell you . . . because you're more spoiled than a little princess. Your mother felt it was an imposition for her little girl to have to breathe. So no man could be up to the expectations of a spoiled, conceited, pampered little in-love-with-yourself Miss-can-do-no-wrong.

DELLA: I've come here for one reason and only one, to take Brice home with me.

WILLIAM: You have no home. You have a roadhouse and even the poorest young man in the world isn't poor enough to live with you and your roustabouts in that disorderly house you call a home. Do you think I don't know what goes on under your roof.

DELLA: But nobody tries to rape young women in my house. You're not fit to be Brice's father. And I won't stop until the court gives me jurisdiction over him.

WILLIAM: Then the court will hear from me what goes on in your roadhouse.

DELLA: Hear from a man like you when everyone in town knows what you did to Miss Reece.

WILLIAM: Trying to steal a kiss from a girl who would have been an unwed mother if she hadn't had an abortion in New York! You call that rape! Is kissing a crime. Then every man who wears pants is unfit to raise his son!

DELLA: I half admire your mendacity, Will. Why couldn't you have argued and fought with me when we were married. We might have gone on together then as man and wife.

WILLIAM: Not a chance, Della. My eyes have been opened to the whole race of womankind. I don't want any of you. You think because you harbor a child in your womb for nine months, mankind itself must bow the knee to you for the rest of your life and grant you every wish and whim, give you every excuse for your own misdeeds, and finally crown you queen of the heavens. No thank you. You can take your divorce papers and frame them in your Garden of Memories.

DELLA: You not only sicken me, you would horrify me if I had not been already horrified to death by your miserable character, and your shiftless years of idling and failure.

WILLIAM: While all you've ever had to do was sit at home and weep and moan so Melissa would reach again into her bank account and shower you with more of her support and inexhaustible cash.

DELLA: And Melissa never bankrupted herself did she helping you out of every one of your financial scrapes. . . . Now listen to me, and listen good and proper. I'm going to put you behind bars if Brice isn't turned over to me. Rape all the women who are fool enough to come to your rooms at midnight but you shan't have Brice to misguide and corrupt.

WILLIAM: I'm sure they have a place in hell for women like you who live only to rejoice in their feeling they have been wronged and mistreated by the race of men, when every shower of blessing has been poured down on your every yearning, want, and desire. You would feel neglected and abused if Melissa handed you a million dollars in gold every livelong day. For feeling sorry for yourself is your only pleasure. I would rather see Brice dead than have to live with a deranged virago like you. . . . Go back to poor Melissa and get her to shower you with more undeserved largesse. . . . There's the door for you if you can keep your mouth shut long enough to pass through it.

DELLA: Now that you've ranted and raved to your heart's content, let me say this: (*She goes directly within inches of his face.*) I'll take Brice away from you if it's the last act I ever perform.

WILLIAM: You mean you'd take away the only thing left to me.

DELLA: Willingly and without the least regret.

Scene 6

DELLA and DEREK.

DEREK: (*calling*) Della! Della! (*comes over closer to her*) Don't you know me.

DELLA: For heaven's sake. I'd know your voice anywhere, Derek. But you look so different. What on earth are you doing here?

DEREK: (*echoing*) What am I doing here? I saw you go into Will's house. I thought I'd wait. If you don't mind my saying so, I thought you'd want someone to walk you home.

DELLA: Derek, have you any idea how you've changed in appearance. I wouldn't have known you except for your voice.

DEREK: It's that noticeable, is it? (*a pause*) I gave up drink you know, for one thing. But Della, *you've* changed.

DELLA: Yes, for the worse I suppose. But Derek, you look . . . a sight for sore eyes as they say here.

DEREK: (*going back to the subject*) Do you want to tell me, Della.

DELLA: (*hopelessly*) No. (*pauses*) What good would it do to tell anyone.

DEREK: I've known you longer than Will. In fact, I can't remember the day I didn't know you.

DELLA: It's true, what you say. After all, didn't we go to the first grade together. Old Bess Jordan taught us.

DEREK: What did Will say, if I don't sound too nosey. Della, excuse me, but I'd do anything to help you.

DELLA: *What did Will say*, you ask. I wish I could remember. What did Will ever say to anyone they could remember. (*begins to cry*)

DEREK: I can't bear to see you cry, Della.

DELLA: (*bitter*) Don't you know tears are good for one, Derek. I find they're more refreshing than smiles.

DEREK: Let me walk you home. It's pretty late.

DELLA: That would be nice for two old schoolmates.

DEREK: You'll pardon me again, Della, but what did you tell one another? You and Will—I don't want to press you, but I'm concerned, Della, more than you'll ever know.

DELLA: All right, Derek, let me tell you. (*pause*) We talked around Robin Hood's barn as usual and said nothing. Nothing I can remember. Now I've told you.

DEREK: They say Will won't contest the suit.

DELLA: So that's all over town too, along with the story of Miss Reece. And did they say too what a fool I was ever to institute divorce proceedings. Does one institute a suit against a dead man.

DEREK: He won't contest the suit?

DELLA: That's right. He won't.

DEREK: (*unbelieving*) He's giving you up then.

DELLA: Oh, Derek. I'm the bigger fool, for though I never want to see his face again, all I see and think about is him, Will Hawkins!

DEREK: (*shocked*) Della, you sound like a woman in love.

DELLA: Is it love to think all the time about someone who never gave me one hour of happiness, one moment's respite, one peaceful hour.

DEREK: I daresay it's one kind of love.

DELLA: I hate Will Hawkins, that's all I know.

DEREK: And you can't forget him. (*as he says this* DELLA *moves closer to* DEREK *and hardly realizing it, she is in his arms,* DEREK *kisses her, then as they break away)* I always loved you, Della. Maybe that's why I had my problem.

DELLA: I'd hate to think it was because of me, Derek, you had your . . . problem.

DEREK: No, no, Della, it wasn't on account of you I went down.

DELLA: If Will and I could only have talked things through. But he was always . . . dreaming. Yes that's the right word. His thoughts were always a thousand miles away. Like he was expecting some miracle from somewhere, from nowhere, say. I and our boy were not as real as his dreams. And we never knew what his dreams were. He did not share them, as he did not share himself with us. I went tonight to see him, oh I hardly know why. . . . I went to see if we could say something at last that would open the door on all we have been through together. But come to think of it, I guess we were never together. There we were all during our marriage, seeing one another, hearing one another but ten thousand miles apart. He with his dreams and his unspoken hopes, I with my longing to be loved and told I was his all.

DEREK: And your boy, Della. *(waits a while)* Your boy Brice.

DELLA: Yes, my boy. He too is ten thousand miles away with his own dreams and longing to be gone.

DEREK: Let me walk you home then, Della. I'll walk you tenderly. I'll hear every word you say because the truth is I've always cared only for you.

DELLA: Oh, Derek. Thank you. I'd love to pour out my thanks to you.

DEREK: It's too late for thank yous, Della. Just let me walk you home. That'll be more than my reward.

DELLA: I don't know what I'd done had I not run into you tonight, Derek. (DELLA *and* DEREK *begin to walk off together, stage right.*) I swear I don't.

DEREK: The good fortune is all mine, Della.

Scene 7

SIMEON *and* WILLIAM.

WILLIAM: I know, Simeon, I know. Calling an old man out of his bed in the middle of night.

SIMEON: No, Will, you've got it wrong as usual. I'd get out of my grave to help you, and I'm not as old as you like to think.

WILLIAM: All right, all right, be young then, Simeon. I wouldn't have called you at this hour if it wasn't a damned serious matter.

SIMEON: (*almost collapsing in a chair*) I think I know too what your serious matter is, Will.

WILLIAM: I reckon you do. (*brings out a letter from his jacket*)

SIMEON: It's your boy of course.

WILLIAM: (*rather irritated*) My boy of course. . . . Read this, Simeon.

SIMEON: Why don't you read it to me, Will.

WILLIAM: No, you've got to read it.

SIMEON: Well, wait till I find my specs, why don't you. (*reaches in his breast pocket for his reading glasses*) I'm getting blind as a poker. (*slowly fumbling puts on his glasses*)

WILLIAM: Read it for God's sake!

SIMEON: (*stares at him*) Will, sit down, and try to get quiet. (*begins to read*) But it's written to his grandmother.

WILLIAM: For God's sakes read it!

SIMEON: (*nods, bends slowly then looking up occasionally*) Didn't I warn you, Will. (*reads on*) Didn't I warn Della and Melissa. Didn't I warn all of you.

WILLIAM: Haven't you finished that damned letter.

SIMEON: I'm close to the end. (*reads more then finishing he folds the letter and hands it back to* WILLIAM) Yes, Will?

WILLIAM: Well why don't you tell me what to do, Simeon, for Christ's sake and don't look so damned satisfied.

SIMEON: I tell you what to do? I told you what to do ages ago. In one ear out the other. What can I do now. It's ended, Will.

WILLIAM: Can't you tell the sheriff maybe. Can't you do something to find Brice?

SIMEON: Of course I can but I must warn you, we have a lot more pressing matters, Will, than to locate a runaway boy.

WILLIAM: (*said in a stinging anger*) Name one more pressing matter than to find a boy like Brice for his dad, will you. You surprise me.

SIMEON: In any case he's out of town, the sheriff, Will.

WILLIAM: And how about the police chief and his deputies.

SIMEON: When did you see your boy last?

WILLIAM: It must have been yesterday.

SIMEON: And when did you first notice this letter?

WILLIAM: I laid eyes on it just before I called you.

SIMEON: I'll tell the police what's happened. . . . But Will, your boy could be a day's journey from here by now, or he could be . . .

WILLIAM: Don't guess in front of me. I can't take anyone else's guess-work and suspicions. I won't be able to get a wink of sleep now that I've read this letter. (*SIMEON rises to go.*) Don't tell me you're leaving.

SIMEON: But, what more is there to do here, Will.

WILLIAM: (*calming down*) Don't go. Listen, I want you to stay until Della and Melissa get here. Simeon, believe me.

SIMEON: You won't need my help with two ladies like them around. All right, I catch your drift. I can keep them, you mean, from cutting you into fine mincemeat.

WILLIAM: I wish to God somebody would shoot me.

SIMEON: I said I'd stay and I will, but I don't want to hear any more of such gab from you. Act like the man you are.

WILLIAM: What man are you talking about. There is no man now! I've lost my boy. What more can I lose and still call myself a man. (*There is a knocking at the door.*) That must be them.

SIMEON: Let me go, Will. You sit still and don't get up when the ladies come in. Keep seated. (*He soon returns ushering in* DELLA *and* MELISSA.)

MELISSA: We came as soon as we could, Will. But what is it? Why couldn't you have let us know on the phone what this emergency was. You've frightened both of us to death.

WILLIAM: (*not rising*) You can't be as frightened then as I am. The fact is I felt I had to let you know in person. (*cold*) Della, good evening.

DELLA: I think I know what's happened. (*turning to* SIMEON) Thank God you're here, Simeon. You should keep us on an even keel.

WILLIAM: (*producing Brice's letter*) This is the news, this is what has brought us all together when as Simeon has put it, it's too late. Melissa, take it please. (*hands* MELISSA *the letter*)

MELISSA: I'd know that handwriting anywhere. Oh, Will, I am scared to read it. Can't you tell us what it's about. What has happened to Brice, Will?

WILLIAM: I asked you, Mother, to read the letter.

MELISSA: I can't see very well in this poor illumination.

SIMEON: Sit over here, Melissa, why don't you, where there's a strong light.

MELISSA: Thank you, Simeon, but I can begin to make it out now. Let me remain standing.

DELLA: (*when* MELISSA *hesitates*) Do you want me to read it for you, Mother.

MELISSA: No, dear, I can see perfectly well now. It's a short message. (*her voice trembles*) Why is it so many fearful messages are short.

(*reads*) And why, this one, Will, is addressed to me I see. I had missed the fact the envelope had my name on it.

DELLA: (*angry*) Read, Mother, for God's sake!

MELISSA: (*reading*)

Dear Grandma,

Just think of me as if I had never been born. I know if I stay here any longer I'll choke to death. I have learned from the wild horses how I can be free. They looked at me as if they really seen me and knew who I was. So I must run if I need to, to the ends of the earth. I've got to change my name every time the sun goes down from now on. Or maybe I'll be like the waves of the ocean which haven't got any name. If you care about me at all, please don't try to find me. All I want is to be away from here forever and I've got to forget, everything and everybody except maybe you. Yes, I've got to forget!

Goodbye,

Brice

(*She turns to* WILLIAM.) The wild horses, Will. Did you note that?

DELLA: (*sits down silently overwhelmed then concerned for* MELISSA) Mother, dear, please come over here and sit down beside me. Mother, did you hear?

MELISSA: I'm all right, Della. Don't worry about me. I'll sit right here, if you don't mind. (*sits apart from everyone*) Did you hear the words. I'm not the best of readers as you know by now.

DELLA: We must find him, Simeon. He's no more than a child. Do you realize the danger he must be in. And where could he go. He has no money. He doesn't know his way around.

SIMEON: We can't do anything until the morning. Melissa, if I'm to go to the police here as Will has asked me, I'll need that letter.

(MELISSA *does not respond as if in deep slumber.*)

DELLA: Mother, didn't you hear what Simeon is asking you.

MELISSA: I hate to part with the letter, for it's the last thing we may have from him.

DELLA: (*irritated*) But, Mother, the police will want to know why we think he has run off.

SIMEON: That's right, Melissa. They can't just go on our word that Brice has left us.

MELISSA: I see. It's to be his word supporting ours. (*turns to* DELLA) I hate so to part with his letter, Della.

DELLA: I understand.

MELISSA: (*almost inaudible*) You do?

SIMEON: (*coming over to* MELISSA) I will take the very best care of it and I promise to return it to you the first thing in the morning. Won't that do?

MELISSA: It will have to. It's a strange thing, all, but I feel now I never want his letter to be out of my sight and touch.

DELLA: (*more annoyed still*) Mother, for pity's sake. It's only pen and ink after all.

MELISSA: How can you say that. Look what it has done to all of us. (*looking over at* WILLIAM) Look what it's done to his father.

DELLA: It's clear, Mother, where your sympathies lie. Where they've always lain. As if we all were not crushed . . . by Brice's words.

MELISSA: Come, Simeon, I'll give you what Brice has written. But you must promise me as if on the Good Book you'll be back with it tomorrow morning.

SIMEON: In all the years we've known one another, Melissa, have I ever gone back on a promise.

MELISSA: No, you haven't. But this is a different matter. (SIMEON *advances and takes the letter slowly, almost delicately from* MELISSA *as if he was grasping something fragile.*)

DELLA: (*rising*) Will, this is a very sad occasion I'm sure for everyone here. (*She goes over to* WILLIAM.) You may not believe me, Will, but I know what you're going through. But you must not blame yourself now.

WILLIAM: (*coming out of a deep reverie*) I must not?

DELLA: Believe me, Will. (*with difficulty*) I do not blame you.

WILLIAM: Then I'm hearing something new.

DELLA: Please don't take it so hard, Will. . . . We did what we could do, after all.

WILLIAM: Don't include me in that, if you please. And I wish God himself would thunder as he blames me. . . . Look after your Mother, Della, she's in a bad way.

SIMEON: Can't I accompany you ladies home, Della.

DELLA: Cy Bancroft's car is waiting outside for us, Simeon. Otherwise I'd be happy to accept your offer . . . (*calls nervously*) Mother. (*goes over to her*) We are leaving now.

MELISSA: You needn't shout as if I was ninety or a hundred. My hearing is better than many young folks.

DELLA: (*taken aback*) I'm sorry. Listen, Mother, he's become more real than when he was amongst us, so much closer . . .

MELISSA: Exactly. Thank fortune you feel it too.

DELLA: But take my arm. . . . The car is waiting below. (*They begin to go out; DELLA suddenly turns back to look at WILLIAM.*) Goodbye Will, for now. . . . Try to remember all the good times you and Brice enjoyed together.

(WILLIAM *sunk in deep sorrow does not respond nor looks at* DELLA.)

MELISSA: Until tomorrow, Simeon. . . . And don't forget his letter, whatever you do.

(DELLA *and* MELISSA *exit.*)

SIMEON: (*stands looking after the departing ladies for a lengthy time, then turns back to stare at* WILLIAM) Will, what do you, need?

WILLIAM: A new heart I guess. (*almost inaudible*) This one's busted. (*pause*) You lost a son I believe in the last war, Simeon, ain't that right?

SIMEON: (*after a pause*) That's so.

WILLIAM: And how did it take you? I mean, did you get over it at last.

SIMEON: Will, there is an old saying time heals all wounds. It's a bit wide of the mark.

WILLIAM: (*becoming agitated*) How so. Wide of the mark.

SIMEON: I speak only for myself of course.

WILLIAM: What are you telling me. That some sorrow cannot be healed.

SIMEON: Oh that's one way of putting it, Will. But see here, I think I should hurry on to the police station now on my way home.

WILLIAM: But what do you mean saying time don't heal all wounds. That some sorrow can't be healed. . . . Of course your boy is dead, so you can at least visit where they have laid him.

SIMEON: (*standing up*) Well, as I say I want to show this letter to the men at the police station. If you'll excuse me, then. But be sure to call me, Will, should you need anything. I want to stand by you, believe me.

WILLIAM: Thank you, Simeon. Pardon me if I don't get up to bid you goodnight. And thanks, thanks. Thanks for all you do. My thanks.

SIMEON: (*goes up to* WILLIAM *and takes his hand, which is limp as a wet cloth*) Till tomorrow. (*exit*)

WILLIAM: (*talking aloud*) You can tend a dead soldier like his boy is, I see. But then what did he mean by that remark, giving it to me at a time like this. What's wrong with him? *Time don't heal all wounds.* What a thing to say to a man who's just lost his boy. Time don't heal? Then to hell with time. (*He lowers his head into his hands.*)

Scene 8

HARRIET *and* MELISSA *are with their sewing. However, the sewing lies untended in their laps.*

HARRIET: You're sure, Melissa, that Simeon is coming this morning.

MELISSA: He swore he'd be here to return the letter.

HARRIET: That letter, Melissa . . .

MELISSA: What is it you want to say?

HARRIET: It's so . . . precious.

MELISSA: That's the right word for it, *precious.*

HARRIET: But what if the police want to keep it?

MELISSA: Then I'll go to the station and take it away from them. It belongs nowhere but here. With me. My letter.

HARRIET: He's usually on time.

MELISSA: They've probably put the poor old man through hell and high water. I hope nothing has happened to him.

HARRIET: I never think of Simeon as old.

MELISSA: (*absentmindedly*) No?

HARRIET: I've seen him going down the main street at a clip a young man might envy. And he toils from sunup to sundown.

MELISSA: Thank God. Then he'll not forget to bring me the letter.

HARRIET: If he doesn't I'll go to the station and get it for you.

MELISSA: Thank you for saying that. I know you'd go too. You and Simeon are cut out from the same cloth. You're close to perfection . . . both of you. You are perfection.

(*The bell rings.*)

HARRIET: That must be our friend. Let me go to the door.

MELISSA: (*speaking unlike herself*) I must never let anyone take that letter from me again. I must never part with it ever.

(SIMEON *enters ushered in by* HARRIET.)

SIMEON: Don't get up, Melissa. Stay right where you are.

MELISSA: (*almost frantic*) Have you brought my letter?

SIMEON: (*joking*) What do you think. It's right here. (*points to the breast pocket of his jacket*)

MELISSA: Then give it to me, Sim. (SIMEON *takes the letter from his pocket and hands it to her; she takes the paper from the envelope.*) Ah, yes, it's all here. You kept your promise. I wish everybody was like you, Sim. Sit down, don't leave us now. Sit down over here close to me. Has there been any news about our boy?

SIMEON: As yet Melissa there's none. But it's too soon really to expect any. I can't stay, my dear. I've got a thousand things waiting to be tended to.

MELISSA: That's all everybody always says to me, *they can't stay* when they come to see me. *Hello and goodbye, Melissa.* So you're no different.

SIMEON: It's Will I'm worried about, Melissa . . .

HARRIET: (*interrupting*) May I bring you something to drink, Simeon?

SIMEON: No, no please, and don't stand on ceremony. Regretfully as I've told Melissa, I'm needed in the station to answer questions about Brice's disappearance. And I've got to look in on Will.

MELISSA: (*almost angrily*) What's wrong with him. Isn't he satisfied?

SIMEON: (*somewhat taken aback*) Satisfied?

MELISSA: Aren't both Della and he satisfied, yes, satisfied with their handiwork.

SIMEON: I'm sorry, I don't quite know how to answer you there. I can tell you though Will is not himself. He didn't go to bed last night. He can't sleep a wink he says. As to satisfied, well . . .

MELISSA: Forget I said it, then, Simeon. Harriet, bring in the bottle of elderberry wine. Simeon dare not refuse a taste of that.

SIMEON: (*chuckles*) I certainly dare not.

MELISSA: You can't leave with a dry throat, as my own mother used to tell visitors who were in a hurry.

SIMEON: Melissa, you are a caution. What would we do without you.

(HARRIET *returns with a bottle of the wine, three glasses on a tray; they drink in silence for a while.*)

MELISSA: I often had a strange daydream, and I seem to have it now, Simeon, Harriet. I think I understand it now . . . this dream. I see Brice and me in a large sun-drenched room. As if he had never left. And Brice is speaking to me in this strange daydream. I think he says, *we have always been alone together, Grandma, haven't we.* And now we can be alone together for always and always.

HARRIET: (*shocked*) You never told me your dream, Melissa.

MELISSA: I once read in a gypsy fortune teller's little book, decorated with moons and stars and planets, a queer sentence. It said, *In death all dreams come true.*

SIMEON: (*rousing himself*) Melissa, my dear friend, we must hope for the best. Mustn't we, Harriet. Let's drink to better times, to happiness, all of us. There is always more good we can do, you know that, Melissa.

HARRIET: Oh I believe that too.

MELISSA: I will drink on that. (*They all drink.*) Except for one thing, Simeon, Harriet. (*She drinks and helps herself to a little more wine.* HARRIET *pours* SIMEON *another drink.*)

SIMEON: And what is that *except for one thing,* Melissa?

MELISSA: Brice will never return. No, no, don't tell me I am wrong. Do you think I would say such a thing about the dearest boy in the world. True, Simeon, we must go on, but we must face what the truth is. He won't ever return. That's what the wild horses must have given him.

HARRIET: Melissa, let me put the softer pillow behind your back. (*She goes to a nearby chair and brings out a pillow and gently arranges it behind* MELISSA's *back.*) There, isn't that better.

MELISSA: Of course, of course it's better. What would I do without Harriet, Simeon, or you. You are my two dearest friends—now. My only dearest ones.

SIMEON: (*rising*) I want to say something, Melissa, and I want you to be silent while I say it. There is a great deal of hope we can find your Brice. Do you hear me, my friend. There is a great deal of hope.

MELISSA: You're wrong there. He won't allow himself to be found. Not Brice. Not a boy like Brice. But I hear you, Simeon. Of course I hear you. And God has been good to me in giving me two friends like you.

SIMEON: Goodbye, my friend. Goodbye, Harriet.

(*HARRIET ushers him to the door and then returns.*)

MELISSA: I knew Simeon's boy, Harriet. Do you remember him too.

HARRIET: Who could forget him, Melissa. Todd was his first name.

MELISSA: Such a handsome chap. I almost bit my tongue off when I started to mention Todd to Simeon. He was his pride and joy. His whole life was in Todd.

HARRIET: Can I pour you another small glass, Melissa.

MELISSA: If you want another taste, why not. Go ahead, I'll join you.

HARRIET: (*pours*) Where do you want me to put his letter?

MELISSA: Where? Oh, let me think about it. A very safe place of course.

HARRIET: There's the little music stand with the sheet music.

MELISSA: The lock's broken on it, though.

HARRIET: The hall safe.

MELISSA: I thought of that. But it's too cold and ugly. No, Harriet, I plan to keep it right against (*points to her bosom*) *here.* I won't part with it ever again. Not ever. Every so often I feel I see him on the deck of a ship somewhere going far from land. How dark it always is on the sea even by day. . . . I used to take the longest sea voyages. Now I'm too old and yet the sea seems everywhere.

HARRIET: But what about Sadie Patterson's new gown. We've hardly touched it lately and there's a long day ahead of us.

MELISSA: And a long evening. (*After a pause, she suddenly brightens a little.*)

HARRIET: What is it Melissa?

MELISSA: I have suddenly a strange feeling that our Brice has found his chance. Yes, I have a feeling he's free at last. For after all what could they offer him here.

HARRIET: But Brice wouldn't want us to sit here and pine for him.

MELISSA: Heaven knows he wouldn't. He'd want us to carry on and never shed useless tears.

HARRIET: Then shan't we pitch in and finish Sadie's dress before she beats the door down to know why it's not done.

(HARRIET *picks up the gown and brings it over to* MELISSA *who smiles at her.*)

THE PARADISE CIRCUS

CHARACTERS and ages at the play's beginning

ARTHUR RAWLINGS, 65
JOEL RAWLINGS, 18
GREGORY RAWLINGS, 20
ALDA PENNINGTON, 50
DR. HALLAM, 58
GIUSEPPE ONOFRIO, 50
GONZAGO, 40
MINNIE CRUIKSHANK, 40
EPHRAIM, 25
BOAKE, 20

The farm country near a Midwestern village, 1919.

ACT I

Scene 1

A large room in a sprawling farmhouse. ARTHUR RAWLINGS *and his two young sons live here.* ARTHUR *is speaking with a journalist who has dropped in.*

RAWLINGS: I'll be open with you. I don't like the idea of anybody writing about my own flesh and blood, despite the fact that Rainforth died for his country and as you say has reached some degree of notability . . .

EPHRAIM: It's only a short paragraph or so we would be putting in the book on soldiers from the Revolution down to the present concluded conflict, and your son did receive many citations and medals. . . . There's no way of leaving him out, Mr. Rawlings . . .

RAWLINGS: My two youngest boys can't hold a candle to their brother, that's certain. Have you spoke to them about their brother.

EPHRAIM: No but I would like to.

RAWLINGS: You're welcome to talk to them of course. But they can tell you very little . . .

EPHRAIM: With your permission, sir . . . I'd like to go speak to them then.

RAWLINGS: (*almost belligerent*) They're retarded boys. Never finished school . . . (*going back to the important subject*) On the other hand, people have also criticized me for naming my oldest boy Rainforth. Said it didn't sound like a Christian name. That Rainforth

Rawlings had a dismal sound. They would have preferred I guess Jim Jack or Fred. Maybe even then he was too much a leader. People were a little afraid of him, in fact. Never even talked about him behind his back. He was a star athlete in college, and I wasn't at all surprised to learn he won the Distinguished Service Cross, and all the rest of the medals they ever thought of for heroism . . .

EPHRAIM: What did people call your son then?

RAWLINGS: (*astounded*) What?

EPHRAIM: I mean, sir, did they call him Rainforth.

RAWLINGS: No. (*pausing*) They called him always Rawlings, even when he was still a lad. It seemed to people like a first name maybe. More than Rainforth.

EPHRAIM: Do you feel you misnamed him?

RAWLINGS: (*astounded*) Of course not!

EPHRAIM: I mean, sir, if nobody ever called him *Rainforth*, do you feel now you might have chosen an easier name for people to pronounce.

RAWLINGS: I get your drift. (*thinking some time*) I tell you what. The world wants everything ordinary. And both his name and his character were extraordinary. Rainforth was right for him, whether people liked it or not.

EPHRAIM: Do you suppose they called him Rainforth in the army . . .

RAWLINGS: I have no idea whatsoever. He didn't write to me too frequently. . . . He was made captain just the day before he was . . . killed. I do know that.

EPHRAIM: (*rising*) With your permission now, sir, I'll go talk with your two other sons.

RAWLINGS: Go ahead if it suits you. . . . But they know next to nothing about Rainforth. . . . They were so much younger than him. They lived sort of in awe of him though, to tell the truth. . . . But go ahead if you want to, talk to them. . . . I've already warned you they are none too bright . . .

Scene 2

EPHRAIM *enters the carpentry shop of the two* RAWLINGS *boys. The two young men,* JOEL *and* GREGORY, *ages 18 and 20, respectively, are putting the finishing touches on some merry-go-round wooden horses, highly ornamented and bedizened with flashing glass jewels.*

EPHRAIM: (*clearing his throat*) Excuse me, boys. . . . Your father has given me permission . . . to have a word with you.

GREGORY: Come in, sir. I am Gregory and this is my brother Joel. (*He points to the younger boy.*)

JOEL: (*stopping work*) How do you do. (*He speaks in a voice which is close to a stutter.*)

EPHRAIM: As I said, boys, your father has very kindly consented to let me talk with you about your older brother Rainforth who died a hero. (*As he speaks the two boys exchange meaningful looks with one another.*)

GREGORY: We barely knew him.

EPHRAIM: But still he *was* your brother.

JOEL: So far as we can find out.

EPHRAIM: Certainly he was a hero.

(JOEL *and* GREGORY *exchange glances again. It is clear they are very close to one another.*)

EPHRAIM: Of course if you would prefer not to talk about him.

JOEL: What do you intend to do with the information, if I can ask. . . . I mean what will come of all your questioning us about . . . him . . .

EPHRAIM: I'm writing a book about the heroes of America. . . . Your brother's name would figure in it prominently . . . in the chapter on the last war.

GREGORY: First of all he was gone for a good many years while we were growing up. (*more cooperative now though still diffident and untrusting*) But outside of the days when we were little and went

89

fishing with him, we don't remember too much about him. Except he was Father's favorite and was more like a second father to us because he was so much older you know . . .

EPHRAIM: I understand.

Scene 3

Lights up on first part of stage. DR. HALLAM, *an M.D. of 58, is standing near the elder* RAWLINGS, *a small weathered black bag in his right hand. He is listening absentmindedly to* RAWLINGS's *rambling speech.*

RAWLINGS: I have to think about winding up my affairs, Doc. . . . I can't last forever, and those boys out there in the paint shed don't amount to a tinker's damn compared with the firstborn who lies thousands of miles across the ocean. . . . I do not know how they'll make out once I'm gone . . .

HALLAM: Rubbish, you'll last another quarter century and you know it!

RAWLINGS: (*as if he had not heard* HALLAM's *interpolation*) The younger of the two, Joel, can barely add up a column of figures. . . . And Greg is subject to brooding fits. . . . Both are lazybones and dreamers. They're content to putter and do nothing all day! The ways of the universe! One cannot fathom why the finest and the best, the flower of manhood are taken, and the infirm and feeble are left behind. Search me, Doctor . . .

HALLAM: I am a bit worried, to tell you the truth, about the boys' health. . . . They're constantly inhaling the fumes from the paint, you know, and the youngest boy has developed asthma.

RAWLINGS: It doesn't surprise me in the least. . . . I've told them to stick to carpentry, but they are crazy about refinishing these old merry-go-round horses. . . . The circus and the carnival people are always sending the wood horses over here to be refurbished and repaired. . . . Well, if you want to see them go along then. You know where to find the barn. But let me warn you, there's a busy-body of a reporter fellow in there already. He's come to ask all of us what we know about Rainforth.

HALLAM: Rawlings, might I venture a suggestion in this matter?

RAWLINGS: A suggestion or another of your confounded sermons on my shortcomings . . .

HALLAM: (*laughs*) I'm not always sure where the one leaves off and the other begins in my practice. (*after a lengthy pause*) Sometimes young men can get sick for sheer want of a little encouragement and downright affection, Rawlings. . . . And all they hear from you, if you will pardon my frankness, is a steady diet of praise for Rainforth.

RAWLINGS: (*stung, angry*) You treat them for the paint fumes, Doc, and let me bring up my boys in my own way.

HALLAM: Good enough, Rawlings. I'll see them then.

RAWLINGS: (*shaking his finger at him*) But you get one thing straight now. . . . I've done all any father can do for those two boys. . . . They don't have to raise a hand if they don't want to, and you know it. Free grub, free lodgings, clothing and accessories. . . . It ain't my fault they're dull-witted . . .

HALLAM: They work hard.

RAWLINGS: I told you before. They putter all day in the carpentry shop or the paint room, but what comes of it?

HALLAM: I was talking with the carnival and circus people the other day. They say they have never seen such fine merry-go-round horses as after your boys paint and repair them.

RAWLINGS: (*resentful*) As I say, they're fond of puttering around, and that's all.

HALLAM: And as I say, Rawlings, a word of encouragement or praise sometimes makes all the difference in a young man's outlook, and his health.

RAWLINGS: Then since you're the doctor supposin' you give them that along with your prescriptions that cost an arm and a leg . . . (*mus-*

ing, silent for awhile) No, they've been a bitter disappointment to me. . . . They failed miserably in school, as you probably remember . . .

HALLAM: And it couldn't have been maybe the school's fault?

RAWLINGS: How could I know whose fault? I've almost come to the conclusion it's destiny. . . . We are so and so and such and such, and we will be what we came into the world to be, no more, no less.

HALLAM: That's a very gloomy philosophy you have there.

RAWLINGS: Can you give me a better one?

HALLAM: My job is to make people well.

RAWLINGS: You'll never make those boys of mine any better than they are now. You can count on that right now. (DR. HALLAM *shrugs his shoulders and begins to move off toward the carpentry shop.* RAWL-INGS *continues talking as if he were already alone.*) Sometimes I wonder if they *are* my sons. My firstborn I was sure of. But these two are more like what my superstitious Grandmother called *changelings.* Oh well. . . . (*He looks up to see that the doctor has left the room.*)

Scene 4

Scene shifts to DR. HALLAM *entering the barn.*

HALLAM: Gregory! Joel! (*The boys stop painting the merry-go-round horses.* GREGORY *advances to greet the doctor.*)

GREGORY: Good evening, Dr. Hallam.

HALLAM: And what is your trouble today, son.

JOEL: (*advancing*) Doctor, I'm having a little trouble with my breathing again.

HALLAM: Just a little? Sit down, my boy . . . open your mouth . . . Yes, there's a little congestion there. . . . Do you boys get out in the open air regularly. . . . (*They do not reply.*) Well, you should. Don't stay cooped up here so much. Take more hikes.

GREGORY: We have lots of pressing orders you know from carnivals and circus people.

(EPHRAIM *steps forward.*)

EPHRAIM: Let me introduce myself, Dr. Hallam. . . . I'm writing a book on the heroes of this vicinity, going back to the Revolutionary War and coming through the just-completed conflict.

HALLAM: (*indifferent*) I see.

EPHRAIM: Do you know anything about the older Rawlings boy. . . . I've been able to find out very little here, though these boys are the politest fellows I've ever met.

HALLAM: (*balking*) Well, I suppose I could give you a fact or two. . . . But I'm afraid I wouldn't be much help for anything sustained or detailed.

EPHRAIM: And I'm ashamed to say so, but I'm stumped when it comes to Rainforth Rawlings. . . . His own family seems to be able to give me so little.

HALLAM: These boys were much too young to have remembered their brother, sir. . . . Excuse me. . . . I'm going to write you out a new prescription, Joel, and you take this down to the druggist and have it filled the first thing in the morning . . . (*writes*) Then I want you to come to my office in a day or so. . . . Is that clear . . . (*hands him the prescription*) Now then, good morning to you all, and follow my instructions about getting out in the fresh air more often, boys . . .

EPHRAIM: I will go along with the Doctor, boys, but if you will allow me to do so I would like to make a return visit one day. Perhaps by then your memory will have been jogged a bit and you can tell me something about Rainforth.

GREGORY and JOEL: Whatever you say, Ephraim.

(DR. HALLAM *and* EPHRAIM *exit. When they have gone out, the two young men jump up and down and let out wild Indian cries of relief and high spirits.*)

JOEL: If they only knew! If they could only see into our thoughts.

GREGORY: That's the thrill of it, isn't it. . . . Nobody knows our real life, least of all our father. (*They both laugh almost hysterically, and uncontrollably.*)

(*The circus owner,* GIUSEPPE ONOFRIO, *appears.*)

ONOFRIO: (*who has been watching their antics, suddenly applauds*) Wonderful! Beautiful! Inspired! As I said in my visit last year, you boys should not waste your lives here but join our circus. . . . You would make your fortune.

(GREGORY *and* JOEL *stare at the circus owner with amazement, and also with fear.*)

GREGORY: We are too much attached to our carpentry shop here.

ONOFRIO: Rubbish. . . . If you traveled about a bit you'd find there is no better life. Always seeing new sights and new people. . . . We travel over almost the entire globe. . . . You would get so attached to travel and change, you would wonder why you ever stayed here, painting wooden horses in this backwater!

JOEL: Our father would never allow us to leave.

ONOFRIO: Would you allow me to speak to your father about it.

GREGORY: If you want to. . . . But it won't do you any good. . . . (*Both boys laugh.*)

ONOFRIO: Where is the gentleman.

GREGORY: Just go down the hall there, to your right, he is sitting in his study.

JOEL: (*in a low but distinguishable voice*) Counting his money.

ONOFRIO: I will speak to him and be back directly . . .

(ONOFRIO *goes to the elder* RAWLINGS's *study, raps on the opened door, clears his throat, and waits to be recognized.*)

ONOFRIO: Mr. Rawlings, sir.

RAWLINGS: Have you come about purchasing the quarry.

ONOFRIO: My name is Giuseppe Onofrio. I own the circus which is passing through your town.

RAWLINGS: You do not wish to buy the stone quarry.

ONOFRIO: As I say I am the owner of the Paradise Circus.

RAWLINGS: I'm afraid you and I then will have little to talk about. (*stares at him suspiciously*) Indeed nothing. You will have to excuse me, I'm very busy. (*He goes back to looking through his ledger.*)

ONOFRIO: I would like to buy your sons. I mean the service of your sons.

RAWLINGS: What?

ONOFRIO: You heard me right. I know the proposition sounds incredible, but I have never dealt in ordinary ways with people. All I am and have ever done is the extraordinary.

RAWLINGS: Only a madman or a criminal would mention such a thing. . . . Buying sons!

ONOFRIO: I am neither mad nor a criminal. . . . I am like you a sharp businessman. I repeat. I wish to buy your sons.

RAWLINGS: Well, allow me to inquire, although they are not a commodity or for sale, how much do you offer me.

ONOFRIO: How much do you think they are worth.

RAWLINGS: (*bemused*) I'd take ten thousand for the two.

ONOFRIO: Agreed, Mr. Rawlings, agreed. . . . I will pay you that in cash. (*takes out his money*)

RAWLINGS: (*staring at the money which* ONOFRIO *has produced*) God in heaven, you can't be serious.

ONOFRIO: There is no God in heaven and you know it. . . . There is at this moment only you and me, and we are sealing a bargain.

RAWLINGS: After all, they have been a bitter disappointment to me, both of them. (*absent-minded, almost forgetting he has a visitor who has made him such an offer*) It was their older brother who was my hope, my promise, my life. . . . These boys have never loved me, or respected me. . . . All they have ever thought of doing was tomfoolery, going on long hikes and frequently absent in the summer looking for mushrooms, and in the winter they repair merry-go-round horses. No interest in their brother's memory or in their father . . .

ONOFRIO: Then their leaving you will be no sorrow at all.

RAWLINGS: None at all. . . . But my duty and my honor will not allow me to accept your . . . more than generous offer. I must ask you therefore to depart.

ONOFRIO: Take the money then as a deposit only. . . . If the boys do not work out in my circus, I will return them to you, and you will return the money. . . . Understand?

RAWLINGS: You are a very persuasive man. But we must ask the boys, must we not . . .

ONOFRIO: We should certainly inform them of the offer. . . . Agreed.

RAWLINGS: (*calls*) Gregory, Joel. . . . You are wanted in here. . . . At once, do you hear. On the double. (*The boys come quickly to the study.*) This good gentleman has agreed to accept your services with the circus. Would you care to accept his offer. . . . Speak up, boys.

JOEL: We would prefer to stay here with you, sir, if you don't mind.

RAWLINGS: It is a matter of indifference to me. . . . After all, you have not found yourselves so far as careers are concerned, and you both eat a great deal. Your consumption of fresh fruit and vegetables alone comes to a small fortune. (*consulting his ledger*)

GREGORY: If you are commanding us to go with Señor Onofrio, of course we will obey you. . . . We know also that the memory of Rainforth will cheer you more than our absence will cause you to grieve.

RAWLINGS: True. My grief for Rainforth has been the principal occupation of my time.

JOEL: Then, Gregory, I suspect we had best take Señor Onofrio's advice and sign up with the circus.

GREGORY: Since Father does not oppose our going, I agree.

RAWLINGS: Just a minute. . . . Are you aware how stupid these boys are, Señor Onofrio. They both failed all the way through the public schools here. They were truants and smoked forbidden drugs, and were constantly in hot water. Although I beat them incessantly, they never improved.

ONOFRIO: I am perfectly aware, sir, of their character, and their abilities. I am satisfied with the sale.

RAWLINGS: Then I will wash my hands of them. . . . If you come through town again, however, let them come to see me. In your company of course. I believe that would be the correct thing to do.

GREGORY and JOEL: Goodbye then, Father. . . . We will join Señor Onofrio and the circus, as you have advised.

RAWLINGS: Take good care of them, Señor Onofrio. Although they were not my favorite sons, still, for all I know, they are my own flesh and blood. . . . But they do not earn their keep and I am an old man who must look out for himself. . . . So, my blessing on all of you. . . . Goodbye! (*He turns after they leave and counts the money.*)

Scene 5

Three years have passed since the sons GREGORY *and* JOEL *have joined the circus of* SEÑOR ONOFRIO. *It is night.* DR. HALLAM *is sitting talking with the elder* RAWLINGS.

RAWLINGS: You say I should not blame myself, but I do. . . . I have thought of them everyday. And have not had so much as a word from them in all the three years they've been gone. I don't know what came over me to allow such a decision.

HALLAM: If you did not love your sons, you did not love them, that's all there is to it. We must face what we are.

RAWLINGS: I can't agree with you. I should have pretended I loved them. It would have cost me less suffering.

HALLAM: I wonder how much you loved your firstborn, Rawlings.

RAWLINGS: Oh I have no doubts about that.

HALLAM: It's easy to love the dead. They make so few demands on us. But the living try our patience beyond endurance. The dead are perfect and we forget how far short they fell in life of our expectations. The living present us with all their faults and tiresome weaknesses . . .

RAWLINGS: I have missed them more than I can say. And contrary to what you preach, I miss their faults! Rainforth was too perfect. When he lived he was so faultless. . . . I was afraid of him.

HALLAM: (*eager*) Go on.

RAWLINGS: In retrospect, I think I would have not been happy with him had he lived, had he been part of my life. . . . Do you understand.

HALLAM: But so vital and energetic a young man would not have remained here with you.

RAWLINGS: Why not?

HALLAM: Simply because he would not. He would have established a carpentry shop of his own. He would have married.

RAWLINGS: Married perhaps but he would have remained in business with me. Father and son.

HALLAM: Never the Rainforth I knew. He was much too self-willed and indeed headstrong. He would never have remained in this backwater hamlet. You know that!

RAWLINGS: What are you trying to tell me. That Rainforth did not love me.

HALLAM: (*rises, looking at his watch*) The time has run away while I've been talking. I have many other calls to make.

RAWLINGS: Sit down, Doctor. And answer my question. You saw a good deal of him. More than I did.

HALLAM: I merely treated his aches and pains from his football injuries. The time he broke his leg playing hockey. He was not a confiding young man.

RAWLINGS: But you are a keen student of human nature. . . . You saw something.

HALLAM: (*disturbed*) Rainforth is dead.

RAWLINGS: You shall not trifle with me like this, Hallam. . . . You shall not . . .

HALLAM: But I know nothing of what he felt for you.

RAWLINGS: You lie, damn you. . . . You lie . . . (*his voice breaking*) You have never liked me. You think I am a miser, cold, selfish, unloving . . .

HALLAM: (*rising*) And unloved.

RAWLINGS: Hallam, how can I get back my sons.

HALLAM: I am going to tell you something, Rawlings. Pay close attention. Your younger boys loved you a thousand times more than Rainforth. Or they would have, had you permitted them to.

RAWLINGS: Go on, Doctor, plunge the knife deeper. Don't spare me.

HALLAM: I have said my say.

RAWLINGS: No, damn you, you haven't. . . . You know, it seems, what Rainforth really felt for me.

HALLAM: Rawlings, I have some really sick people waiting to see me.

RAWLINGS: You don't have anybody sicker in the world waiting than me.

HALLAM: I never dreamed, Arthur, you would open your confidence to me even if you were facing death.

RAWLINGS: This is worse than death. . . . Hallam. . . . This is the nothingness that comes to people in life. . . . Living death . . .

HALLAM: I suppose (*preparing to go*) you could find your sons if you searched for them. Even though you sold them like livestock . . .

But that was three years ago. Would they be the same sons now as they were when they lived here. The sons who hoped one day you would return their love . . .

RAWLINGS: You have spared me nothing. Go, go to your other patients.

HALLAM: Perhaps the world has taught them what folly it is to love, to offer affection where it is not wanted. Perhaps they too have turned to rock.

RAWLINGS: Go, go, Doctor. . . . And never come again.

HALLAM: You will call me another time. . . . After all there's not another doctor for fifty miles around.

RAWLINGS: There's Alda Pennington . . . the old midwife who dabbles in herbs and magic and is, they say, a witch. She will be kinder to me than you.

HALLAM: Goodbye, Arthur.

RAWLINGS: (*pleading*) If I humbled myself, Doctor, should they come back, do you think they would be able to love me . . .

HALLAM: (*watching him*) Anything can happen in this life, I suppose. Anything and nothing. (*exits*)

RAWLINGS: (*alone*) His treating the sick and dying for forty years has turned his heart to stone. Life and death alike mean nothing to him. . . . Every man is just another patient and another prescription to him, another exorbitant fee to pay.

Scene 6

Another year has passed. The same scene as the first, MR. RAWLINGS's study and office. DR. HALLAM enters.

HALLAM: I thought I'd drop by as long as I was in the vicinity. I haven't seen you in nearly a year.

RAWLINGS: It could be a year. . . . it could be ten. You don't fool me none, Doctor. . . . I know damned well you came clear over here to see if I was dead or not.

HALLAM: (*sitting down*) You'll outlive the whole county and you know it. . . . I'll tell you. . . . I did come on purpose.

RAWLINGS: Well there's nothin' wrong with me, Doc. No more now than there ever was . . .

HALLAM: The Paradise Circus and Carnival has opened in Hebblethwaite. (RAWLINGS, *too moved to speak*) I went over there the other night. They're there, your boys. They're bareback riders. . . . Horsemen . . .

RAWLINGS: You're sure it's them.

HALLAM: I spoke to them.

RAWLINGS: They're coming to see me, I suppose. . . . (*HALLAM evasive, looks at his hat.*) Well, are they?

HALLAM: I asked them that as a matter of fact . . .

RAWLINGS: And?

HALLAM: Rawlings, they've changed so you would hardly know them. . . . They're men now, with beards, and powerful arms and chests. . . . But they use your name!

RAWLINGS: Why ain't they coming . . .

HALLAM: I think they've forgotten everything. . . . Not that they weren't polite. They were politer than ever. Your boys were always so polite! Rawlings. . . . But it was as though their mind was changed as well as their bodies.

RAWLINGS: (*as if to himself*) I don't understand it. . . . How long is this god damned circus going to be there.

HALLAM: A few days more, I daresay.

RAWLINGS: I'll go see them and bring them back here.

HALLAM: Rawlings, listen to me. . . . Your heart isn't what it used to be. The trip might . . . (*stops at a look from RAWLINGS*)

RAWLINGS: I'll see them if it's the last thing I ever do. . . . And they will come back home. Circus performers! I thought they went to repair the wooden horses on the merry-go-round and the rest . . .

HALLAM: They don't seem to remember anything. . . . As if they had been born in the circus, Rawlings . . . (*then, emphatic*) Don't go. . . . I'll go see them again and urge them to come here. . . . Do you hear?

RAWLINGS: But what if they won't. . . . What if like you say they've lost their memory for their own blood and kin. . . . Don't say it, Hallam. . . . I know what you're thinking but don't say it. That I sold them to Onofrio. . . . All right, damn it, go and ask them to come.

HALLAM: That's better, Rawlings. . . . I'll go right now . . . (*exits*)

RAWLINGS: Circus horsemen . . . Beards . . . Arms like gladiators . . . We'll see though when they get here if they've forgotten as much as the Doc says. We'll see . . .

Scene 7

Same room. Late in the day. DR. HALLAM *enters first.* JOEL *and* GREGORY *follow hesitantly behind the doctor, but they are not as timid as when they lived at home and their bearing is magisterial.*

HALLAM: Your boys have come to visit you, Rawlings . . .

RAWLINGS: You should have give me more notice they was coming, Doc. . . . I'd have been ready for them then . . . (*stares at his sons*) Gregory, Joel . . . Come on in, why don't you. . . . Sit down . . .

GREGORY and JOEL: How do you do, Father . . . (*They shake hands with him. They exchange looks with one another, and are shocked at how he has "failed."*)

RAWLINGS: (*after an awkward pause*) I'm glad to know that you use your own name, boys. . . . Though I'd never have dreamed you'd become horseback riders and athletes. . . . I think Rainforth would have sort of liked the idea, come to think of it.

JOEL: (*as if piqued by the reference*) We can't stay long, Father. . . . The circus is leaving tonight for the West . . .

RAWLINGS: But you just got here, Joel. . . . I don't think I would have recognized you boys if I had met you on the street. . . . When I study you of course I know you're . . . my sons . . .

GREGORY: Are you in need of anything, Father?

RAWLINGS: Why, no. . . . You wouldn't change your mind would you now and let Minnie heat you up something . . . she's still cooking for me, and the grub is good as ever.

GREGORY: As Joel has said, Father, the circus is leaving in just a little less than an hour . . .

RAWLINGS: I see. . . . Just tell me one thing, though, boys, you were planning to come to see me weren't you anyhow. . . . I mean you didn't have to wait for Doc Hallam here to drag you back home now . . .

JOEL: Yes, we'd thought of visiting you, Father. . . . But we weren't sure you would want to see us. . . . (*The boys make impatient gestures to be gone.*)

RAWLINGS: I see. . . . Well, it's good anyhow we got to see one another again . . . however briefly . . . (*tries to stand up, and* DR. HALLAM *has to assist him*) Don't stay away so long the next time, lads. . . . And when you come home, plan to spend a week or so, will you.

GREGORY and JOEL: We will, Father.

RAWLINGS: And write, why don't you. . . . Just a postcard will do. . . . Just to let me know you're all right and doing well . . .

(GREGORY *and* JOEL *shake hands with their father and go out.*)

HALLAM: Rawlings, are you all right . . . (*goes hurriedly to the sink and draws some water, picks up a glass, and puts some medicine in it and brings it back to* RAWLINGS) Drink this, Rawlings, right down now. . . . 'Twill make you feel a little easier.

RAWLINGS: What are you making me swallow this time? (*but drinks it nonetheless*) Mmm. You were right, Hallam. . . . I would never have recognized them in a blue moon. I wouldn't have knowed them from Adam . . .

HALLAM: (*takes his pulse*) I want you to get a good night's sleep, now, Rawlings. . . . Ten hours or so.

RAWLINGS: You know I never sleep, you old son of a bitch. . . . And another thing. We both know damned well they would never have

set foot in this house if you hadn't a dragged them. . . . Ain't that
so. . . . They were strangers came tonight, Hallam. They weren't
my sons anymore. I have no sons. No sons at all.

HALLAM: I want you to, sleep, get a good night's sleep now. . . . I'll be
over the first thing in the morning. Minnie's staying here tonight,
isn't she.

RAWLINGS: (*after a long pause*) So far as I know, Doc.

HALLAM: Goodnight, then.

RAWLINGS: They no more would have come to see me than the sun
will rise in the West . . .

HALLAM: I'll look in on you in the morning, Arthur.

(*HALLAM exits.*)

RAWLINGS: Doctors . . . I have my fill of them. . . . Or least this one. . . .
I'd be better off going to see the Witch of Hebblethwaite. (*thinking
over what he has said*) By God, what if I did go see her. How could
she fail me any more than everybody else! And because she's what
she is, and has never pretended to be more than she is, she may
give me the help I need. (*He says this last looking out with indigna-
tion and rage. The lights go out.*)

Scene 8

Lights go on and we see RAWLINGS *standing in front of* ALDA PENNING-
TON's *house. He has forgotten how late it is. Raps at the door. Lights go
on revealing* ALDA PENNINGTON *crocheting a new doily or dresser cover
for her fastidiously kept home. Antique furniture everywhere, beautiful
carpets and mirrors. Fresh flowers. An air of restrained wealth and comfort, not the house one would associate with a midwife or "witch."*

ALDA: Who is it?

RAWLINGS: Someone you never expected to see again who stands in
need of your counsel.

ALDA: What a pretentious apology for arriving in the dead of night.
Come in. The door's open. (*aside*) I never lock it. What's the good.

All know me, including the ones bent on evil, and all can get in if they wish to in any case. Hence the door is open, if not wide, half ajar. (*RAWLINGS enters.*) You've gotten spare and bent since I saw you last. You could live quite a while yet though. . . . You're tough like an old walnut orchard. Sit down. . . . Do you know how late it is, Mr. Rawlings? It's three o'clock in the morning.

RAWLINGS: I had no idea!

ALDA: You never had an idea! You were born with more ideas than you've gathered up in all your mature years. . . . What do you want?

RAWLINGS: Your counsel and advice.

ALDA: Oh that's easily given. . . . I thought you wanted some herbs or medicinal teas perhaps . . . (*looks at him sharply while going on with her crocheting*) What's wrong, Mr. Rawlings. . . . What's really wrong. Or do you know? (*laughs*) Of course you don't. . . . No man ever knew what was really wrong. . . . You know nothing! Men, I mean. . . . You act but you don't know why you act. . . . I hate all of you. . . . Come, come, what do you want. . . . It's past even my bedtime.

RAWLINGS: I have made a hash of everything, Alda Pennington. . . . Dr. Hallam . . .

ALDA: (*contemptuous, bitter*) Dr. Hallam! That mountebank! Pill-choker! Sawbones . . . He tried to get me ridden out of town on a rail years ago, for curing the patients he was trying to kill. . . . Don't talk to me of old Doc Hallam.

RAWLINGS: I thought he loved you in his youth.

ALDA: You thought . . . Doc Hallam be damned. . . . What do you want from me, Arthur . . . (*She has known him, as she's known DR. HALLAM, since her youth.*)

RAWLINGS: I drove away my sons.

ALDA: I heard you sold them.

RAWLINGS: All right, sold them. . . . I made a terrible mistake. . . . Now all I can think of is them.

ALDA: (*biting the thread*) Mmm. (*glowers at him*) Go on. Tell me more.

RAWLINGS: They did come to see me. . . . But without wanting to. . . . They were cold as the brook after a snowfall. . . . Hardly said a word.

ALDA: Just as they were trained.

RAWLINGS: (*controlling his anger*) So you are going to talk to me just like Doc Hallam.

ALDA: So they returned and were cold to you. . . . What did you expect them to be when you had sold them to a crooked circus proprietor. . . . Why didn't you kill them in the first place and sell them to the renderer to be made into tallow while you were about it. . . . You should be in jail, Arthur Rawlings. . . . You have no right to go about a free man.

RAWLINGS: So, go ahead and abuse me. Out Hallam — Hallam.

ALDA: Go on with your story.

RAWLINGS: There is no more to tell. . . . I preferred my dead son to my living boys. . . . I sold them. . . . I have nothing in life left.

ALDA: What did you do with the money that came out of the sale.

RAWLINGS: (*shocked into remembrance*) The money.

ALDA: The money! (*angry, irritable*) Didn't Onofrio pay you in money.

RAWLINGS: Of course.

ALDA: Well, then, what did you do with it.

RAWLINGS: (*Shocked, he has never remembered it before.*) Why, I hardly know . . .

ALDA: Did you spend it?

RAWLINGS: No, I'm sure I didn't spend it.

ALDA: (*shouts*) Well, where is it then. . . . Don't you know, you old fool?

RAWLINGS: (*stammers*) I . . . I . . .

ALDA: I wouldn't be at all surprised they would be carting you off to the county lunatic asylum. . . . Sold his own boys and don't even know where the money from the sale is . . . (*rises*) remember while I fix you a cup of coffee.

RAWLINGS: Not coffee. . . . I would never sleep then again in my life.

ALDA: (*going up to him*) You came here for advice, didn't you . . . (RAWLINGS *nods, frightened.*) Then damn it you shall drink coffee. . . . Strong coffee. (*goes over to a small stove, heats the coffee*) And did you bring any money to pay for my advice. . . . For I charge more than old Doc Hallam nowadays . . .

RAWLINGS: I'll pay you twice what I pay him and more . . .

ALDA: And what will you have in your coffee.

RAWLINGS: Sugar, white sugar will do.

ALDA: And you can't remember what you did with the blood money . . . (*laughs stridently*) It's a wonderful story. I can't remember a story that is quite so shameful, or quite so unbelievable. . . . One would have expected it to happen a thousand years ago, but not today. . . . Just like that, he sold his own sons to Onofrio. . . . (*She laughs. The coffee heated, she brings it over to him.*) Drink this down to the bottom of the cup and we'll talk.

RAWLINGS: What's in this besides coffee.

ALDA: What does a desperate old fool with one foot in the grave care at this time. . . . Do you want advice or do you want to die in your chair, with your bad conscience. . . . Drink it.

(RAWLINGS, *cowed, drinks the coffee.*)

ALDA: Drink all of it, and there's more in the pot.

RAWLINGS: A second cup of this brew would kill me. . . . My heart is already pounding like a trip hammer.

ALDA: You'll drink it or I'll never open my mouth again.

(*He hands her his empty cup. She takes it, refills it, and brings it back to him. She sits down.*)

ALDA: And how much did Onofrio pay you for your sons.

RAWLINGS: (*coming out of a reverie*) Not enough.

ALDA: (*exasperated*) If you want my counsel and advice, you will answer my questions directly. Is that clear?

RAWLINGS: You should have been born an empress. You only come alive when you command.

ALDA: Answer my questions directly or get out. I have no time for those who cavil and evade, pretend and cover up, like some silly heiress who lies about her age. *How much were you paid for selling your sons!*

RAWLINGS: (*in a whisper*) Ten thousand dollars.

ALDA: All of that for two feeble-minded yokels?

RAWLINGS: Watch out, Alda, watch your venomous tongue!

ALDA: You think they were worth more? Then why didn't you demand more!

RAWLINGS: Nothing would be enough. (*His own words surprise him. Even* ALDA *is shocked into silence by his statement.*)

ALDA: (*more reasonable, almost kind*) And where is this money.

RAWLINGS: Why don't you say blood money as before.

ALDA: Yes. Good. (*as if corrected by a prompter*) Where is this blood money?

RAWLINGS: (*sleepily, as if hypnotized, despite the strong coffee*) It is in a deserted rat's nest.

ALDA: Rat's nest?

RAWLINGS: That is what I said.

ALDA: (*indignant*) And where is this rat's nest.

RAWLINGS: In the attic above my late wife's bedroom.

ALDA: Where she died of grief and humiliation.

RAWLINGS: I should never have come here. . . . You take away the very little I have . . .

ALDA: Little? *Little!* You do not have little. You have nothing! Nothing. . . . Sit down. . . . You came for my counsel and advice, and you shall have it. S-i-t d-o-w-n, I say. . . . (*He sits.*) We have only commenced. You killed your wife Dora. Had you cut her throat you could not have been more guilty. And you invented your first son . . . Rainforth. . . . Don't say anything. . . . We will come to him later if you live. . . . You sold your younger sons to Onofrio. . . . And I am expected to help you. . . . Is that right, you expect my help.

RAWLINGS: I expect nothing.

ALDA: You lie. . . . I see still in your mind a famished desire to go on living. In fact you will never die.

RAWLINGS: You raving bitch! I should strangle you . . .

ALDA: (*as if she had not heard him*) The very first thing you must do in order to regain your hold on life and in fact bring back the boys you have lost, is to burn Onofrio's money. . . . Here, before my eyes. . . . (RAWLINGS *stares at her horrified, but unsure now whether she is sane*) Did you hear what I said. . . . You must bring the ten thousand dollars from its hiding place, and we will burn it together . . .

RAWLINGS: No!

ALDA: Good. . . . Then we have achieved that much. You will keep the money and the Devil can keep your sons.

RAWLINGS: Couldn't it be given to charity.

ALDA: Blood money given to charity? Who would accept it.

RAWLINGS: Somebody certainly who needed it.

ALDA: Who would accept money from a man who sold his own flesh and blood. . . . Rawlings, I've done . . . You owe me a hundred dollars. . . . And don't ever come here again, do you hear. . . . I never want to see you again. You disgust me . . .

Scene 9

Dressing room of the circus. JOEL, *the younger, and* GREGORY, *the older of the boys, are in the midst of an altercation.*

JOEL: You, of all people, Gregory! Wanting to go home, wanting to leave the circus. I can't believe my own ears . . .

GREGORY: I can't help it, Joel. . . . I've got to go home. . . . I can barely go through my act in the circus any longer. When we go through the flamin' hoop, I want to be consumed in the flames. . . . I want to die.

JOEL: It was you who hated Father the most.

GREGORY: But it's home, don't you see. . . . It's home. . . . This is all a dream, a dream that goes on and on less real every day. With no nourishment in it for me. . . . I feel like a painted doll of a horse-back rider instead of a man. (*wipes off some of his makeup*) I want to be a man, Joel, not a toy for an audience to applaud and drivel over. . . . I want to go back where I came from. . . . Will you come with me, Joel . . .

JOEL: I don't know how I could stay without you. . . . But what will we tell Onofrio . . .

GREGORY: We need not tell him a thing. After all, what do we get out of it. . . . He's never paid us because he says he paid our father a fortune . . .

JOEL: We've had our keep though.

GREGORY: Our keep! We are the stars of his circus if you ask me. . . . And when we ask for money, he won't shell out a dime. . . . Joel, what do you suppose Father did with that money. . . . Are you listening to me. (*takes him in his arms*) You look so troubled. . . . Don't be. . . . I will never leave you, count on me, Joel . . .

JOEL: But what'll we do if we go back to that sleepy village that we came from. . . . These past five years, we've had a sort of exciting life, haven't we, Greg.

GREGORY: You know better. . . . It's all tinsel and make-believe. . . . You know too we'll never be great horsemen and riders. . . . We learned too late. . . . We're just handsome young men the audience admires. . . . We look pretty good in tights. (*looks down at himself*) We're toys.

JOEL: (*throws himself again into* GREGORY'*s arms*) We'll never part though.

GREGORY: Never . . .

JOEL: But Father . . . To go back to Father . . . It's a nightmare.

GREGORY: (*rapt*) What has he done with all that money . . .

JOEL: Who cares about the money, Greg.

GREGORY: It should be ours. . . . It's a fortune, . . . It's blood money. . . . It should belong to us. . . . Supposing he is dead. . . . Supposing someone else should inherit it all. . . . Think of it! For all his neglect of us, all his sternness, and his coldness, his jibing us, his always preferring Rainforth to us, praising him while he looked down on us, extolling Rainforth as a god while we were no better than niggers in his eyes, bastards. . . . He once called me a shitass. That is what we were . . . to him . . .

JOEL: Then why go back there.

GREGORY: Because he must be dead or dying. . . . And that fortune is ours. . . . We've earned it. . . . Don't you see Onofrio has treated us the same way Father did. . . . We're no better than slaves, working for nothing, and yet like Father he depends on us. . . . Let's go home, Joel. . . . And if we don't like it there, we can run off and be vagabonds. . . . After all we've always lived on nothing all our lives. . . . Joel, tell me you'll agree. . . . We'll leave tonight.

JOEL: Without a word?

GREGORY: Without a word.

JOEL: We're a long way from home, Greg.

GREGORY: Then if you're afraid, stay . . . stay with Onofrio, but I'm going. If you're a coward, you're a coward. (*turns from him*)

JOEL: Oh, Greg, what are you talking about? You know without you I am no good. . . . I couldn't even get on the horse if you weren't there to spur me on. . . . Of course I'll go with you. Don't doubt me, Greg. . . . I only somehow fear Father more than Onofrio.

GREGORY: They're the same stripe, ain't they? Murderers at heart. Slave drivers.

JOEL: (*puzzled*) Why murderers?

GREGORY: Because they killed what we might have been, Joel. Father began it and Onofrio finished it . . .

JOEL: And we can't ever be . . . ourselves. . . . Be men?

GREGORY: You trust me. . . . But the main thing is to go home and claim what is ours. . . . Don't you see, that money is ours . . . well, call it birthright, call it anything, but it is ours. . . . We've slaved for it. They both owe it to us!

Scene 10

In the tent of GIUSEPPE ONOFRIO, GONZAGO, *his handyman and "barker" enters in alarm.*

GONZAGO: They've cleared out. I tell you. Joel and Greg . . . Their tent is vacant.

ONOFRIO: You're either drunk or you're crazy. . . . Go back and search. They can't have cleared out. They have to be somewhere in the immediate vicinity, or they're lying drunk behind the tiger cage again.

GONZAGO: I'm telling you, they've lit out. Their belongings are all gone.

ONOFRIO: They had no belongings, only the clothes I put on their back.

GONZAGO: Their trinkets are gone.

ONOFRIO: Trinkets?

GONZAGO: They had a box full of photographs of their home, their mother, pieces from the merry-go-round horses, the glass eyes from the horses, and little jewels.

ONOFRIO: You've memorized their possessions, I see. . . . How do I know you haven't had a hand in their disappearance, that they're lying in a ditch somewhere their throats cut by you . . .

GONZAGO: (*insulted*) Go have the ditches searched then.

ONOFRIO: What will we do for the bareback and horsemanship act tonight.

GONZAGO: You'll find some other pair to obey your wishes . . .

ONOFRIO: Look. Go back and have all the grounds searched one more time.

GONZAGO: We have already done that, Señor Onofrio. I tell you there's no trace of them.

ONOFRIO: How could they leave me. . . . I am their rightful owner, their own father handed them over to me. . . . Were they dissatisfied?

GONZAGO: (*his disgust and anger breaking through*) Dissatisfied is hardly the word!

ONOFRIO: (*missing the "barker's" contempt and pent-up hatred for him*) They had everything. Could have remained with me and my carnival forever. . . . They have nowhere to go.

GONZAGO: (*too low to be heard*) That is exactly where they headed.

ONOFRIO: What are you mumbling about! I'm surprised you did not go with them. You acted smitten enough on them.

GONZAGO: (*lofty, gelid*) I will have the grounds searched again.

ONOFRIO: Wait a moment, Gonzago. . . . You are right. . . . They've decamped. I've known it was coming for some time. They had no more interest in riding bareback and jumping through flaming rings than they cared about hearing their old man's yarns about their hero brother. . . . Their old man had it right about them. . . . All they wanted to do was putter, and paint wooden horses. When I gave them real horses to ride, they were bored!

GONZAGO: They were good horsemen, Señor, and you know it.

ONOFRIO: Perhaps to those blinded by admiration . . .

GONZAGO: They rode as if the horse and they were one animal and you know it . . .

ONOFRIO: Call that simpleton who does the act with the tigers. . . . He can ride. . . . We'll never miss them in a week or so. . . . But their father, Gonzago, he must give me back my purchase money! For I've kept them in grub and clothes and shelter these five years, and they've not earned it! The old man must cough up the purchase money . . .

GONZAGO: We're a thousand miles from where he lives, if he lives, Señor Onofrio.

ONOFRIO: Then we'll change our itinerary and go as the crow flies toward the other direction instead of where we're headed.

Scene 11

ARTHUR RAWLINGS *and* ALDA PENNINGTON. *He is standing in the door-way of her house. It is nightfall.*

ALDA: I would have staked everything on your not returning.

RAWLINGS: (*coming in*) You don't look surprised or amazed.

ALDA: I'm disappointed.

RAWLINGS: (*almost outraged*) Disappointed!

ALDA: Yes. I thought you at least would go on being yourself, resisting everything and everybody, that not even the lightning would touch your pride.

RAWLINGS: Well, rejoice then in my fall. (*falls into a chair*) I've come to capitulate.

ALDA: Did you bring the money. (*She has become even more strong than usual after his statement about capitulation.*)

RAWLINGS: (*mournful, sullen, sardonic*) I have indeed.

ALDA: You see how wrong I am occasionally about everything. I got it psychically you would never find it.

RAWLINGS: (*lifts a thick filthy looking envelope from a box*) Oh it took days to find it, don't you worry. And a bad fall . . . Even Minnie could not locate it.

ALDA: Minnie deals entirely in the things of the world, that's why.

RAWLINGS: And money is not a thing of the world, Alda Pennington!

ALDA: Not that money. No, it's not, Arthur.

RAWLINGS: (*almost enthusiastically, certainly not angry*) You hellion.

ALDA: Blood money is not of this world. It has its own kingdom. (*suddenly angry again, at least imperious*) Well! Shan't we begin.

RAWLINGS: (*expecting mercy, at least delay*) Begin what.

ALDA: He asks me *what*. What did you come for? Do you think this is a savings bank!

RAWLINGS: Somebody once called you the portress of hell-gate.

ALDA: Oh I've been called worse than that, by far. . . . (*suddenly*) Let me see that money. Do you hear me?

RAWLINGS: (*very gradually rising, hobbling over to her like a much older man*) Take it, Alda, and be damned.

ALDA: (*chuckling*) Hear him. (*She takes an envelope from the box; mutters.*) Chewed by rats all right, but even they you see cared not to tear open such money! Even the rats have avoided you, Arthur Rawlings!

RAWLINGS: Croak on, exult over me, go on . . .

ALDA: (*She tears open the envelope.*) Arthur Rawlings . . .

RAWLINGS: What is it now? . . . I've had enough of you.

ALDA: (*rising, and towering over him*) You count it. Go ahead. Count it.

RAWLINGS: (*taking the money with trepidation*) One thousand . . . Two thousand. Three . . . Four . . . Five . . . (*counts now without speaking*) . . . Ten thousand . . .

ALDA: Despite their having been put in a rat's nest, they're crisp almost brand new and *genuine* U.S. bills . . .

RAWLINGS: Oh, Alda, what shall we do?

ALDA: There's only one thing to do . . .

RAWLINGS: I can't think, Alda. . . . My mind is like, like frozen.

ALDA: Oh, don't try to embellish the facts. Frozen . . . Do you want your sons back or don't you.

RAWLINGS: I can only think of the money, Alda . . .

ALDA: (*picking up the bills*) And there's a lot to think about certainly. . . . But you have no choice.

RAWLINGS: Just black and white again, eh? (*He speaks more like the old RAWLINGS.*)

ALDA: (*holding up the money*) You can either burn it, and let your sons come home to you, or you can keep it and even the rats will leave you in peace . . .

RAWLINGS: My brains . . . my poor brains.

ALDA: Then let me burn it. . . . (*She advances over to the burning grate fire.*)

RAWLINGS: No, no!

ALDA: Do you want your sons to come back or do you want to lose them forever.

RAWLINGS: It's not a fair choice.

ALDA: Nothin's fair in this life. . . . I asked you a question. . . . Do you want your sons to be lost to you forever or do you want to put your money where even the rats and the spiders will spurn it . . .

RAWLINGS: Burn it, burn it. . . . Burn all ten thousand.

(*ALDA goes to the fire, and throws in some of the money.*)

(*RAWLINGS rises, screams, rushes toward the grate and tries to extricate the burning money. ALDA pushes him away. He falls on the floor, his clothes partly set afire by his trying to rescue the thousand dollar notes.)*

(ALDA *goes on throwing in the money.)*

RAWLINGS: Have pity, Alda. . . . Spare me some. . . . Just a thousand even.

ALDA: *(implacable)* No, nothing. . . . You made your choice . . . *(picking up a heavy poker, threatening him)* Go back to that chair while I burn your blood money. . . . Do you hear? (RAWLINGS *obeys.* ALDA *goes on burning the money quietly, while from the chair* RAWLINGS *makes terrible outcries like those of a dying animal.)*

ACT II

Scene 1

GREGORY *and* JOEL *on a crossways, their few belongings in two small valises.*

GREGORY: To tell you the truth, Joel, I don't ever want to reach home.

JOEL: You're not sorry though we left the circus.

GREGORY: Not a whit. But I don't want to go home neither.

JOEL: Then couldn't we just wander . . .

GREGORY: (*deeply disturbed, speaks haltingly, huskily*) Wander, Joel.

JOEL: Yes, just go from place to place.

GREGORY: As beggars . . . ?

JOEL: (*beginning to see what he has said*) Well.

GREGORY: We'd have to eat, after all. . . . We can't live on air.

JOEL: Well, Father couldn't deny us a crust of bread . . . if we did go home.

GREGORY: If he's alive, Joel. . . . Old men sometimes go like a puff of smoke. . . . And we never kept in touch with him.

JOEL: I don't see that we have any choice but to go home. . . . At least folks know us there, they can't turn us completely from their door like the strangers we've met on the road. . . . So, let's go on, Greg, and see what our chances are at least back there . . .

GREGORY: I don't like to turn back! I like to keep going. . . . It's not good luck to turn back . . . had we made our fortune, Joel, we would come home like victors. . . . But what have we got to show for our five years with the circus. . . . We'll be greeted as runaways . . .

JOEL: Greeted! We are runaways. . . . And he owes us, Greg. . . . He owes us . . .

GREGORY: You say that as if you could . . . kill him, Joel. . . . I've never seen you so fierce.

JOEL: It don't matter what name people give to our homecoming or us. . . . We have that one home. . . . Every man belongs somewhere, and that place where we painted the merry-go-round horses is ours. . . . A tramp is only called a tramp after all when he's not in his birthplace.

GREGORY: I never heard you talk like this before, Joel. . . . I do marvel at it. . . . You sound like an orator.

JOEL: I spoke the truth though didn't I? Didn't I, Greg.

GREGORY: You bet. It's a mouthful of truth, little Joel. . . . I take my hat off to you. . . . All right, we'll go on. We'll go home . . . if he's dead, he's dead. . . . If we have no home, we have no home. . . . But don't forget, we've a good five hundred miles to walk or hitch a ride. . . . And Joel, we're almost out of money. . . . So bear up. . . . But I say you're right. . . . It's right we go home, kid. . . . It's right. (*They embrace.*)

Scene 2

ARTHUR RAWLINGS *comes staggering into his living room.* MINNIE, *a woman of 40, is tidying up the room.*

MINNIE: (*looking up*) For God's sake, Mr. Rawlings. . . . What's happened to you. You look like you'd been speaking with . . . the dead.

RAWLINGS: (*falling down into a chair*) Worse, Minnie, much worse. . . . What can the dead do after all . . .

MINNIE: Can I bring you something.

RAWLINGS: I don't think so.

MINNIE: There's still some bourbon in the cupboard.

RAWLINGS: No, nothing . . . (*after a long pause*) I've been to the witch of Hebblethwaite, Minnie . . .

MINNIE: I'm disappointed, sir.

RAWLINGS: Disappointed? (*turning to look at her full in the face*) Whatever for . . .

MINNIE: I only mean, sir, I think it was beneath you to visit her.

RAWLINGS: If it had only been beneath me, I wouldn't look the way you say I do.

(MINNIE *goes unbidden to the cupboard and pours him a drink of bourbon, brings it back, offers it to him. He takes it matter-of-fact like one who had ordered it; sips it.*)

RAWLINGS: Thank you, Minnie. . . . Thank you. . . . I must be in my second childhood.

MINNIE: You're too young for that, Mr. Rawlings.

RAWLINGS: Then perhaps I have softening of the brain. . . . But what I have done tonight even a lunatic would not have done. . . . Do you hear, Minnie. . . . The most raving lunatic in the most dangerous ward of the craziest crazy house would not have done what I did tonight. . . . I let Alda Pennington burn ten thousand worth of money . . . (MINNIE *is speechless.*) Do you hear me. . . . Did you hear me.

MINNIE: I heard the words.

RAWLINGS: And I participated in the deed, and neither of us, you nor I, are convinced. We are never convinced I guess by what life brings to us. Later we get used to it and call it the truth. . . . Alda Pennington has burned up our future . . .

MINNIE: But what would you let her do such a thing for. . . . Or did she steal it from you.

RAWLINGS: No, I gave it to her. . . . She said it was blood money, it was the money from Giuseppe Onofrio, the circus owner, I accepted in exchange for his taking my sons into his service. Indemnity money you might call it. Or as she called it, money for the sale of my sons.

MINNIE: But that part's not true surely. (*As he stares at her, she continues.*) You didn't sell your boys.

RAWLINGS: What does it matter what you call it, after all. . . . I see now the intention was evil. So why not say I sold them. Yes, Alda Pennington may be in contact with the Devil, but she speaks the truth.

MINNIE: But to burn . . . a fortune.

RAWLINGS: I will never get over it. . . . Now I feel that I have not only killed my sons but burned the money that belonged to them. That is I have murdered them twice! I have killed their past and their future!

MINNIE: You must get into bed, sir, and rest! It's been too much for you.

RAWLINGS: But I wanted you to know, Minnie. . . . You have been more than just the hired girl in this house . . .

MINNIE: I hope so, Mr. Rawlings . . .

RAWLINGS: I don't excuse myself. . . . I can say it now. . . . I sold my own boys, and now I have destroyed their birthright and their fortune. . . . But she persuaded me, that if I got rid of the money, they would come back to me. . . . Do you see . . . I don't excuse myself. . . . But I felt at the moment she said that, that I must burn the dirty money to have my boys back home with me. . . . But I see now that it was merely another folly. Once we commit one folly, we must commit another and another, and another. . . . One folly must follow after another, until there is nothing but folly. . . . Do you follow me . . .

MINNIE: I believe one can repair almost any part of bad fortune.

RAWLINGS: (*Kindled, amazed he advances toward her and takes both her hands in his and kisses them.*) Minnie! Minnie . . .

Scene 3

ALDA *opening the door on* MINNIE.

ALDA: I didn't need foresight to know you'd be coming. . . . Well, come in. Don't stand there gaping as if you were as crazy as your employer. (*leaves her, and goes to her big chair; sighs*) I haven't seen you Minnie since your last miscarriage . . .

MINNIE: (*coming in*) You said it was an abortion at the time. . . . At least you charged enough . . .

ALDA: I gave you as I give everybody your choice, have the baby . . .

MINNIE: Or let it die by your hands.

ALDA: I merely carried out your instructions.

MINNIE: You took advantage of my need, as you take advantage of everyone's . . . Of poor old Rawlings . . .

ALDA: He's only acting old. He's as stout and wiry and tough as a walnut tree. He may never die. He could bury all of us . . .

MINNIE: Is that your foresight speaking or only your choler and hate.

ALDA: Perhaps the two mix, in-ex-tri-cab-ly, Minnie.

MINNIE: Oh, I daresay.

ALDA: (*angry*) So you hate me, and you come for no other purpose. Don't try to pull the wool over my eyes. You're not here to sue for old Rawlings or his whelps . . . you're here to cry for your murdered babes. You cowardly whores, who want your cake and eat it too! Go hang yourselves on one of the sassafras trees by the river, why don't you . . . come here to act the pious devout slut, and throw up to me my crimes and wrongdoings. . . . Do I ask people to come here to be helped?

MINNIE: You're here, though, aren't you. . . . And you let us in. . . . You're available, and you work for us, don't you?

ALDA: Whores always turn to preaching and moralizing when they lose their good looks . . . you're no exception.

MINNIE: Give me back that money to take to him. . . . He's gone stark raving mad.

ALDA: *Gone.* Yes, twenty years ago he went . . .

MINNIE: Alda, the money.

ALDA: You shall never have one penny of it. It's burned to ashes. (*motions toward the grate*)

MINNIE: The oldest gypsy trick in the world. Pretending the money some rattled and delirious old man handed you has disappeared. . . . I am surprised even at you . . .

ALDA: I'm glad something may have stirred your corpse-like physiognomy . . .

MINNIE: (*taking out a gun*) Alda, look here.

ALDA: (*only half-looking*) I see it. . . . Why don't you shoot. . . . They'll find in my ledger book the record of your abortions so you'll be put down as a child murderer before you're hanged for killing me.

MINNIE: Almighty Christ. (*lowers the gun*)

ALDA: (*leaping up, wrests the gun away from her*) You simpleton. (*She strikes her.*) I should shoot you and bury you. The county would secretly thank me for sparing them the trouble of getting rid of you.

MINNIE: See here, at least admit it. You've still got the ten thousand.

ALDA: Unlike some reformed whores, I'm not afraid to admit anything.

MINNIE: Admit you did not burn the money. Admit it's here, waiting to fulfill some damnable plan you are fomenting and brewing. . . . Admit it. (*She strikes* ALDA *hard, knocking her almost to the floor.*)

ALDA: You'll regret that, Minnie Cruikshank . . .

MINNIE: I have no doubt. I only wish I had killed you while I had the gun.

ALDA: (*herself again*) Your whole life is whining out your regrets: You didn't do this, you didn't do that, or the other. . . . Why don't you do something once you want to do and then die! Why are all you fools so afraid of the only thing you are good for, the grave! A real woman would have had her bastard sons instead of trying to murder them one way or another, in the woods, by the brook . . .

MINNIE: And in the house of an old retired whore and abortionist like yourself!

ALDA: I am always blamed for other people's follies. . . . There *is* no money. There's only ashes. You're welcome to them. (*ALDA motions to the grate. She goes and puts the gun in a little commode and locks the drawer. MINNIE goes over to the grate and searches through the ashes for any remaining bills, extricates a charred piece of a thousand dollar bill, examines it and then bursts into tears.*)

MINNIE: It's true. It's true. You've burned the money.

Scene 4

MINNIE *and* RAWLINGS.

MINNIE: She doesn't have the money. It's all ashes.

RAWLINGS: Remember I saw her burn it myself. . . . I burned my fingers trying to extricate the bills. So your trip to see her was in vain.

MINNIE: (*bitterly*) Yes, she convinced me against my will.

RAWLINGS: A burden has been partially lifted from my heart.

MINNIE: I don't see why or how . . . (*almost to herself*) To think your fortune has all gone up in smoke at the hands of a gypsy. (*There is a long silence, in which both are lost in thought. MINNIE has seated herself at the other end of the room from RAWLINGS. She is mending some curtains.*)

RAWLINGS: Listen. Listen to me! They are coming back, Minnie. The boys.

MINNIE: What makes you think so?

RAWLINGS: Here I am talking like the old hag from Hebblethwaite herself. . . . But it's true. . . . I feel their presence. . . . They are coming back.

MINNIE: (*drops her work; then as if to herself*) How will it be, our reunion.

RAWLINGS: Yes, how will it be. Will they come home as the masters. Will they come home full of hate and rage and pride, Minnie.

MINNIE: They were such good boys. Obedient, quiet, industrious.

RAWLINGS: That's the trouble. When good and obedient quiet boys turn, watch out. . . . They were kept down too long! (*as if to himself*) I say watch out. . . . Anything can happen if they come back. I warn you. By you, Minnie, I mean everyone!

MINNIE: We have nothing to fear from Joel and Gregory, and you know it. You've not been yourself since Alda destroyed . . . your fortune . . .

RAWLINGS: The boys shall learn of it, Minnie, and have it out with me.

MINNIE: (*rising*) There, there, now, you must not take on so. . . . Remember, what Dr. Hallam warned you against. Unusual excitement.

RAWLINGS: That is all life amounts to, unusual excitement. Even in the grave there must be turmoil and uneasiness. Everything is sickening motion and ceaseless unrest. . . . (*A knocking is heard outside. At first they both take it that it is the wind, that a storm is arising in the West. . . . But the knocking continues. Then, looking at the door:*) Would you go and ask who it is, Minnie.

MINNIE: (*MINNIE rises and goes toward the door, which is some distance away. She is heard talking. . . . Then she returns.*) While we were speaking of them, they were outside all the time.

RAWLINGS: You can't mean it, Minnie. By they, you could only mean them. Only the boys . . . My God . . . Do I look too terrible and old . . .

MINNIE: (*studying him kindly*) You look like their father. . . . And think from how far off they've come! Shall I open the door. (*RAWLINGS nods.*) Come in, boys. . . . Your father is expecting you.

RAWLINGS: Welcome back. . . . I don't know that you can believe I would welcome you on account of the way we parted. . . . Gregory, Joel . . . Joel, Gregory! It was as if someone else commanded me, do you understand.

JOEL: We don't care about your explanations, Father. . . . We have not come home to see you or even be your sons. . . . We feel we've lost all those rights.

GREGORY: We've come home or rather back because we had no other place to come to, and we could not stand the circus and that slave driver Onofrio, who after all, I suppose, is our real owner and father. . . . We broke our bargain. . . . We've traipsed and wandered all those countless miles!

RAWLINGS: (*disturbed*) But I don't understand, Joel. . . . I admit the wrong I've done you, and I know you cannot forgive me. . . . But when you say you haven't come home or back to see me, what exactly do you mean by that.

JOEL: We ask only that you give us back our carpentry shop. . . . We will not disturb you or bother you or engage you in conversation. After all neither you nor we have any claim upon the other. You . . . sold us to Onofrio, and we have escaped from him, as slaves used to escape their white masters. . . . In time of course he will come for us.

RAWLINGS: (*sitting down*) You didn't return to see me. . . . You have no claim on me. . . . Did you hear that, Minnie . . . you will be lodgers in this house, nothing more?

GREGORY: We will stay until he arrives here, and has it out with us about the future.

RAWLINGS: He will never dare come into this house . . . he has used all of us!

MINNIE: You will take some food with us at least, though you say you are only here as lodgers.

JOEL: We would prefer to eat alone, or prepare our own food.

MINNIE: Then if you plan to be so distant to us, never to speak or see us why did you come back? Why did you not just live in some house in the woods.

JOEL: As we have already explained, we had no other place to go, and after all this house is the start of our life, and maybe the finish.

RAWLINGS: (*to* MINNIE *or to* God *perhaps*) You see they have not forgiven me. . . . They have come home like spirits, not sons.

JOEL: We are not your sons. . . . You had only one son, Rainforth . . . he satisfied all your longings. We never pleased you, and when you sold us to Onofrio, you lost all claim upon us. . . . But you cannot very well turn us out in the street . . . fugitives though we be . . .

RAWLINGS: I suppose your real master will be here then any day.

GREGORY: He will surely come for his money, if not for us!

RAWLINGS: Minnie, we will have to tell them how that matter stands.

(MINNIE *nods.*)

GREGORY: (*interested*) I suppose you have made it grow a hundred-fold.

RAWLINGS: A hundred fold of ashes! . . . I have lost your money.

JOEL: Your money. Nothing that belonged to you was ever ours, sir.

RAWLINGS: After I lost you boys, my worship and longing for Rainforth died out. . . . I realized then that Rainforth was always too perfect and did not require my love. . . . I saw that it was you two I should have cared for, and not him. . . . My sin was that I worshipped him when I might have loved you. . . . Now I have lost all three of you . . . as to the blood money as it is called, it is burned to ashes. . . . All burned to nothing.

GREGORY: Burned. In a fire or an explosion.

RAWLINGS: Unable to sleep or eat, guilty of what I did with respect to you young men, I went in my desperate plight to see Alda Pennington. . . . She is, as you know, said to possess supernatural powers. Her powers, though, are maybe more those of a witch. . . . It was she who persuaded me. She threw it all in the fire in her grate. . . . With my compliance, let it be known. . . . I tried to extricate a few bills and was badly burned. . . . I wished to God I could have thrown myself in with the rest of your fortune and gone up like it in black smoke. . . . So I have told you all. . . . Have you ever met or read about a greater old fool or botcher, a worse specimen of a man than Arthur Rawlings. . . . I would not blame you if you killed me, but you will not. I can see it in your eyes. . . . You do not respect or honor me enough to punish me for my bad deeds. . . . I think Rainforth would have killed me.

GREGORY: You see, Rainforth again! Even in your fall you throw him up to us.

RAWLINGS: I swear to you boys I will never mention his name again then. . . . For I no longer love him. . . . As I said he was too perfect. . . . I never loved him. . . . I only worshipped his perfection which to tell the truth I now see made me feel abashed and unworthy. . . . And now I am not worthy of *your* love. . . . Well, let things stand as they stand. . . . You may go to your room and be fed there. . . . Do whatever you wish. . . . You have complete freedom here!

JOEL: We would respond to you, Father, if we could, but when you sold us and when we were in bondage to the circus master all these years something happened to us inside . . .

RAWLINGS: Inside?

JOEL: Yes, inside. . . . Tell him Greg, finish what I can't put in words.

GREGORY: All he means, sir, is, and we often spoke of it late at night when we could not sleep . . . that our hearts which were here warm and outpouring, if you will believe me, our hearts—and we tested the symptoms a hundred times, listening at one another's heartbeat—were turned to stone. . . . We feel nothing now toward any other human being.

RAWLINGS: This can't be true. . . . Minnie, it can't be true.

GREGORY: We are calm now, but we have no feelings, as if a stone had been substituted for our heart. . . . So when he comes, you can tell him this. . . . There is nothing for him to take back to the circus, and you can give him, perhaps, if you can collect them, the ashes from Alda Pennington's grate.

RAWLINGS: He shall not have you boys! I will not part with you, if I have to raise the money by terrible deeds.

JOEL: Whatever you wish, sir.

GREGORY: Goodnight, then, sir. . . . Goodnight, Minnie. . . . We are very tired from our long journey . . .

JOEL: Goodnight.

Scene 5

GREGORY *and* JOEL *in their old workroom.*

JOEL: But it looks so little, Greg! When we lived here we always remarked on how big it was, and when we were with the circus it still seemed such a big place. We've been back more than a week now and the room seems to be shrinking more every day. . . . Even the merry-go-round horses (*He approaches them cautiously.*) seem to have shrunk to little colts of no account.

GREGORY: Maybe it's because we are still tired from our journey, Joel.

JOEL: Do you think Father is glad we're back . . .

GREGORY: His only interest seems to be in the money he claims he burned . . .

JOEL: How could such a story be true, Greg . . .

GREGORY: I guess age has caught up with him . . . or I guess he was always crazy . . .

JOEL: He was, wasn't he?

GREGORY: Oh, Joel . . .

JOEL: Of course he was . . . he's always got one thing on his mind and then he worries it to death. . . . Once it was Rainforth. . . . Now it's the money he burned. . . . He don't see life like it is . . .

GREGORY: (*bitter*) And how is life seen, Joel . . .

JOEL: It ought to be like the sun, pouring down from everywhere, all sides, drenching down upon us . . .

(*Spotlight goes off boys.*)

Scene 6

Lights come up on RAWLINGS *and* MINNIE. *It is several nights later. The sound of heavy knocking.*

MINNIE: There's someone at the door, sir . . .

RAWLINGS: It's too late for visitors, Minnie. . . . Don't admit whoever it may be.

MINNIE: But he's been hammering out there for half an hour.

RAWLINGS: I know. . . . I heard him.

MINNIE: You know who it is.

RAWLINGS: I have more than a faint suspicion, Minnie. . . . Keep the door bolted. (*The pounding at the door has now become almost maniacal.*) Go tell the boys to hide, do you hear. . . . Don't stand there, like a disobedient idiot. . . . Go! Warn them . . . (MINNIE *exits*. RAWLINGS *shouts.*) I hear you. . . . Beat your knuckles raw.

ONOFRIO: (*calling from outside*) If you won't let me in you'll let in the sheriff by God, if I go for him.

RAWLINGS: And what if I let you in and burn you like I did your filthy money. (*then to himself*) Killing would be too good for someone who hoodwinked a crazy old man. . . . People should be punished for tempting men like me. . . . We should be kept out of temptation, and away from crooked roustabouts. . . . God damn you, Onofrio. (*goes to the door but does not open it*) Go back to your wild animal show, your fire-eaters and sword-swallowers and naked ladies on horseback. . . . This is a white man's house you're trying to break into.

ONOFRIO: You can let me in or I'll bring the sheriff.

RAWLINGS: (*throws open the door*) Don't come in. (*bars further entrance to him*) You can speak your piece from the threshold.

ONOFRIO: I want my money back or turn over to me your no-account brats.

RAWLINGS: If they was so no-account what did you put such a big down payment on them for . . .

ONOFRIO: Fork over the money or I'm going to the law.

RAWLINGS: (*He turns his back on him.* ONOFRIO *enters the room.*) Your money's burnt.

ONOFRIO: (*misunderstanding*) You wouldn't blow in money if you was starving to death. A skinflint like you.

RAWLINGS: I wish I had blowed it in now on almost anything except the way it went.

ONOFRIO: I know Arthur Rawlings, the greatest miser in eighty counties, would never mislay or foolishly spend one half buck . . .

RAWLINGS: Oh but someone *cleverer* and *evil-er* and *hellish-er* might have did it for him. . . . That never occurred to you . . .

ONOFRIO: Enough of your riddles, you old four-flusher. . . . And where are your cursed brats.

RAWLINGS: You'll never set eyes on them again, so give them up. . . . It's money we're talking of . . .

ONOFRIO: You haven't killed your boys have you rather than keep them in grub and shelter and heat. . . . I wouldn't put it past you! (*looks around suspiciously*)

RAWLINGS: I killed them when I sold them to you.

ONOFRIO: Sold, hell. . . . That was a bargain. . . . Don't you pin kidnapping or shady deals on me. . . . The sheriff knows me!

RAWLINGS: All that is left of your money lies in the fireplace grate of Alda Pennington. . . . Ashes and soot! And here's proof of it . . . (*takes from his pocket a half-consumed thousand dollar bill*)

See! (*suddenly rolls up his sleeve and exposes his burns and scars*)
See those.

ONOFRIO: (*credulous and shocked in spite of himself*) What are you
ranting and raving about old Alda Pennington . . .

RAWLINGS: You heard me, you moulting old fox. . . . Alda Pennington!
She told me, she threatened me (*bemused, insane*) that if I did not
burn your blood money, I would never see my boys again. . . . She
had given me some brew or potion which disordered my brains,
but even without the brew, I swear to you she would have made
me do it!

ONOFRIO: You can't con me with such a story. . . . You probably paid
her to make her swear she burned the money . . .

RAWLINGS: Believe anything you will . . . your money is no more, and
you won't take back my boys. . . . You paid them nothing while they
were with you. They have told me how you treated them!

ONOFRIO: I'll give you till tomorrow morning to return the money,
and then by God if you don't have it we'll see who'll have the upper hand. . . . I'm warning you, you two-faced old bastard. . . . You
who've posed as a pillar of honesty and upright dealing.

RAWLINGS: Where is your proof you ever gave me a dime . . .

ONOFRIO: My word against that of a crack-brain! My word . . .

RAWLINGS: You half-breed Gypsy . . . who would believe you. . . .
You never associated with anybody but pimps and cardsharpers,
pickpockets and dope fiends till you spirited away my boys. . . . Get
out, and don't you ever come back (*seizes* ONOFRIO *and throws him
to his knees*) Out, you rotten greaser . . . (*kicks him*)

ONOFRIO: (*rising*) I'm glad you did that, Rawlings. . . . NOW we'll
fight on my terms, and you will never win.

RAWLINGS: There's nothing you can win from me. . . . Money or boys
or proof . . . I'll keep all I have and you'll crawl back to your wild
animal menagerie on all fours. (*chases* ONOFRIO *out of the room*)

Scene 7

ALDA PENNINGTON's. *She is reading the cards for a young workingman, who has dressed up in his Sunday best, and who is awkwardly seated and fidgeting as she "reads."*

ALDA: You cannot resist the girls, can you. Indeed I see almost nothing else in your life. (*looks up at him almost in awe*) You should have lived in the time of harems. Yes, you should have been a sheik. You were born at the wrong time.

BOAKE: But, Alda!

ALDA: Silence! Do not disturb the presiding forces, my dear. . . . Now you have rattled me.

BOAKE: I'm sorry, but . . .

ALDA: Quiet, I say. . . . Quiet. (*She meditates.*) You should avoid strong drink. Drink nothing hard. . . . You have a violent disposition. . . . You must bridle your animal instincts. . . . You need a guiding hand to your strong appetites. (*As she says this* ONOFRIO *enters and stands noiselessly listening, with slightly bowed head, and wry amused mouth.*) You are very strong physically, but you have no control of your temper. . . . For this reason I recommend that you engage daily in hard physical exercise . . .

BOAKE: But . . .

ALDA: (*stopping him with an outstretched hand*) You have got four or five girls in the family way the past year alone. . . . And your own birth . . .

BOAKE: (*trying to stop her*) No . . . no.

ALDA: (*going on*) Your own birth. . . . Your parents were not married. (BOAKE *bows his head, and holds his fist to his eye.*) I see lots of trouble unless you learn to control your emotions. . . . Can't you go to . . . sporting houses instead of involving local girls. . . . Can't you . . .

BOAKE: Sporting houses! Nobody says that today . . .

ALDA: Your mother loved you deeply. . . . It is her love alone which has saved you. . . . She is near you . . .

BOAKE: I don't believe in the other side . . .

ALDA: Again you have insisted on interrupting me. . . . If you speak again I will terminate this session. (*BOAKE bows his head.*) You are very fond of fine things which you cannot afford. . . . The classic case of champagne tastes and beer pocketbook. . . . You must never marry! Better ruin the village and farm girls than risk your disposition to the yoke of matrimony. . . . Work out your animal heat daily. . . . In effect, persecute your body and make it know hard labor that you will be free of its imperious demands. . . . Make your body sweat and groan in severe trials for it!

BOAKE: (*disappointed in his reading*) Oh, oh, oh . . . (*throws down his money and turns to face ONOFRIO*) Why, where did you spring out of!

ONOFRIO: I could not help hearing Alda's fortune-telling . . .

ALDA: (*scornful, bored*) You again! These things go in cycles always. Some days I see only women past their youth who confess to having murdered their unborn babes years ago. . . . Then old men who have acquired fortunes by devious means. . . . Then young men stung by the incessant promptings of their flesh and animal nature. . . . And then the Devil himself. (*She bows sarcastically to ONOFRIO.*)

ONOFRIO: Still at it, aren't you . . . (*As he says this, he puts his arm around young BOAKE.*)

ALDA: I am at nothing. . . . People are at me. . . . They have worn the pathway to my house into a broad highway.

ONOFRIO: Which leads to destruction.

ALDA: Boake, flee men like Onofrio. . . . He is a greater danger to you than the girls who spread their legs for you. . . . Flee all such men, and you may live peaceably yet . . .

BOAKE: I thank you Alda Pennington. (*goes out*)

ONOFRIO: You make a good living, Alda, dispensing moonshine. . . . And very little overhead . . .

ALDA: They receive the wisdom of a lifetime of study and meditation on the human heart. . . . That is preciouser than the overhead even of a palace . . . (*throwing down some cards and reading*) You are in great danger. . . . My advice to you is *flee* while there is yet time.

ONOFRIO: Wouldn't that be applicable to everybody. The moment we come screaming from our mother's bodies shouldn't we turn tail and run if we could . . . stop breathing . . .

ALDA: There would be no work for the Devil then.

ONOFRIO: Where is my money! (*roars this and throws the cards on the floor*)

ALDA: Pick those cards up. (*She says this in such a murderous and frightening voice that* ONOFRIO, *though he struggles hard with himself, slowly obeys her.*) Don't you ever dare offer me insult of any kind in my own house. . . . Knowing too what I know about you. . . . Is that clear . . .

ONOFRIO: Alda, forgive me.

ALDA: And how dare you come here without advance communication with me . . . (*simmering down a little; then, craftily*) What do you want.

ONOFRIO: I told you. . . . I want my money . . .

ALDA: Your money has been burnt. Ashes and smithereens.

ONOFRIO: You expect me to believe that.

ALDA: I expect everybody to believe what I say. . . . That is how I earn my living. If they don't believe it, I keep their money anyhow.

ONOFRIO: (*throwing down money*) Then tell my fortune . . .

ALDA: Oh I am far too tired to give one reading after another!

ONOFRIO: Even if I double (*throws down more money*) or triple (*throwing down more*) or quadruple (*throws more*) or blind you with what I have. (*throws down whole fistfuls of money*)

ALDA: (*picking it up*) Oh you were always a boaster and a showoff. . . . Yes money comes to you like leaves grow on trees . . . (*throwing down the cards*) I see nothing but trouble lately. . . . Trouble trouble . . .

ONOFRIO: Where is my money?

ALDA: Remember what I told the young man. . . . Never interrupt the medium when she is "reading". . . . What is wrong with your manhood, Onofrio!

ONOFRIO: What do you mean.

ALDA: I ask you, how long have you been unable to be with a woman.

ONOFRIO: You are supposed to answer the questions and know everything. . . . You tell me . . . then . . .

ALDA: Good enough. . . . You have been without your manly prowess . . . since you stole two boys for your circus! (*She throws down the cards, and then slowly picks them up again, shuffles and begins laying them out for a complete fortune.*) These two young men have the answer to your manhood . . .

ONOFRIO: (*rising*) And my money!

ALDA: Sit down, you boor. . . . You have less seed than a man of eighty. Because of your sins! Because of your . . . stealing . . . boys.

ONOFRIO: They were of age.

ALDA: You should confine your thieving to horses, which is how you began, remember. . . . Horseflesh . . . Not human flesh . . .

ONOFRIO: Why don't you cure me. Since you're so powerful.

ALDA: The cure is sometimes worse than the . . . liability . . .

ONOFRIO: You hellion!

ALDA: I will cure you for a price . . .

ONOFRIO: I bet. . . . Well, tell me . . .

ALDA: Bend your head over toward my mouth, Onofrio. . . . Quickly! The night's more than half spent . . .

ONOFRIO: (*He bends his head—she whispers, and his eyes grow large in amazement or perhaps horror. He rises.*) You expect me to believe your hocus-pocus.

ALDA: Believe! You're past the shred of hope for believing. You have no more cards to play. Shut up. Don't speak. All you want need or hope for is in my hands. You know it, and now you believe it. Silence. Wait till I'm finished and then you can mewl and cry like a newborn babe. You want your manhood back. For without it you will soon have nothing. You've gotten by for the past few years despite the fact you stole two young boys. But they're beyond your power now. You'll never get them back. And you'll never get your money back. I'll see to both of those factors.

ONOFRIO: You! You—

ALDA: Will you be silent or shall I wash my hands of you. Then listen. Your manhood will come back to you as simply and as silently as dawn streaks over the east. Provided . . . (ONOFRIO *beats his forehead violently with one hand.*) Provided—one, that you renounce any claim to the boys, and abandon likewise any hope of regaining the ten thousand dollar blood money. And finally I want you to take this potion and keep drinking it sparingly and often until you're out of town. (*She opens a bottle containing an opiate and hands it to him. He drinks a small amount.*)

ONOFRIO: Look at a licked man, rather a licked cur. (*rises*) I don't believe you. I believe nothing.

ALDA: Don't you feel something already, just the same, Onofrio.

ONOFRIO: What do you mean. (ALDA *touches the left side of his chest with one hand.*) What do you . . . (*A strange look comes over him.*)

ALDA: I know you feel something.

ONOFRIO: (*drinks again from the potion*) My blood has been curdling just sitting here with you. And . . .

ALDA: And?

ONOFRIO: (*touches the left side of his chest where she's touched*) Yes, yes, maybe something is stealing over my veins and arteries. (*drinks more potion*)

ALDA: (*rising*) And will continue to. . . . Now my last instructions and then go out of here and never return.

ONOFRIO: Well. (*a strange, peculiar look on his face as he touches the flesh over his heart*)

ALDA: Once you are out of this community you'll see what I've done for you. . . . And then . . . are you listening. You are to depart at once, without any word more to anybody. The minute you leave this place, your manhood will be in your possession again . . . (*whispers*) You'll have the testicles of an eighteen-year-old!

ONOFRIO: I must be as soft in the brain as you are, Alda, for I believe you. . . . And I do feel something coursing through every tissue of my body . . .

ALDA: Then don't waste anymore time.

ONOFRIO: (*turning away from her*) I can feel it, God is my witness, or Satan in his hellish kingdom. I feel it! God knows what I've drunk. Probably my death. (*He rushes from the room.*)

(ALDA *laughs maniacally until she lays her head down on the table in her mirth.*)

Scene 8

ALDA *is alone,* ONOFRIO *and her other clients having departed. She pokes the fire occasionally, grinning at it. The sound of a great clock is heard striking faintly from some other room.*

ALDA: Men always think they can stop the inevitable progression of events, events that were being propelled from before there were men. And they convince themselves they are altering the universe, the progression of time. . . . That is what keeps them at work. They believe they are the true gods. . . . No matter what they do, nonetheless, they are overruled. (*noise like that of a door opening sounds and frightens her*) What was that? (*She turns 'round.*) The trees talking to themselves. They wait until humankind are sleeping or dead, then they assume their true being . . . (*humming*)

> The leaves
> and the trees
> exchange words together

(*falls to sleep, then wakes with a start*) Who is it? (*listens intently*) I saw a fox the other night. . . . Of all animals it has the most appraising expression in its eyes. Of all animals it is the one least impressed by mankind. It's beyond cynicism. I don't think the fox was ever taken in by man. The horse, the dog, even the cat. . . . The fox knows our number is up . . . (*hears a noise again*) My God! (*she shudders again; reaches for a gun under her shawl*) Now come out of there, whoever you are. . . . Do you hear. . . . (*The door opens and* JOEL *enters.*) I knew it, I knew it! You had to come. I sent all kinds of unspoken messages. Do you know why you came, dear boy? Do you? I thought though your older brother would be the one who would come. Go ahead, sit down. I see you're weary.

(JOEL *slumps down in a chair, and looks around in a kind of wonder at what he sees before him.*)

ALDA: I knew your mother from the time she was as young as you.

JOEL: My father—he's very low, ma'am.

ALDA: Call me Alda.

JOEL: Alda, yes. He's been stricken. Dr. Hallam—

ALDA: Don't mention him. I knew your father was ill.

JOEL: Yes, they say you know everything. (*He covers his eyes with his right hand.*)

ALDA: But you didn't come here to speak of your father's illness.

JOEL: I don't know, Ma'am, Alda, that is, why I came. I felt, well like in a dream I felt you would want me to come.

ALDA: You were right. You had to come, Joel. (*She rises and goes toward the back of the room.*)

JOEL: Where are you going?

ALDA: (*looking back at him*) I think we should have a cordial to celebrate your coming.

JOEL: A cordial? Well, yes, thank you, of course.

ALDA: (*bringing back two glasses*) Here, Joel. It's from a recipe my own grandmother had from her grandmother. Huckleberry cordial. (*She raises her glass.*)

JOEL: To you, Alda, and to the memory of my mother.

ALDA: To you, also, Joel, for coming here tonight as my visitor. (*They drink silently for a while.*)

JOEL: This is the most delicious drink I have ever tasted. But why do I say that. I have never had a cordial before.

ALDA: It clears the mind, Joel, and calms the spirit.

JOEL: I believe you. I feel better already.

ALDA: I have something for you, Joel. Something that belongs to you and Gregory. I have kept it safely, carefully, securely. Now it is time that it should be yours, and your brother's. Don't move, and don't leave. I will be back directly. (*exits*)

JOEL: Something that belongs to us both. This cordial makes me see everything in a different light. Do you suppose it is true she is an enchantress? Well, then, so what. Let me be enchanted! (*He drinks some more.*)

ALDA: (*returning with a box which* JOEL *eyes lengthily*) Your father and I had a strange conference some while back. I am afraid I disturbed him very much. But it was a thing which had to be done. The forces commanded it, Joel. The forces are those spirits which often advise and inform me, urge me and confide in me. They propelled me to do to your father what I believe the true spirits wished. Yes, (*turning to pour more cordial in her glass and rising, pouring more in* JOEL*'s*) your father, bless his soul (*She crosses herself.*) had lost you boys.

JOEL: (*in anguish*) Oh please, please, must we speak of his faults at this time.

ALDA: Your father came to me in the greatest anguish. The greatest desperation. Are you listening?

JOEL: (*in torment*) Go on, Ma'am. Go on, Alda.

ALDA: I made him see how he had lost the only beings dear to him.

JOEL: Who were they?

ALDA: (*somewhat taken aback*) Who were they? Who but you, you and Gregory.

JOEL: You are mistaken. He only loved Rainforth, his eldest.

ALDA: You stand corrected. He worshipped Rainforth, but that worship was hollow. He only loved you.

(JOEL *puts his hand over his eyes again and lets a sob escape.*)

ALDA: I told your father, for the forces spoke through me, that the only way he would ever see you boys alive again was if he destroyed the money which Onofrio had paid for you.

JOEL: Oh God! God.

ALDA: I commanded him to bring the money he had stored away . . . in a rat's nest.

JOEL: A what? (*spoken with horror*)

ALDA: You heard me. Let me be brief. He fetched the money, some ten thousand dollars all in thousand dollar bills.

JOEL: What? . . . You said a rat's nest?

ALDA: We burned it.

JOEL: Burned it.

ALDA: I told him unless he burned the money, the blood money, he would never see you boys alive again. . . . This he could not bear. I saw then before me the man made of steel or ice break like dry twigs. He burned his greed and avarice. And you boys were returned to him.

JOEL: Why are you talking in riddles.

ALDA: Don't you see, I had to force him to give up what he thought he loved in order for him to confess what he truly loved but had forsaken, you and Gregory. Here, (*opening the box*) here are the ashes of his fortune. Go on, take it, then finish your cordial and go home.

JOEL: (*looking at the ashes*) I can still catch sight of pieces of the thousand dollar bills. I don't know, Alda, I am afraid to touch it.

ALDA: It is yours. It is no longer blood money. And Onofrio is gone too while your father, as you say, lies on his deathbed. . . . Go home, don't waste time. He won't last the night.

JOEL: (*rising*) May I have one more glass of . . . your huckleberry cordial.

ALDA: (*nods, goes to the back, brings out the bottle, and pours it in his glass*) It is the hardest ordeal of all for a man who is all steel to admit he is flesh and blood. Hard, hard to admit love! Go on now and comfort him before it's too late. (*JOEL embraces ALDA, and then leaves.*)

Scene 9

RAWLINGS's *bedroom. He lies propped up slightly in a large king-sized bed.* DR. HALLAM *is looking anxiously at his patient. He takes his pulse, and with a cloth wipes the perspiration from* RAWLINGS's *face and brow.*

RAWLINGS: Well, Doc, tell me now. How much longer have I got.

HALLAM: Why can't you be quiet.

RAWLINGS: Why can't you doctors ever answer a direct question. How much time, I said, have I got.

HALLAM: I told you not ten minutes ago, Arthur, you could go at any moment, or you could last a few hours, even days. Does that satisfy you?

RAWLINGS: (*as if not having heard him*) Where are my boys, Doc?

HALLAM: Gregory is outside. I don't know where Joel is.

RAWLINGS: You don't think Onofrio took him do you.

HALLAM: No, I don't. Let's not let ourselves be bothered with him again.

RAWLINGS: (*again probably not having heard*) I wonder what I'll say to them, Doc.

HALLAM: You mean Greg and Joel?

RAWLINGS: Greg and Joel. What can I say, what can I give them.

HALLAM: You want my opinion?

RAWLINGS: Oh I suppose, though your opinions always take the wind out of my sails. . . . Well go on give it to me, give me your unvarnished say-so why don't you. Though I'll probably choke on the words when I hear them.

HALLAM: (*pacing the room, his head lowered*) I can only tell you what I think, I'd say if I had two fine boys like you have, if also I had done to them what you have done.

RAWLINGS: Sold them like cattle you said once.

HALLAM: Did I now? Ah, well . . .

RAWLINGS: And what would you say if you was in my stead, Doc.

HALLAM: I would say . . . (*hesitates*) I would hope one day they would find it in their hearts to overlook my failings, and that when they were my age they would understand how hard it is to tell those we love how much we love them.

RAWLINGS: (*perhaps not having quite heard it all*) But you never would have done what I did, Doc. You would never have . . . give your loved ones away to a circus owner.

HALLAM: Oh I reckon I did things almost as bad, or maybe worse. But you have no time, Arthur. You must know it too. . . . Let me call in your eldest boy. Say something to him. Give him something to make him feel you were after all his dad, and that he won't have another . . .

RAWLINGS: I don't know how to say it to him.

HALLAM: Shall I call Greg in.

RAWLINGS: Call him in. (*HALLAM goes out*) They can't know. Youth can't know. They'll never know till they be fathers. Even then maybe not.

(*Enter HALLAM and GREGORY.*)

GREGORY: (*advancing to the bed*) Hello, Father.

RAWLINGS: (*faintly*) Gregory. I guess Doc Hallam did a good job coaxing you to come in. . . . Where is your younger brother.

GREGORY: (*nervous, upset*) He had to run some errands, Father. He should be back though any minute now.

RAWLINGS: (*weakly*) What would we do if we couldn't run errands, eh, Greg.

GREGORY: (*anguished*) Father, you are going to be all right, aren't you?

(*HALLAM admonishes GREGORY to be careful what he says by putting his finger to his lips.*)

RAWLINGS: It's nice of you to hope so, Gregory. Nice of you to be here. But I feel, well, how can I explain it. I seem to feel a partition is opening around me, so that I'm looking into something more spacious and brighter than where we are if you can follow me.

GREGORY: (*frightened*) Yes, Father.

RAWLINGS: Well, since Joel is running an errand supposin' I say all there is to say, Greg, my boy, and you can tell Joel afterwards.

(*HALLAM offers to leave the room.*)

RAWLINGS: No, no, Doctor, don't go. What I'm going to say can be said in front of company. So, stay Doctor. You won't be a bad witness. Now where was I? Yes, you are to tell Joel what I'm about to say to you, and you will, I know you will. I leave it to you. Oh if there was only time to tell you. And if I had the words. We never seem to find the time to tell those closest to us the important things. The grains of sand run too low, always. Tell Joel then and keep this in your memory too—I'm glad I burned the blood money at Alda Pennington's. I'm relieved and glad, maybe not happy, but satisfied, there's a difference. It has took one burden from my shoulders. But it hasn't made me forget the things you boys said to me the day you come back.

GREGORY: What things was those, Father.

RAWLINGS: (*sadly*) *Father* he says. . . . Why, Gregory that you and Joel's hearts had turned to stone because I gave you to Onofrio.

GREGORY: Oh well, Father, we spoke out of disappointment I suppose, and we was tired from the long journey back home.

RAWLINGS: But you're young, Gregory, and your heart should be light and blithesome. Not stone hearts! I want to take away the stone from your hearts, don't you see? Tell me how I can, Greg.

GREGORY: Oh, Father.

RAWLINGS: Burning the ten thousand wasn't enough. You knew I burned the blood money, Hallam, didn't you.

(*HALLAM bows and then looks away.*)

(*GREGORY kneels down at his father's side.*)

RAWLINGS: Let me put my hand through your hair, will you? (*GREGORY nods and buries his face in the comforters.*) There must be some medicine, Doc, to cure hearts of stone! In time, I do believe you and Joel . . . your hearts will return to be just as they was when you was young boys. . . . That is my hope . . . to see the stone removed from your hearts.

GREGORY: We spoke that day Father in haste. You must forget our speaking of stone hearts. . . . We didn't mean to make you sorrow over it so long.

HALLAM: Gregory, Gregory.

GREGORY: (*somewhat angrily*) What is it?

HALLAM: (*going over to where* GREGORY *is kneeling*) Please, he can't hear you now, Greg. Please get up. Gregory, (*shaking him gently*) your father's gone.

(*GREGORY rises and throws himself in the doctor's arms.*)

Scene 10

JOEL *enters his father's house.* GREGORY *looks up from where he is seated. Leaps up in a kind of paroxysm of relief and rage.*

GREGORY: Where was you all this time? I have been calling every neighbor in town about you. Do you know what you left me with. Do you know what has happened. What on earth is wrong with you.

JOEL: Oh, Gregory. (*in a flash of hysteria*) Everything's wrong with me. How's Father?

GREGORY: How's Father, he says. You've been gone most of the night. Have you been in the saloons, what's wrong with you I repeat . . . where in tarnation have you been?

JOEL: Let up will you. Let up. I've been through too much to be scolded. Where's Father?

GREGORY: Joel . . . listen! He went while you was gone. . . . Father's gone. He died with Dr. Hallam in the bedroom.

JOEL: Did he ask for me? Did he talk at all.

GREGORY: Father fretted as he was saying his last words about the time when we came home we told him our hearts had turned to stone. He took on and on about it. I tried to tell him we hadn't meant it like it sounded. But I guess my explanation came too late. Anyhow I felt he sort of blessed us in his own strange way at the very last. One thing sure, Joel, he said he was glad he burned the blood money, the ten thousand dollars.

JOEL: And I can't see him.

GREGORY: I'm afraid not. Not here. Doc Hallam had him taken to the Barstow Funeral Parlor.

JOEL: (*in a reverie*) Poor Father. He never seemed . . .

GREGORY: What? (*said angrily, impatiently*)

JOEL: I mean, he seemed like God, distant and cross and displeased all the time. If God died I suppose he would be hard to miss too.

GREGORY: What do you keep clutching at that box for. What is it.

JOEL: Oh yes, the box. (*stares at it*)

GREGORY: Joel, are you all right. You ain't really drunk are you.

JOEL: A little maybe. I run into Onofrio on the way home.

GREGORY: (*as if scandalized*) Onofrio. No!

JOEL: But before I go into Onofrio and the line of hokum he handed to me . . . (*brings out a crumpled piece of paper*)

GREGORY: Joel, I am going to heat up this pot of coffee and you're going to drink it all down.

JOEL: (*absentmindedly*) Gregory, ain't you sad Father's gone.

GREGORY: (*preparing the coffee*) Yes, I guess so. But it's sort of as though a mountain that always was everywhere you looked when you looked was suddenly gone and there was only sky and level ground to look back at you.

JOEL: I see.

(GREGORY *goes over to* JOEL *and touches his brow to see if he has fever, then takes his pulse.*)

JOEL: I'll need the pot of coffee to tell you what I've got to tell. Then maybe we will go or at least me and look at Father in the undertaker parlor.

GREGORY: You should never have gone to see old Alda. Minnie told me where she thought you went. (*goes over to stove and brings a king-size cup of coffee*) This is as strong as some of the brew she gives her clients I daresay. Drink it down.

JOEL: (*taking cup*) Oh I could drink an even stronger dish.

GREGORY: Oh, Joel, Joel. You'll always be my little kid brother. You'll never grow up, will you.

JOEL: Alda, I'll begin with Alda, then you can say or do what you want to with what I've got to tell you. Well, to make a stab at a long story, she did burn Father's money. Told him unless he burned the money Onofrio give him for him selling us boys to the circus, he'd never set eyes on us again. . . . It was a hard bargain but Father, who was master of hard bargains, rather than never set eyes on us again, give her the ten thousand from Onofrio. He had kept it she said in a rat's nest.

GREGORY: In a rat's nest?! Go on.

JOEL: Well, here it is. She give me the ashes from the burning of the blood money.

GREGORY: (*taking the box*) Well I'll be. (*begins to count it*) You can see from a charred piece or two it was real thousand dollar bills all right. (*puts down the box and places the piece of bill back in it*) We must be dreaming. We must be back at the circus. We must have fallen off the horses and damaged our brains.

JOEL: And now speaking of the circus, here comes the rest of my tale. Onofrio! As I was headed home, somebody whistles at me. He comes out of this saloon. He was drunk, and sort of undressed. A woman followed him out and called to him. "You wait your turn," he calls back to her. But, Gregory, he didn't look like himself. His voice was deeper, and his face was as smooth as a young man. And his hair didn't look gray, at least not in that light coming from the saloon. "You look like a younger man, Onofrio," I said. "Let me tell you something," he replied, "I am younger maybe. The Onofrio you knowed is no more." And he laughed then like a couple of jackasses, and drug me into the tavern.

GREGORY: So I can see.

JOEL: Oh no, Greg, I am not drunk on liquor, I am drunk on what I've heard this day and night. Well, I listened to him for hours, and then he gives me this paper he calls a Document. Read it and tell me I'm not daydreaming. (*hands him a crumpled paper*)

GREGORY: Why it looks legal all right. As if it was notarized. (*reads*) "Joel, Gregory, be free now. Be men! Adíos. Goodbye forever, Giuseppe Onofrio." (*begins to cry*)

JOEL: What are you bawling for?

GREGORY: I don't know. Too much has transpired. Lost fortunes, old men turning into young, death. My brain is turned. It's hard to take all this in, isn't it. So much has happened it's hard to keep things straight.

JOEL: I told you I wasn't acting this way from drink. It's too much to take in. I want you to take me to the Undertaker's Parlor. Did you hear me.

GREGORY: I heard you. I'll go with you, when I'm settled down a little.

JOEL: It will be like saying goodbye to someone we only knowed briefly and casually, but who all the same made a deep impression on us before he left us.

(*Enter* MINNIE.)

MINNIE: Oh, boys, I've been so worried about you. (*They rise and embrace her.*) Are you boys alright? I heard the sad news of course, and have been to the funeral parlor.

JOEL: Maybe Minnie can go with us after a while.

GREGORY: Yes, by and by. We have lots of news, Minnie, other news.

MINNIE: Do I smell a fresh brew of coffee on the stove, Gregory.

GREGORY: You do. Help yourself, here let me heat it for you.

JOEL: (*speaking to himself*) It's so hard to straighten all these things out. It's not the wine I drank. No I would feel this way if Onofrio had plied me with spring water. Too much has happened to get it all straight.

GREGORY: Joel! What are you talkin' to yourself for like that. Come over here and join us.

MINNIE: Oh let him be, Greg. You boss the poor lad too much.

GREGORY: I suppose, poor devil.

(JOEL *joins them near the stove and* GREGORY *embraces him, and then* MINNIE *embraces them both.*)

WHERE QUENTIN GOES

CHARACTERS

GAMALIEL ENDORS
QUENTIN WYATT
GWENDOLYN LUDWORTH
MEG BATTERSHELL
DANA
LILY MAE CRAMER
SADIE
JULIA
NEALE ASTOR

ACT I

Scene 1

The law office of GAMALIEL ENDORS. QUENTIN WYATT *is standing. The two men have been arguing quite fiercely.*

ENDORS: Cool off, Quentin. I'm only doing my duty.

QUENTIN: If you ask me, you've gone way beyond your duty. Into shame.

ENDORS: Now, my boy, think before you speak. Your father would be heartsick to hear you speak like this.

QUENTIN: I'm afraid I don't care much by now what he'd think about anything.

ENDORS: You're still bitter.

QUENTIN: Call it what you will.

(*He almost falls into the chair that does not face* MR. ENDORS, *but is instead at an angle to him, facing more directly the audience.*)

ENDORS: Quents, let me read your grandfather's will again.

QUENTIN: (*wheeling about*) Haven't I heard it enough?

ENDORS: You act as if I'd been the author and *had* drawn it up.

QUENTIN: And you didn't?

ENDORS: I merely drew up what he very emphatically commanded.

QUENTIN: And didn't you point out to him what a mistake he was making, to foist upon his second boy, poor Dana, the humiliation of having to acknowledge as his mother a woman who . . . ?

ENDORS: Be careful, Quentin.

QUENTIN: A woman of the lowest moral character one could find, and who today is operating what you lawyers designate I suppose as a house of ill *repute!*

ENDORS: You are very hard on everyone, Quentin.

QUENTIN: Everyone! Do you call what she is *everyone?*

ENDORS: Whatever we may call her, she is the mother of your half-brother, Dana, whom you care for so deeply.

QUENTIN: And what do you mean by that? (*He turns the chair now to face the lawyer more directly.*)

ENDORS: I mean since you care so deeply for Dana, and are indeed like a second father to him, though you are half-brothers, some good must have come to him from his mother. She can't be all you say.

QUENTIN: (*picking up the sheets of documents from the table*) But for a will made out with the proviso that, before Dana can come into his inheritance, he must make the acquaintance of his mother! It's little short of blackmail. (*He reads more from the will aloud.*) *That he should make known who he is to his mother, and if possible get to know her within so far as this is within the sensibilities of both parties. .*

ENDORS: Yes, I warned your grandfather about that paragraph in the will. In fact, though you won't believe me, I told him this had no business being in the will. . . . But he was so earnest about it.

QUENTIN: How . . . earnest?

ENDORS: Passionate.

QUENTIN: (*throws down the will and mutters something under his breath*) And supposing, Mr. Endors, that my brother refuses to go see his alleged mother?

ENDORS: I will have to reflect on that, my boy.

QUENTIN: You don't mean to tell me that unless he pays a call on a common strumpet, he will be prevented from coming into his inheritance?

ENDORS: I should hope not. I feel your grandfather may have come to think his treatment of Dana's mother was harsh. And since your father is dead—since he was a hero also in the late war—I think we all owe him the honor to try to understand his feelings toward this woman. I feel we should obey your grandfather's written instructions to the letter.

QUENTIN: Even when obeying those instructions places his son in moral jeopardy?

ENDORS: Which son are you referring to?

QUENTIN: I am surprised you should try to be witty at such a serious matter.

ENDORS: Though I advised your grandfather not to leave this stipulation in the will, I feel he was right.

QUENTIN: (*bitterly*) Right, I see.

ENDORS: He felt—your grandfather, that is—he'd made a mistake in forcing Julia Lessard to give up her child when his own son had had every intention of marrying her. Also, bear in mind that when she became Dana's mother, she was not the proprietress of the place you call a *house of ill repute*.

QUENTIN: And what do you call it, Mr. Endors? . . . A hotel?

ENDORS: As a matter of fact, I only recently learned that Miss Lessard is the proprietress of such a place.

QUENTIN: It would seem to me that, as my grandfather's attorney, you might have known that one day Dana would be compelled to make her friendship.

ENDORS: My boy, you're making of your granddad's simple request a thorny, complicated, even diabolical plot. Listen to me. (*moving toward* QUENTIN) I have known you since you were a small child.

In fact, I've known you ever since you were born. Listen to me, Quentin. You are too good, too noble, and too wrathful.

QUENTIN: (*stung to fury*) Too wrathful? You mean I am to take my brother to a house of prostitution as if we were going to an 11 o'clock church service?

ENDORS: I thought, as your grandfather's attorney, I would do that. It would be a visit, I decided, of some ten or fifteen minutes.

QUENTIN: I believe that duty, sir, should be mine.

ENDORS: (*somewhat disconcerted, and almost angry*) Very well, then, but Quentin I insist that you do pay her this visit, and (*searching for the will again*) within four or five days after he reaches the age of eighteen.

QUENTIN: I'll obey what the will says, Mr. Endors. You can count on me.

ENDORS: I merely thought, Quentin, that if I were to go I would spare your very tender feelings.

QUENTIN: Your irony is wasted on me, Mr. Endors. (*rising*) I will say good morning, then. And thank you for your solicitude and your exactitude, your—

ENDORS: (*cutting him short*) You don't owe me thanks for carrying out your grandfather's wishes.

QUENTIN: (*angry again*) I see. Then thanks be damned! Good morning. (*He leaves.*)

ENDORS: (*said after him*) Wait, Quentin, until life has tried you a little. I would like to meet you then, when you are not so lily-white pure. But if anger is a deadly sin, then you are the best of sinners!

Scene 2

GWENDOLYN LUDWORTH, *grandmother to* DANA *and* QUENTIN, *is in her front parlor, with her female attendant,* MEG BATTERSHELL. *The room is one of tarnished splendor fast going to complete decay. It houses many mirrors, elegant handmade chairs in need of repair, a small wind organ (harmonium) at stage right, a few straw fans hung on the wall, and an ingrain CHK carpet under the two ladies' feet.* MEG *is pouring* MRS. LUDWORTH *her coffee, then helps her light a long cigarette, which* GWEN *has trouble drawing.*

GWEN: (*drawing on her cigarette*) You said today was the day?

MEG: I did, dear. He should be here any moment.

GWEN: I adore the way you say *he*, Meg. I couldn't do it better myself.

MEG: How, Ma'am?

GWEN: Oh, go on with you. You know how. . . . I dread this visit. I dread him.

MEG: But he's such a handsome fellow.

GWEN: (*sighing*) Yes, and what use does he make of his good looks? (MEG *coughs nervously.*) He should have married years ago. And he doesn't have to be a blacksmith. He has enough money from his grandfather and his poor father. (*She indulges some unhappy memories and puffs harder on her cigarette.*)

MEG: I didn't know he was an actual blacksmith.

GWEN: (*almost angrily*) Don't doubt my word. Of course he is. Call it a *foundry* if you will. Always raising and lowering hammers, and with the forge burning like the fires of hell. I've visited him many a time, Meg. He always acts sheepish when he sees me. *This is no place for a lady,* he always says. I don't like the way he says *lady.* . . . Or of course the way he watches over poor Dana. He's the boy's jailer as much as his brother. And he's only his half-brother at that! Watches the boy's every move. He once said to me at his blacksmith's shop or *forge*, as you want me to call it, *He's got to be prevented from going the wrong way!* And he says that like some wandering evangelist preacher! *The wrong way.* The poor chap, Dana, hardly is allowed to put on his shoes and coat without consulting Quentin.

MEG: But in the end, ma'am, young Dana will grow up and go his own way.

GWEN: Not if Quentin has anything to do with it. He'll never go away because he won't grow up.

MEG: Why, that's a queer thing to say. (*She pours* GWEN *another cup of coffee.*)

GWEN: Quentin has managed his life so that he has no friends except his brother. None of the church people really like him. He knows scripture better than the young preacher himself. Corrects the young pastor all the time. He knows more than God! A proud, arrogant man, with ice water in his veins, but the ice water gives every indication of turning to molten lead! I can hear him in his blacksmith shop, sometimes in my mind, clear over here. Hammering the iron, beating the metal with red-hot hammers.

(*The doorbell rings violently.* GWEN *starts, and puts out her hand to restrain* MEG.)

GWEN: Don't go . . . quite yet.

MEG: But ma'am, he'll pound the door down like the last time if I don't let him in promptly.

GWEN: Wait till I catch my breath. . . . All right, go. . . . Go.

(*She starts to put away her cigarette as* MEG *leaves, then angrily decides to smoke in front of her grandson.* QUENTIN *soon enters, accompanied by* MEG. *He is dressed all in black and carries an expensive new hat in his right hand, which he holds almost over his heart. He waits a moment before speaking.*)

QUENTIN: Grandmother. Good morning.

GWEN: (*acknowledging him by extending her hand, which* QUENTIN *takes absentmindedly*) Sit there (*motioning to a far away chair*) so that my cigarette smoke does not annoy you.

QUENTIN: I told you last time, Grandma, I would not refer again to your . . . cigarettes. At least they're better than the cigars you used to poison the room with.

GWEN: As children, Quentin, we used to smoke the long things hanging from the catalpa trees. We called them *cigares*. Perhaps in time I'll give up cigarettes and smoke the catalpa.

QUENTIN: Oh, I've other worries today. I'll let you off about your smoking.

GWEN: Have you ever tried tobacco in any form?

QUENTIN: Yes, I'm ashamed to say Cy Farley, the man whose blacksmith shop I bought ours from, used to insist I chew a plug with him. I thought I had to! (*He acts almost as if he were confessing to a misdeed or crime.*) (*dreamily*) I thought I had to, you see.

GWEN: (*almost under the same spell as he tells of his temptation*) Did you enjoy it?

QUENTIN: Enjoy it? What are you talking about?

GWEN: My dear Grandson, tell me, have you ever enjoyed anything?

QUENTIN: Now, Grandma, are we going off into another of your digressions about my never having any fun out of life? Enjoyed chewing tobacco? No, I didn't. I chewed it to please him and because I wanted to buy him out.

GWEN: (*persisting*) But did you never enjoy anything, truly and wholeheartedly?

QUENTIN: (*beginning to get angry*) Grandma! (*He puts his hat on the floor.*)

GWEN: (*to* MEG) Put his hat away, Meg. I'm surprised at you!

MEG: (*apologetically*) I already asked him if I could, ma'am.

QUENTIN: I can't stay that long, Grandma.

GWEN: Pour Quentin a cup of coffee.

QUENTIN: No, no, I don't want any, thank you.

GWEN: I insist you have some, Quents. . . . For my sake. (*She signals that* MEG *should pour him a cup.*)

QUENTIN: (*splenetically*) All right, all right. And I suppose you've got some whiskey you'd like me to swallow this early in the morning?

GWEN: (*watching him drink the coffee as if he were required to taste the medicine*) What's on your mind, Quentin? You're dressed like a young king today, not at all like a blacksmith.

QUENTIN: Grandma, you know very well why I'm here. Don't force me to make it any harder for myself than it is.

GWEN: I have never deliberately made things hard for you, Quentin.

QUENTIN: We have not very often seen eye-to-eye, though.

GWEN: But I have always respected you, Quents, and loved you.

QUENTIN: You've never loved me, Grandma. You loved Dana, who's not even your real grandson. Never me.

GWEN: (astounded) How can you say that, Quents? You are my own and in a way my dearest.

QUENTIN: (choking) Not so. But that is not why I'm here.

GWEN: But I do love you, Quents, dearly, whether you believe it or not. I wish I could make you see that I do.

QUENTIN: The matter at hand is Dana.

GWEN: And what has he done this time?

QUENTIN: Done? He's done nothing. It is what they expect him to do that is the matter. You certainly must know of it.

GWEN: I presume I do if it has to do with you and Dana.

QUENTIN: It has nothing, Grandma, to do with me. Please don't act as if this were all a surprise. I told you the last time we met.

GWEN: Quents, you are shouting at me as if I were on trial! Just tell me—and lower your voice—how I can help you, and what you have come for.

QUENTIN: (trying to control his anger) I have been to see that old shyster Endors.

GWEN: Pardon me, but he is not a shyster, he is . . .

QUENTIN: Shyster! I say shyster. . . . And do you know what he expects Dana to do?

GWEN: Quietly, Quents, quietly. Please.

QUENTIN: Have another cigarette, Grandma. (takes out the copy of the will and hands it to her) You have seen this, I believe. Look on page five, where I have underlined the passage in red ink. (GWEN *takes the will and stares at it.*) Don't you need spectacles, Grandma?

GWEN: The print is very large, Quents, and I have read the will many times. Many times.

QUENTIN: And you are not angry, Grandma?

GWEN: Why should I be angry?

QUENTIN: That the will requires Dana to see his mother before he can be given his inheritance?

GWEN: Yes, but why should I be angry?

QUENTIN: Grandma! For the love of . . . (*stops himself*) Do you know what kind of woman Dana's mother is? (*standing*) Do you know how she earns her livelihood? How she's always earned it? Do you know what such a woman is called? Even in these loose-living days.

GWEN: Sit down, dear. Try to lower your voice, at least, if you cannot be calm.

QUENTIN: (*sits down, but is so agitated he is trembling, and fiercely loosens his tight necktie*) She runs a house of prostitution. The men call it . . .

GWEN: A *whorehouse.*

QUENTIN: (*He is too agitated to hear her at first. Then, almost hysterically.*) What did you say?

GWEN: I don't think it is.

QUENTIN: Don't think it's what?

GWEN: (*not using the word*) A bad house.

QUENTIN: (*almost babbling*) Bad . . . You don't, Grandma! What kind of house is it then I am to take him to?

GWEN: (*icily, majestically*) It is a roadhouse. She puts up traveling salesmen, with room and board. That is all it is. I too have made investigations, Quentin.

QUENTIN: Then your investigations weren't completely comprehensive, as mine were.

GWEN: Many things happen in inns and roadhouses, for which the proprietress is hardly responsible. After all, your father died leaving her with nothing but . . . an illegitimate child. She has done what she could do.

QUENTIN: You're apologizing for her!

GWEN: I see nothing wrong with this will. It is a little strange, perhaps, for a legal document. But it is very human. You know Julia, Dana's mother, refused to marry your father in France. So some have said she was in a way the cause of her own misfortune.

QUENTIN: That is not the way I heard it! (*He starts to rise again, but after a sign from* GWEN, *he sits down again.*)

GWEN: How did you hear it?

QUENTIN: I heard that, before he got himself blown up, he found out what she was and would not consent to marry her.

GWEN: Then you heard wrong. Julia came here herself and told me she did not want to marry him when he was still to fight in the trenches. . . . She said she would wait! He sent her back here and intended to marry her when he returned home.

QUENTIN: I see. Or I don't see . . . (*rising with dignity and some studied calm*) Very well, I will obey the terms of the will. I will take him to see his mother.

GWEN: Quentin, why don't you let me take Dana to see her?

QUENTIN: (*confused and almost incoherent*) Why? It's a man's job to do so. To protect him. To see that nothing goes amiss. To bring him back safely.

GWEN: Your trouble, Quentin, is you are too close to this boy. You care for him too deeply.

QUENTIN: Do I, Grandma? Very well, then . . . I do. . . . But I will obey the terms of the will. I will show the world that, at least. And I will protect him. Goodbye, Grandma.

GWEN: Quentin!

(*He rushes out of the room.*)

Scene 3

The stark, almost bare front room of QUENTIN's *house, where he lives with* DANA. *At stage left is an unfurled American flag. A large table, to which people might sit down at a banquet, is at the rear wall. Chairs are placed haphazardly around this table. A kind of collection of antique and even modern guns hangs from the wall facing the audience.* DANA *is a handsome boy of about 18, with features somewhat different than those of his half-brother. Still, despite* QUENTIN's *dark complexion and strong physique, there is a marked family resemblance.* DANA *appears deep in thought, seated in one of the more uncomfortable chairs. Occasionally, he lets his head fall into his outstretched hands.*

(*Enter* QUENTIN, *whose face relaxes a bit as he catches sight of* DANA. *Then as* DANA *looks up at him,* QUENTIN *assumes his more familiar scowling and irritable expression.*)

DANA: What kept you so long, Quents?

QUENTIN: You can ask! (*almost savagely*) They kept me. They're all in the same plot, if you ask me. (DANA *rises eagerly, as if he would embrace* QUENTIN, *who turns away immediately.*) You know damned well who they are. Your damned old rip of a grandmother for one. Then of course there is the lawyer. There's always a lawyer!

DANA: I told you, Quents, I don't care about the money. They can keep it. I want always to stay here . . .

QUENTIN: (*the struggle with his feelings becomes harder, more severe*) You'll do what you're told to do!

DANA: But you're so against me going there, you said. I don't want to see her, Quents. You know that. I always want to please you, Quents.

QUENTIN: Those days are over, Dana. You're becoming a young man. You can't stay here with me forever, for cripes' sake, in any case. (*He looks away wildly in front of him.*)

DANA: I don't care about the money. I don't want to see her!

QUENTIN: Dana, that's all me talking through you. Don't you understand? I've been too much of an influence on you. I see it all clear now. Guess your grandma and the lawyer are right. You'll have to go—you've got to come into your inheritance. . . . (*almost savagely*) I have nothing for you. Your future is not with me.

DANA: That's a very harsh thing to say after all we've been through together. You're all I have, Quents.

QUENTIN: That's the trouble. That's why I suppose you haven't done very well in school or got to know more people. People are always saying, *That surly, morose blacksmith and that fine young friendly young Dana.*

DANA: Don't speak that way about yourself. (*with a sudden, almost wild change of mood and voice*) Why can't I stay with you? What's out there for me?

QUENTIN: We must think carefully—carefully. But first I must get you ready to meet her. Your mother. Your real mother. I'm only your half-brother, Dana. She is your full-blooded mother. But I have to get you ready. . . . You're so ignorant. That's my fault, too. I've kept you ignorant.

DANA: I don't understand what you're driving at.

QUENTIN: The church is always saying it's so easy to know right from wrong. A lot the church knows, don't it? Once you've closed the Scriptures, you're as lost as before. I don't know right from wrong here.

DANA: (*frightened*) I've never seen you so upset. Shan't I fetch you some of the mulled wine the housekeeper left for us?

QUENTIN: What good will mulled wine do, Dana? (*seeing the boy's disappointment*) Oh, all right, if you want some. Go get it.

(DANA *hurries out to the kitchen, stage right.* QUENTIN *throws his arms behind his back and pulls his chest backwards, then shakes his head violently. He is a man who would prefer to live in his body, but he is always tormented by thoughts that give his body no rest.*)

DANA: (*bringing in two steaming cups of mulled wine*) It was left on the fire so it would be warm for you.

QUENTIN: (*takes a cup from* DANA) Well, if this won't chase our troubles away . . . (*He makes a kind of toasting gesture, and the two drink.*)

DANA: So, Quents why don't we just ignore the lawyer and . . . ?

QUENTIN: I told you no. I won't be held responsible for ruining your life anymore than I have already.

DANA: Ruined my life, Quents? What do you mean by that?

QUENTIN: That's what people say. I've kept you here all by yourself, out in the country, and turned you into a man as unfriendly a man as myself. And now they are saying I'm trying to spoil your chances of coming into your inheritance. The first thing you know, the sheriff will come here and take me in.

DANA: Oh, Quents. Don't you know I liked all these years with you? If that's lonely—being with you—I want always to be lonely.

QUENTIN: I'm afraid what people say is true. Yet who did you have? Our dad went out and died in war, and before that my mother died when she had me. Gwen is not really a blood relation to you. Your grandfather didn't know what to do with you. He finally realized he didn't know how to raise a boy alone. So, there was only me. And somebody, they say—anybody, they say—is better than nobody.

DANA: I don't think my own dad and yours could have done so much for me as you, Quents.

QUENTIN: You don't know what you're saying, Dana, 'cause you didn't know your dad. And up 'til now you have not known her. Your mother . . . Dana listen to me. Do you know what you are in terms of the law? I don't know why I didn't speak to you about it earlier, but, well, I did not.

DANA: I don't know what the law has to do with what I am.

QUENTIN: Dana, according to the law . . . (*uncertain how to proceed*) you are without a name. Without . . . legally . . . a father or a mother.

DANA: I know that.

QUENTIN: I thought maybe I hadn't ever made it clear.

DANA: They made it clear at school times enough.

QUENTIN: You never told me.

DANA: They told me. A thousand times.

QUENTIN: Yes, of course, I might have guessed they would. So you only felt, I guess, you had a half-brother to not tell you. But there's more, Dana, for Christ's sake there's more.

DANA: Maybe I know that, too.

QUENTIN: No, I doubt it. But when you go to see her with me . . .

DANA: I'll go alone.

QUENTIN: No, you won't. If I ever exercised my authority over you at any time I must exercise it now, Dana. You'll not go to her alone. If you ever needed me you'll need me then.

DANA: What is she then, Quents, that's so terrible I need your protection?

QUENTIN: Dana, your mother . . . (*stops*)

DANA: I've heard that too, Quents. I know I am without a name, and my mother keeps a house. I know all that, Quents.

(*QUENTIN turns away from him.*)

Scene 4

As before. DANA, *alone, is busy cleaning his brother's rifle. His face is more relaxed, but still brooding and almost wrathful at times. He whistles and occasionally shakes his head. Then he puts down the rifle with the long Garland barrel.*

DANA: If I had the nerve I ought to have, I'd light out and never come back. That's what Quents don't know. I'm ready to light out. I dream of it so—just picking up and going out into the furthest stretch of mountains and woods. (*shrugs and picks up the Garand rifle again. There's a knocking at the door at stage left.*) Wouldn't you know it, when I'm cleaning this (*he touches the rifle almost as if it were a person*) some nosy neighbor wants to come in. (*shouting*) All right, all right. (*He hesitates about what to do with the rifle, then angrily throws it down on the big dining room table.*) So let you rest there. (*He pats the rifle again as if it were alive and opens the door for* LILY MAE CRAMER, *a handsome girl of about 22, who is carrying a bag she holds carefully.*)

DANA: Oh, it's only you, Lily. Come on in, then.

LILY: What do you mean, it's only me? Ain't I more than that to you? (*kisses him wetly*) Look how grown up you're getting, Dana. You must have sprouted up another inch since I saw you a month ago. (*She puts the bag on the table, near the gun.*) I brought you two-dozen fresh eggs. (*stares at the Garand*) Why, Dana, what's this doing out?

DANA: (*belligerently*) I'm cleaning it . . . for Quents.

LILY: (*confounded*) And he lets you. (*She takes him by both hands.*) I don't believe you.

DANA: (*lying*) I thought I'd clean it for him. He's going hunting in a few days . . . (*lying again*) I wanted to surprise him.

LILY: I've heard him say a hundred times you're never to touch his firearms, Dana. (*Dana pulls his hand from her.*) He's so afraid of an accident.

DANA: He's afraid of everything.

LILY: Quents is afraid of everything? (*She laughs boisterously.*) That's news to me. He's afraid of nothing, if you ask me.

DANA: You don't live with him. Just wait. Just wait.

LILY: (*Sitting down, she starts going through the bag of provisions.*) Just tell me what the big lummox is afraid of and I'll give you a twenty-dollar gold piece.

DANA: He's shaking in his boots because . . . he's going to take me to see . . . my mother.

LILY: Your mother?

DANA: Didn't you know I had one, Lily?

LILY: Dana, are you telling me the truth . . . ?

DANA: I'm telling you what Quents told me. It seems I have this mother, about fifty miles away, on the way to Chicago. . . . (*He moves toward* LILY *and takes her hand in his.*) And she has a big, big sprawling house she lives in, and fancy curtains, and rich upholstered furniture, and music, Lily. Music pours out of all the rooms night and day. Why she must be as rich as Croesus!

LILY: Have you been drinking some of Quents' homemade *moonshine*?

DANA: (*mischievously*) Smell my breath, Lily. (*He bends down and kisses her.*)

LILY: My God, you're growing into the very spit-and-image of your dad.

DANA: You can remember him?

LILY: I was only five or six, but I remember him as clear as yesterday afternoon. In his marine dress uniform.

DANA: (*suddenly pained*) That's enough, Lily.

LILY: What is wrong, Dana? What is wrong? Can I brew you some tea, dear? It'll only take a minute. Dana! Yes, I will. (*She goes to the stove, stage right, and starts getting everything ready to make tea.*)

DANA: Did you know her, too, Lily?

LILY: (*turning around*) Who, dear?

DANA: Never mind, never mind. . . . I'd better put away the gun before Quents comes in on us. (*He begins to gather up the gun.*)

LILY: Who did you mean, dear, by her? . . . For God's sake, don't point that thing at me, Dana.

DANA: Oh excuse me, but don't be scared because it's not loaded. Who did I mean by her, but my mother!

(*Having prepared the tea,* LILY *brings the teapot to the table and sets it down where the gun was.*)

LILY: Drink some, dear . . . (*Talking as if alone now, her eyes looking out into the indefinite space.*) Just once, I saw her coming out of your grandmother's house. It was a very warm June afternoon. She had on the most beautiful summer white dress I have ever seen, and she carried a faded pink parasol. Just as she was raising the parasol, a flower came loose from her dress and fell to the ground. On an impulse I ran over and picked it up for her. It was a red rambler just off the . . . stem.

DANA: (*also dreamily*) But how did you know that was her, since . . . she never married my dad?

LILY: Your dad was a fool, then.

DANA: (*alarmed*) What?

LILY: I'll speak no more of any of this, Dana. I know nothing about it, anyhow. . . . It's too delicate a thing to speak of—especially before you.

DANA: (*rising*) But why was my dad a fool?

LILY: Excuse me, and drink your tea.

DANA: Why, Lily, why?

LILY: Oh because she was so lovely—like the flower I picked up for her. He should have married her right away—should have stooped a thousand times to pick up all the flowers that were always blooming around her.

DANA: I wonder what you're talking about.

LILY: Listen, Dana, listen. Go to her—go visit you mother. Pay no attention to what anybody else says, do you hear me . . . ? I love your brother very deeply, but pay no attention to what Quents says. I don't.

DANA: I'm to go then.

LILY: Yes, yes.

DANA: And be damned?

LILY: (*outraged*) What? What on earth are you talking about?

DANA: That's what Quents says we'll both be after the visit.

LILY: Damned to see you own mother! (*She comes over and takes DANA in her arms.*) You should have gone years ago—years and years ago.

DANA: But I didn't know there was any. . . . Mother then.

LILY: You're not drinking your tea. And it's good. (*She dries her eyes on her handkerchief.*)

Scene 5

The only House of Pleasure in the vicinity. Faded damask curtains separate Julia's private sitting room from the rest of the house. There are two settees and a rosewood desk, at which she writes checks and answers letters. Music and laughter drift in from adjoining rooms. JULIA is reading a letter.

SADIE: What is it, Julia? You look worried to death.

JULIA: (*putting the letter in a large pocket of her red velvet gown*) Oh, well, Sadie.

SADIE: I've never seen you so agitated, so unlike your old sweet self. Surely—

JULIA: (*as if to herself*) I knew this day would come, but I thought—well yes, to tell the truth, I thought maybe I'd be in my grave when it did come. And so I'd have gotten out of it all. (*looking straight at SADIE*) We never do get out of anything in this life. We pay and pay and pay. (*SADIE now has come to sit down beside JULIA on a small cane-bottom chair. She takes the older woman's hand in hers.*)

SADIE: You're not going to close down the . . . business. (*She looks around her as if to take in all the decaying splendor and its meaning for her.*)

JULIA: (*laughs in spite of herself*) This has nothing to do with my business. (*She takes the letter out of her pocket and hands it to SADIE.*)

Read it for yourself, Sadie. Then you tell me. (*As* SADIE *unfolds the letter,* JULIA *daubs at her face with a sumptuous handmade handkerchief.*)

SADIE: (*stops*) But you never told me—

JULIA: Go on, finish the letter. Read all of it; then we'll talk.

SADIE: (*cries*) My God! (*She repeats this every so often.*)

JULIA: My God! is right. (*She rises, and places her back against the wall facing the audience, as if to testify.*)

SADIE: And they're bringing your boy to meet you after all these years.

JULIA: They? He is. Quentin.

SADIE: Do you know him then?

JULIA: Know him, yes . . . But why now—why now? Why should it all be brought out into the open again?

SADIE: But you surely must want to meet—to see your boy.

JULIA: To tell the truth, I don't know what I think or feel. I know of course I nearly died of grief when they took him from me. But that was like another age! Another woman than me. To relive all that past time in a single *meeting*. What sort of a meeting could that be? All these years, I've thought of my boy as dead. Along with his own father, who was prevented, you see, from marrying me when. . . . Oh why go back into it all? Why come now when I've buried the past—buried father and son with it? They can't force me to see him. And what will it do for the boy—to meet me here under this roof? Isn't it some last humiliation on the part of the old grandfather, who always hated me? Who would have prevented my marrying his son in the first place. . . . You see, Quentin—more terrible even than his old grandfather . . . his mother died, and Jeff and I were to be married. . . . I came across. . . . He thought he'd be back from France. . . . They buried him a hero instead over there. . . . You see, I have been happy in my own way here with you and the girls. It's hard for ordinary people to understand our house and us. But we do live in a kind of perpetual joy, Sadie. Maybe it's not real, but what is real then? Yet to be told after the wound of that long-ago day has healed—or I thought it was healed—that my son is going to be brought to me, and to receive him in this house of pleasure!

SADIE: But then, if the meeting isn't right here—couldn't you go to meet him?

JULIA: Not at all! Not ever. This is how I've had to survive, and I won't dress up like a pious widow in black and go to him on my knees and ask him to forgive me. There is nothing to forgive!

SADIE: But you speak as if it was your boy's fault.

JULIA: No, no. I have been over that a hundred times these past eighteen or nineteen years. I don't know that anything is anybody's fault. The whole of everything is beyond any final understanding. I blame nobody.

SADIE: But, my darling Julia (*taking hold of her*), you are sorrowful still if you aren't bitter and blaming.

JULIA: This should never have been. My sorrows should never have been brought to light again. . . . You remember last year I talked of closing the house.

SADIE: How could I forget?

JULIA: Then I realized what this house was. It was for me not of course the house of sin the world sees in it—even that the men who come here probably see in it. I saw it as the only true house. Greater and happier than any church, because it celebrates men and women the way they are, and are meant to be. The few moments of joy and respite are here and here alone, while the rest of the world is all steel fetters and chains, drudgery, joylessness, emptiness. They do not want us to have joy. This house has at least given us that, and given the men who come here that. So I will never close its doors—especially not now, when they would bring my boy here to make me feel my unworthiness. To make him I suppose never wish to see me again. To prove that his dad never intended from the first to marry me.

SADIE: (*as if she'd not heard any of this, and in a brooding gloomy manner*) And when is your boy coming?

JULIA: (*coming to with a start, as if she'd not heard the question properly*) What?

SADIE: (*studying her a while*) I said, dear, *when is your boy coming to visit you?*

JULIA: Ah yes, when . . . ? (*consults the letter*) Tomorrow.

SADIE: Tomorrow? How can you be ready by tomorrow?

JULIA: Sadie! I am ready today, this moment. What is there to be ready for, after all? You don't think I have time to convert the house into a shrine or that I should dress myself as the preacher's wife! No, I will make no preparations at all. None.

SADIE: There certainly is very little time if it's tomorrow.

JULIA: If he weren't coming for a year, I'd still prepare nothing. Is that clear? I've had to do what I have done in life. How could a boy understand that? And he will not love me.

SADIE: Perhaps you will love him, Julia.

JULIA: Don't go on! I want him to have his inheritance, so I will see him. By now I suppose the money has accumulated so that it is worth something. A young man starting out . . .

SADIE: (*as if to herself*) I am sure he will not know where he is. (*JULIA is very agitated all at once.*) A country boy, living far off from everything, he will think he is in a luxurious home. And a beautiful woman will make him feel welcome.

JULIA: Suddenly nothing is clear to me! (*rattles the letter in her hand*) It's as though we were practicing for a pageant.

SADIE: A pageant?

JULIA: Yes, as if somebody had made it all up for us. For though I have thought of my dead husband, or lover—yes, call him *husband*—I have never thought of my son. I thought—if I did think—that he was lying in the same grave in France with his father. Somehow I had persuaded myself to think they were both dead. That is why I was so industrious in pursuing every form of joy, and insisting that everyone have unstinted joy here. It blotted out everything else for me. It was as if I had created my own realm, and that no other world of sorrow and pain, rancor and disappointment ruined marriages and dead sons. There was only a palace of joy. . . . And now he is coming to spoil it all! To make me remember what I once was. Don't you see?

SADIE: Then tell them you can't see him.

JULIA: It's too late to tell them anything. And why should he lose his inheritance and let it go to the lawyers? I will see him, but I won't let him destroy my realm here. I will make it even more joyful in the future. Just wait and see. I will give everything to making it pure bliss for all those who come here. The world outside can grind itself to powder. I will rule here as I always have, and always will.

Scene 6

QUENTIN's *house again. It is night.* DANA *sits farther away from him than usual, in a large armchair.* QUENTIN *studies him. As* QUENTIN *has been working hard, he takes off his outer jacket. His huge frame and musculature create a kind of heat in the room so that* DANA *looks up.*

QUENTIN: I have to get you ready for our trip to see your mother. . . . What's wrong with you? (DANA *is staring at his half-brother as if seeing for the first time how powerfully he is built, and thinking that if he did not know who he was he'd be afraid.*)

DANA: I'm thinking I don't have anything special to wear, do I?

QUENTIN: Except you see I've bought you a . . . jacket, a pair of trousers, and a shined pair of shoes. (*He goes to the back of the stage and from a clothes press brings out the suit, with its jacket and trousers and the shoes.*) Put these on, Dana. (DANA *rises very slowly like someone suddenly roused from sleep.*) Let me help you. (DANA *takes off his clothes, shivering in the cold from the air coming from outside.*)

DANA: Quents, you wouldn't play a joke on me, would you . . . ? You've always been good and trustworthy.

QUENTIN: Put on the clothes, Dana.

DANA: Answer my question. (*He steps into the trousers.*) Before the other day I always supposed my mother—along with my dad—was dead. . . . Now—

QUENTIN: Now the coat. And look here, the tie. You never wear a tie, you little hick you, do you? (*laughs*)

DANA: (*Near tears, he takes* QUENTIN's *hand.*) Won't you level with me? And it can't be true, is it?, what kind of place she runs.

QUENTIN: It will all be over before you know it. You'll meet this lady, she'll see you're her boy, or we'll show her the papers to prove it, and then you'll come into your inheritance.

DANA: (*fearful*) I won't have to leave you, will I, Quents?

QUENTIN: Not as far as I'm concerned, you won't. I told you you could stay here forever, didn't I?

DANA: I've hardly slept a wink since you told me. I feel we've been to Sycamore Grove Cemetery and dug up . . . (*whispers almost inaudibly*) the dead.

QUENTIN: Let me tie this straight. (*He fixes the necktie carefully.*) Now we'll lick down that cowlick of yours, and you're right out of a bandbox. Go look at yourself in the mirror. . . . Go on. (*He slaps his behind as* DANA *goes toward the mirror.*)

DANA: (*coming back flustered*) It don't look like me. I look like—oh, I don't know who.

QUENTIN: You look like (*wondering deeply*) . . . like somebody I never saw before. Gad, your mother will be proud of you, Dana.

DANA: I don't want to go.

QUENTIN: Look here. I've worked myself up to a pitch to obey their instructions, and don't you back out on me. Do you hear? There's things we have to do, or just stay in bed and pull the covers over our heads and die.

DANA: And what are you going to wear, Quents?

QUENTIN: Oh, I have something upstairs.

DANA: But you're going with me, ain't you?

QUENTIN: Of course I'm going with you. But I don't have to look like I stepped out of a fashion plate. . . . I probably will wait outside, who knows?

DANA: Gosh almighty, I wish it were the day after.

QUENTIN: (*suddenly, as if in premonition*) But what if you liked it? (*said as if alone*) And wanted to stay?

DANA: Ever since you brought me the news, Quents, you've changed.

QUENTIN: (*stirred*) How?

DANA: I don't know how. You look the same, of course. Big and strapping, but your . . . mind is different.

QUENTIN: I want to go there even less than you. I feel we're leaving the country behind us and going overseas.

DANA: It's far, then.

QUENTIN: Not so very. But the roads is bad, and it's located at the end of nowhere. (*sheepishly*) I bought you an overcoat too, Dana.

DANA: What did you go and do that for, Quents? If I'm only going to wear it once.

QUENTIN: (*producing a handsome thick overcoat from a box he'd left at the door*) Who knows, you might be going to a dance before too long. You're growing up before my eyes, you know. (*helps him on with the coat*)

DANA: Don't tell me to go look in the mirror for this one! I'll be embarrassed as all get-out to wear such a thing.

QUENTIN: (*speaks before he thinks*) Nobody will know you where you're going.

DANA: (*laughs before he catches the meaning*) You can say that again . . . (*thinking*) I wish you wouldn't spend so much money on me, Quents. I ain't worth it.

QUENTIN: (*riled*) Don't ever let me hear you say that again, do you hear? If I buy anybody anything, whether it's a coat or a top or a

176

baseball bat, he's worth every cent I put in it. And as to you . . . (*he suddenly takes* DANA *in his arms*) I wish to God it wasn't true.

DANA: What, Quents? (*disturbed by this sudden show of love*)

QUENTIN: The way the world runs. Well, let's go then—let's get it over with once and for all.

Scene 7

JULIA *and* SADIE *greeting* QUENTIN *and* DANA.

JULIA: Come in young gentleman. (*shakes hands with the young men*) This is Miss Sadie Farnsworth, my dear friend and assistant.

(*The young men greet her. They are reserved and obviously ill at ease. But, strangely enough, it is* DANA *who acts more forthcoming than his older half-brother.*)

JULIA: I can't tell you how much I have looked forward to our meeting. I'm especially glad, Dana, that your older brother was kind enough to accompany you. Do be seated presently but first let me look at you both! Dana, Dana. (*She embraces him.*) And Quentin, Quentin. (*embraces him more formally*) How much Quentin you remind me of your father, does he not, Sadie? Now be seated. And let us have a drink in honor of this occasion. (*She rings a bell on the wall.*) Tell me, were the roads in fairly good shape, for I worried a bit at the long trip you were facing?

DANA: (*waits for* QUENTIN *who, however, seems immobilized*) The roads were not too bad, ma'am, were they, Quents?

QUENTIN: (*awkwardly*) No, ma'am, they were in good shape . . . for them. (*They all laugh.*)

JULIA: And did you drive, Quentin?

QUENTIN: Part of the way, ma'am.

DANA: You see, ma'am, Quentin was a bit tired and so I took the wheel, though I don't have a license.

QUENTIN: (*reluctantly*) Yes, ma'am, he drove like a pro, I'll hand it to him.

JULIA: May I ask you young men a favor? Please call me Julia, if you will. (*A young man enters with a tray, a bottle, and some glasses.*) Thank you, Tim. You may serve our guests, if you please. I hope you will enjoy some wine, gentlemen. (*As* TIM *serves the wine, there is a sound of music and laughter from some rooms in the distance.*) They are having a dance this evening. Part of this old house has a small ballroom for dancing.

SADIE: (*rising*) If you will excuse me, I think I have some tasks that need tending to.

JULIA: You needn't leave us, Sadie.

SADIE: I think I should see about things in the ballroom, if you don't absolutely need me here. (*JULIA gives a nod of assent.*) And so nice to meet you young gentlemen! Dana, may I say you are exactly as I pictured you would be! How happy you have made . . . Julia.

JULIA: You are so right, Sadie. Yes, yes, he is exactly as I too pictured him. . . . But your grandmother has filled me in somewhat on both you young men . . .

SADIE: Julia, I will be within calling distance if you need me. Good-bye all. (*Exits . . . meanwhile* TIM *serves each of the guests and* JULIA, *then exits, too.*)

JULIA: To the happiness of us all! (*Raises her glass.* DANA *drinks at once, but* QUENTIN *only sips at his drink.*) Is the wine to your taste, Quentin? (*QUENTIN nods and sips some more.*)

DANA: (*speaking rather loudly*) You see, ma'am, Quentin and I as a matter of fact seldom drink anything except for some mulled wine. Isn't that so, Quents?

QUENTIN: (*blushing, he nods and drinks a little more*) Yes, Dana is right. (*They all laugh.*)

JULIA: You needn't drink it, Quentin, if it's not to your taste.

QUENTIN: I will, ma'am—will drink.

JULIA: As I say, your grandmother, Dana, has told me a great deal about you. So much so that when you came in tonight I felt . . . how shall I put it? . . . I felt all the while we have been far from

178

strangers. And you too, Quentin. Your grandmother has spoken so often of you.

QUENTIN: (*a bit of his old brusque self returns*) I hope she has told you good things, ma'am.

JULIA: Indeed she has. She thinks you are sterling. And of course she thinks the same of Dana here. (*QUENTIN suddenly finishes his glass of wine.*) It is somewhat hard to meet loved ones when they have been, for one reason or other, separated by what someone has called *life's vicissitudes.*

QUENTIN: (*loosening up*) That sounds like Mr. Endors' way of speaking, ma'am.

JULIA: (*springing to agree*) So it does. I'm sure we all know him, don't we, eh Dana! . . . (*drinks*) How handsome you young men are—such wonderful fresh countenances. You have no idea how you liven up the sad gaiety of my home here. (*The music stops for a moment, then begins again.*) We try to be happy here, but we don't always succeed. (*seeing QUENTIN's empty glass*) Quentin, may I sweeten your drink, as we say?

QUENTIN: (*rising and holding out his glass*) You may, ma'am, for it is . . . the kind of drink that asks for more, if you'll excuse my way of putting it.

JULIA: You put it very well. (*pours him some more*) And Dana—ah, you still have some, but let me sweeten yours a bit also. Forgive me, Quentin—and Dana will forgive me also—if I tell you how much you resemble your father. . . . In appearance, Quentin.

QUENTIN: (*drinks*) I believe you, ma'am.

JULIA: *Julia.* Say *Julia,* if you please, both of you.

QUENTIN: (*clearly feeling his drink*) Very well. . . . *Ju-lia.* Say *Julia,* Dana.

(*The music now sounds closer.*)

JULIA: Is the music too loud, gentlemen? We can close one of the other doors if it is.

QUENTIN: I wouldn't care, Julia, even if it was louder. If we opened that heavy door there, perhaps we could hear it better. I've not heard such agreeable sounds, eh, Dana.

(*JULIA nods worriedly and looks down at his drink. QUENTIN goes toward the door and opens it, to the astonishment of both JULIA and DANA.*)

QUENTIN: There! Isn't that better? Oh excuse me, Julia, for such a liberty. You should be the one to open the door. Forgive me. (*He helps himself to the bottle, then drinks.*) But you mustn't believe everything Grandmother says about me, ma'am. Excuse me, Julia. (*He continues standing and looking at Julia.*) I am not quite the cross bear she makes me out to be.

JULIA: Oh, she never said any such thing. Your grandmother is very fond of you. She threw the compliments . . . about both you boys. But, Quentin, if you go in the next room and open the door to it, you can see the dancers . . . dancing.

QUENTIN: Oh can I, ma'am . . . ? I mean Julia. (*He rushes off into the next room and opens the big door, which reveals dancers in the ballroom.*) Julia! Julia! I had no idea. Why, it's a real ballroom, a dancehall. Go and look, Dana. What's the matter? You look as sour as you always say I do. . . . I can't believe it, Julia. A ballroom with live dancers. It makes me . . .

DANA: (*worried*) What, Quents, what?

QUENTIN: I told you not to look so sour, and I mean it.

DANA: But Quents, I am not sour at all. I am so pleased to see you happy for a change.

QUENTIN: (*belligerently*) And what do you mean by that, I wonder?

DANA: I only mean I am always happy when you are happy.

QUENTIN: Good. Then act happy when you *are* happy. Don't sit there scowling.

JULIA: Now, now, boys! Do I hear the beginning of a small domestic argument?

QUENTIN: May I have another glass of this delicious drink, Julia?

JULIA: (*jokingly*) Should Quentin have another glass, Dana?

DANA: You have no idea, ma'am, how happy I always am to see Quentin happy. And this is the first time . . .

QUENTIN: (*as Julia pours him another glass*) You see, ma'am, Dana only knows one side of me: the blacksmith side. He doesn't really like to see me having a gay old time, as now. . . . And actually this may be the first time I have been quite so . . . like I am! (*He raises his glass to* JULIA. *Then sits down and quietly sips his drink.*)

DANA: All I want is for Quents to be happy.

QUENTIN: Then, Dana, let Quentin be happy.

DANA: Amen!

JULIA: The one who is happy, boys, is me. You have no idea. I had so longed for a meeting just like this one, yet I thought it would never be. It was Gwen, your grandmother, who kept the thought and the hope alive in my heart.

QUENTIN: Oh, let's not speak of her, Julia. Let's only speak of you. (*rises, drinking*) Only of you! (*The music blares now very loudly.*) Julia, would you dance with me? Just a few steps. Will you? I know you think perhaps I have tasted too much wine. I know Dana does. Look how he is glaring at us.

JULIA: Of course, Quentin, I will dance with you, if Dana will give the word. (*She winks at* DANA, *who laughs.*)

DANA: Quentin always has my word for anything he chooses.

QUENTIN: I hope you mean that.

JULIA: (*jokingly*) Shall we dance then, Quentin, since Dana has given us permission?

(QUENTIN *and* JULIA *begin to dance. They dance for a while, then Julia breaks off.*)

JULIA: (*laughing*) You are a wonderful dancer! Dana, come here — dance a few steps with me.

QUENTIN: Only with my permission!

JULIA: Ah, very well. Is permission granted, Quentin then?

QUENTIN: (*picking up the bottle and pouring himself another drink*) Granted, granted.

(*JULIA and DANA dance, then finally break off and sit down.*)

QUENTIN: Do you know what, Julia . . . ? I would like to . . . yes, dance alone. Unbeknownst to Dana here, who is my jailer, I often go to the barn dances, and—you know what?—I often at the evening's end dance alone in front of everybody! That's the side to me, you see, Dana does not know!

DANA: Why, Quentin, are you telling the truth?

QUENTIN: Watch me now.

(*He begins to dance in a frenzied but still quite graceful way—especially in view of the fact that he is drunk. JULIA and DANA applaud. QUENTIN dances more and more furiously, then suddenly reels and falls, knocking his head against one of the tables.*)

JULIA: (*frightened*) Oh, Quentin. (*DANA rushes up to his brother.*)

DANA: Oh my God. . . Julia. I fear he has hurt himself.

JULIA: (*bending down*) Oh, Dana, he has hurt himself. Quentin, Quentin, are you all right?

DANA: He's got himself a very bad cut on his head. Quentin, say something.

QUENTIN: Yes, yes what am I to say? I want to dance some more.

JULIA: Quentin, Quentin. Here, I will call Tim. (She rings the bell to the room.) Oh dear, oh dear. (*TIM* enters.) Tim, Quentin has taken a bad fall and hurt himself.

ACT II

Scene 1

After the meeting, JULIA *and* SADIE *are drinking their morning coffee. It is clear they have been having a heart-to-heart talk.* SADIE *is near tears.*

SADIE: But I thought everything went well, Julia. Except the fact young Quentin had had too much to drink.

JULIA: That was the least of it, Sadie. I don't know how you can say it went well, dear.

SADIE: I could hear you tossing and turning all night. But I thought that was due to excitement.

JULIA: Endors should never have allowed both the boys to come. In fact, he could have got round the stipulations of that will and never brought either of the boys here. Or I should have refused to see them.

SADIE: But then the poor boy would have lost his inheritance.

JULIA: No, no. Endors could have found some loophole to prevent the boy from coming here.

SADIE: Julia, I am surprised. You told me, before the boys came here, you were looking forward so eagerly to their seeing you.

JULIA: Did I say that? (*smiles*)

SADIE: You certainly did. Why, you were a different person in the way you were looking forward to seeing your little boy again.

183

JULIA: There is no little boy, Sadie, and there is no Mother. Don't you see, dear? The past cannot be brought back. The dead cannot return to life and joy. . . . Dana was so distant, even cold. Affable, but oh such a stranger!

SADIE: I thought he looked at you, dear, so lovingly.

JULIA: (*bitterly*) You did? Ah well.

SADIE: And how did you think he looked at you, Julia?

JULIA: (*bitterly, wonderingly, and with a kind of crushed disappointment*) His heart has no room for me. And he came only to say *goodbye*. I'll tell you how he looked at me—like someone looking through an album of old photos of someone he had never seen or heard of before, and when he closed the album he would never see again. He came to see a perfect stranger whom he would never meet again.

SADIE: Oh no, no. I beg to differ with you. He looked at you with such tender though bashful longing.

JULIA: Oh if he had only looked at me that way . . .

SADIE: And the other boy, Quentin. He was terribly taken with you.

JULIA: That is where everything went wrong, Sadie.

SADIE: How do you mean, dear?

JULIA: He looked exactly as Dana's father looked when we were sweethearts. He was Dana's father, I thought, when he entered. My heart came to a full stop when he came into the room. He brought back everything that was precious—everything that we can expect from living . . .

SADIE: But one would never have known, Julia, you were feeling such strong emotions.

JULIA: That is because I have learned here in this house of joy never to remember my own smiling happiness, or my own fall. . . . I have become a kind of lady in the waxworks, always bowing and ushering others into happiness when my own has been taken from me forever. No, no, Endors, should have never had them come here.

SADIE: But, Julia, they did come and what is more they want to return! They both said that to me as I was ushering them out.

JULIA: Return? Are you crazy? They shall never return. (*darkly*) Furthermore, while as you say I was tossing and turning in the night, I was thinking of closing this place—this business—and you and I would go far away. Perhaps to some place thousands of miles from here. Who knows where!

SADIE: I believe, Julia, you would pine away if you did not have this house you call a house of joy. And what would we do far away from where we have lived so long . . . ? Listen to me . . . these boys, these young men, you should have them as constant callers.

JULIA: In this house of—as they call it—*house of sin*! Never.

SADIE: You could change its character then. And make it a house just for them.

JULIA: Change the leopard's spots? Listen to me, Sadie, and don't interrupt. I never want to see them again in this life or the life to come.

SADIE: (*breaking down*) Oh, you can't mean it.

JULIA: If each of them had stabbed me a dozen times, I could not have felt greater pain.

SADIE: Yet, looking at you last night, you appeared a young woman who had never known a sorrow in all her days—a woman who was full of happiness and high spirits.

JULIA: That is because I have had eighteen years encouraging others to be happy, ushering in others to feel what it is to be joyful. A dead shell of a woman. . . . They must never see me again. I must never see them again . . .

SADIE: Don't stop now—go on.

JULIA: . . . because all I want is to see them every minute and hour of the day. All I want is to hold them to me and never let them go. Oh, they would bring me greater joy than anyone who ever came to this house. But our joy would end in the most terrible calamity. Their young lives would be consumed in all the pain and sorrow

I have kept in my heart. I would destroy them once they saw into my sorrow and pain.

SADIE: But let's not do anything rash.

JULIA: Oh, Sadie, draw closer. (*She embraces her.*) Isn't our love for one another enough? Why should we let these young men from some dreamland enter our domain? We live in our own shadow-land of joy—not experiencing the joy directly, but savoring some of the joy felt by others. . . . If the young men came here, our lives would be shattered by their strength and vitality, and what could we give them in return? That is, what could *I* give them in return?

SADIE: You could give them everything. Don't you see they want to be with you? How blind can you be? Don't you see they need you?

JULIA: No, no, it's you who are blind. We've fulfilled old Endors' requirements; now let Quentin and Dana go free, Sadie. The past cannot be rekindled and brought to life, save in dreaming. We can dream all we want, Sadie, you and I here. But we can't let in full-bodied life. We can't let our kind of life cast a shadow over theirs. Don't you understand?

Scene 2

QUENTIN *and* DANA *are arguing.*

QUENTIN: I asked you a question and you just stand and stare at me instead of replying.

DANA: All right. You'll have to pardon me, Quents. After last night I can't think straight.

QUENTIN: After last night? When did you ever think straight?

DANA: Thanks, Quents, much obliged for that.

QUENTIN: (*threateningly, after he moves in closely*) I asked you because you told me I was talking to myself in my sleep all night, and I asked you what was I talking about.

DANA: Yes, you did mumble and mutter all night.

QUENTIN: (*wild with anger*) And what did I mutter?

DANA: Don't shout at me like that, Quents. Please don't. You scare me.

QUENTIN: You know something and you won't tell me.

DANA: All right, all right. You were talking about her, the lady we met last night.

QUENTIN: You say that as if you didn't know who she was and cared a damned sight less.

DANA: I'm sorry I ever went there. Sorry she's my mother.

QUENTIN: Oh, so that's where the shoe pinches.

DANA: I should have gone alone and then you wouldn't be in the state you're in.

QUENTIN: What state am I in?

DANA: This is the first time in I don't know when that you haven't gone to work. And last night was the first time you've ever been drunk.

QUENTIN: I'm waiting for my answer.

DANA: Oh, about your muttering. Well, what do you think you muttered about? Her! All you talked about was how much you loved her.

QUENTIN: (*bemused*) I said that?

DANA: You said that over and over again—all night long, all the night through.

QUENTIN: You're not making this up?

DANA: I never make things up. My life has been made up for me.

QUENTIN: And what were my words?

DANA: They turned my stomach, I can tell you that much.

QUENTIN: My words, Dana, my words.

DANA: Ah, well. You said you wanted to hold her to you, cover her beautiful face with warm kisses. And then, at the last, you said *Why can't we go away somewhere far distant together?*

QUENTIN: (*sits down and puts his face in his hands*) Go on.

DANA: Do I have to?

QUENTIN: (*obviously upset by what* DANA *has said*) Suit yourself. But the way you acted, Dana!

DANA: I didn't act. I did nothing. I behaved. I just sat.

QUENTIN: That's what I meant. You paid no attention to her. You acted liked were riding in a train with a stranger.

DANA: Like a stranger? She was, she is a stranger. . . . I hated her. I would have liked to kill her.

QUENTIN: (*shocked*) Dana, for God's sake I've never seen you like this.

DANA: Mother! I have no mother. That whore is not my mother.

QUENTIN: (*rising*) Dana, stop it. Don't say any more. It's been too much for you.

DANA: She's put a spell on you, that's what. She saw she couldn't do anything to me, I guess. Going to see her after all these years, when she refused to be my mother in the beginning!

QUENTIN: Your grandfather made her give you up.

DANA: My grandfather! I bet he had no trouble taking me away from her. She was dying to get back to her House of Joy probably even then.

QUENTIN: What else did I say in my sleep?

DANA: I can't recall. More of the same. *Julia, Julia, Julia,* you called.

QUENTIN: God Almighty. I guess old Endors was right. *He* should have taken you there.

DANA: Nobody should have taken me there. I should have refused to go and given up my inheritance; let the will go to the next beggar in line. I will be sick the rest of my life for having met her. And then, to hear you all night moaning and groaning about wanting to run off with her. For Christ's sake!

QUENTIN: Where are you going?

DANA: Am I going somewhere? Where is there to go? I know, though, where you're going as soon as the shades of night begin to fall.

QUENTIN: (*dreamily*) And where would that be, Dana?

DANA: To Julia's house. To the House of Joy.

(QUENTIN *buries his face in his hands.*)

Scene 3

GWEN *and* QUENTIN *are speaking.*

GWEN: I'm always happy to see you, Quents, so don't apologize for coming at such an early hour. You'd be welcome in the dead of night or at the crack of dawn.

QUENTIN: Ah, Grandma. May I sit down?

GWEN: Quents, what is it. You look so pale and, yes, even thin. Can you tell me, what can I do for you?

QUENTIN: Grandma, do you have something to drink?

GWEN: Something, Quents.

QUENTIN: (*almost shouting in his embarrassment*) Perhaps (*then lowering his voice*) some brandy.

GWEN: Yes. . . . But I thought you didn't ever take any strong drink.

QUENTIN: Then maybe I've changed . . . since the visit. (GWEN *rings, a servant enters, and she says something to him in a lowered voice.*)

GWEN: I want to thank you, Quents, for having gone. I will tell you, I understand how difficult it was for you. I'm grateful.

QUENTIN: Don't go on like that, Grandma, please. After I got there I saw . . . it was all right.

GWEN: (*astounded*) All right?

QUENTIN: (*somewhat like his old self*) Yes, I saw I had been wrong about it all. (*The servant enters and hands* QUENTIN *a drink.*) You aren't going to join me, Grandma?

GWEN: No, dear, not just now. (*watches him, astonished, as he drinks*) I understand you wanting the brandy. Life is full of hard duties, Quents. It never seems to relent on us. But I am worried about Dana.

QUENTIN: (*as if coming out of a deep reverie*) Dana? Why him?

GWEN: He was overwrought on the phone. For the first time ever, he was rude to me.

QUENTIN: How was he rude, Grandma?

GWEN: I can hardly explain it. His voice, so changed. He scolded me.

QUENTIN: Oh, I know.

(GWEN *stares at him.*)

QUENTIN: Go on Grandma. Tell me what he said. (*drinks*)

GWEN: I felt . . . heartbroken after we hung up.

QUENTIN: But what did he say?

GWEN: He said that both you and his . . . mother had behaved badly. That his mother ignored him . . . for you. And that you had got on so well with her. That you had in fact changed . . .

QUENTIN: Go on.

GWEN: . . . *changed character*, I think, is how he put it.

QUENTIN: Grandma, may I have another, do you suppose?

GWEN: (*hesitantly, even fearfully*) Of course you may. (*She rings for the servant, who comes in with the bottle and pours* QUENTIN *a drink.*)

QUENTIN: (*drinking*) Go on, please, Grandma. Don't mind me, please.

GWEN: (*looks at him worriedly*) He told me he hated her. Hated her . . . to the death, he said. I never dreamed Dana would be like this. I can understand it in a way, of course. But he made me see it clearly—as clearly as looking through a bright pane of glass.

QUENTIN: See what?

GWEN: That she was not his mother, for his real mother would have never given him away, or given him up. And this painted Easter egg of a woman . . .

QUENTIN: Be careful, please.

GWEN: (*perhaps not having heard him, or at least so carried away that she does not pay attention*) . . . this painted harlot meant nothing to him. But she meant the world to Quents. So that, he said, he felt he'd forever lost a mother, and lost you, too. Lost you to . . . her.

QUENTIN: (*drinks*) Oh yes, I got that from him . . . direct.

GWEN: Let me tell you, Quents, that the stipulation in the will . . . You were right from the first. Dana should never had had to go there.

QUENTIN: I'm glad I went, Grandma. I'm glad. I want to go again!

GWEN: (*shocked in spite of herself*) Would that be wise?

QUENTIN: I don't know, Grandma. Wise? I don't know. (*drinks*)

GWEN: (*rising*) Everything has changed! Everything has turned inside out.

QUENTIN: Maybe everything has turned right . . . for the first time.

GWEN: I cannot get over Dana changing so. He has broken my heart.

QUENTIN: Your heart will mend, Grandma. Something has happened to me, too. May I speak my mind?

GWEN: I thought you did that from the time you were a small child.

QUENTIN: But I never told you then what I thought or felt.

GWEN: (*worried*) You may tell me anything.

QUENTIN: It was the first time seeing her, sitting in her house there, with all the sounds of music and the brief glimpse of dancers, for I've never seen anyone like her. . . . I did change.

GWEN: And Dana changed, Quents. Don't forget to mention that.

QUENTIN: Now he hates me.

GWEN: You know better.

QUENTIN: (*bitterly*) He has told me he never wants to see me again, because . . . because I told him I wanted to go there again. Again and again!

GWEN: But you won't, Quents. You won't go there. There's nothing to go there for now. You've accomplished your mission. You've satisfied the stipulations of the will, and saved Dana's inheritance. Your work is done.

QUENTIN: (*rising*) No, Grandma, no. I want to go there. Don't you understand? I . . . how can I say it . . . ? I have searched my mind and soul. I love Julia.

GWEN: You don't know what you're saying. Dana complained you were drunk and you are not used to strong drink. That's it. You were right before, never to drink. Tell me you won't go back there.

QUENTIN: No, Grandma, don't make me swear to that and give up the only happiness—no, amend that to *joy*—the only *joy* I've ever had or felt. Don't make me swear to that. I want to go there. Do you hear? (*drawing her to him*) Please listen to me, dear. Please. I belong there with her. It's what I've always wanted. To live in a house where there is joy. Let me go then. Let me live there if I choose—if of course she chooses for me to.

GWEN: My dear boy, you are overwrought. The lawyers have as usual made us do a hard task. When you think it all over, when you are calm and when, Quents, you don't drink anymore. . . . You are not used to it, you know that. You must not! And Dana says you have not gone to work for days now. Quents, I will not allow you to destroy yourself, do you hear? Stay here with me if you like. There is quiet joy here, and comfort. Please, Quents.

QUENTIN: (*kneels before her, takes her hand and kisses it*) I love you Grandma, but now I love her too. I think it is her house more than anything. It has filled my whole body and soul for the first time. She calls it *joy*. I call it *life*. I cannot give that up now that I have felt it. Don't make me give it up.

GWEN: Stay here, dear, until you feel like your old self. That's all I ask.

QUENTIN: I don't want to be my old self now that I have awakened. Can't you understand? I don't want to go back to my old self. I want joy. Joy!

Scene 4

QUENTIN *has broken into the front parlor of* JULIA's *house. He is disheveled, and looks about distractedly in search of* DANA's *mother.* SADIE *enters. At first, she is speechless, finding* QUENTIN *ignores her plea that he leave the house at once. She stands staring at him. He is oblivious to her.*

SADIE: For God's sake, Quentin, will you please listen to me? How many times do I have to tell you, Julia does not want to see you. She cannot see you. And look at you! You are no more the young man who visited us the other evening than you are—

QUENTIN: (*turning to her in anger*) Yes, go on, than I am who? Tell me. That I'm who! Look here, I won't leave this house until I speak with her. You can't just entertain a man lavishly one evening and then bar the door to him the next, as if he was a beggar. Shall I teach both of you some manners? And, after all, who are you to decide who she can see or not see? Let me tell you, I can stay here until all hell freezes over. Go tell her that.

(JULIA *appears.* SADIE *advances to her.*)

SADIE: I'm so sorry, Julia. But our visitor—

JULIA: (*interrupting*) It's all right, Sadie. (*turns to* QUENTIN) You can say what's on your mind, Quentin.

QUENTIN: What's on my mind is only for you to hear, Julia.

JULIA: (*hesitating*) Please, Sadie, I beg you. You may leave. Let Quentin tell me what is on his mind.

(*Exit* SADIE, *reluctantly.*)

JULIA: (*rather grandly*) Good evening, Quentin.

QUENTIN: Good evening is it? I think you have a lot of explaining to do.

JULIA: Listen to me, Quentin. What more do we have to say to each other? We have both fulfilled the strictures of the will and the good counsel of Mr. Endors.

QUENTIN: Oh, so that is all there was to our first evening together. Fulfilling the requirements of Mr. Endors and his will.

JULIA: I'm afraid so.

QUENTIN: And what about the rest of the evening, when we were together for the first time?

JULIA: I'm afraid all that was . . . ceremony and playacting for the occasion.

QUENTIN: Playacting?

JULIA: Oh, call it whatever you like. You followed Mr. Endors' instructions. As did poor wretched Dana. As did I! Now you and I owe no more to anybody. We fulfilled our duty, more than even Mr. Endors or that spiteful will could dictate. We are free now to go about our individual lives.

QUENTIN: You mean, *you* can go about your individual life in this grand palace of yours! As for me—and look at me when I speak—as for me, I will never go about my individual life again after what occurred here.

JULIA: (*deeply moved*) I have done all I can do! For Dana and for you . . . (*grasping at straws*) You have brazenly broken in here today and terrified Sadie. What do you want of me, when you know in your heart there should be no more communication between us?

QUENTIN: (*shocked*) In my *heart*! . . . You do not believe one word you're saying. You talk of housebreaking! *You!* What about what you have done to me? No, don't interrupt. You have broken into me here. (*pointing to his heart*) And now I am to be dismissed as a lackey you have no need for.

JULIA: (*weakly*) I will not allow you to speak to me in this fashion.

QUENTIN: Your mouth says one thing, but your eyes say another. I'm not leaving the premises until you tell me what it is you really feel for me. That you care for me as I care for you. I know you do, Julia. Yes, you may have done your duty to Mr. Endors and perhaps to Dana. What about the duty we owe ourselves? (*from his overwrought condition, he falls to his knees*)

JULIA: For God's sake, get up. What if someone should come in and see you?

QUENTIN: Let the whole town come in and see me. See if I care.

JULIA: Will you get up!

QUENTIN: Not until you tell me I may visit you, speak to you, pour out my heart to you.

JULIA: (*almost beside herself*) Get up then. (*as if to herself*) What do I have on my hands?

QUENTIN: (*rising*) On your hands? What you have made of me, that's what. You have made me love you. And I won't leave until you promise to return some of that love. Not all, perhaps some, (*sotto voce*) maybe.

JULIA: (*almost incoherent with emotion*) What am I to say?

QUENTIN: You are to say that you will allow me to pay you calls here in your home—that I am to be able to see you in what you call your *house of joy*. Oh, you need not fear that I will ask you to say you care for me. I don't expect the impossible. But you can say I will be allowed to pay you calls—that I am to be able to see you here in your (*pause*) beautiful house of joy. Julia, Julia, you do not understand what you have done for me, done to me? You've shown me a glimpse of another world I never knew existed, not even in dream. This beautiful house of yours, the sounds of violins and harps, the girls in their fancy dresses. Do you have any idea what my life has been up until I met you? Of course you don't. Well, it has been nothing but slavish work and duty. My chief task has been living for Dana. And, as you say, following Mr. Endors' many chores, his countless commands. But you and what I believe you call your *house of joy* have shown me an entirely different world. How can you shut me out now when you have given me a glimpse of such a . . . (*gropes for words*) yes, such a paradise?

JULIA: Oh Quentin, Quentin. I am so pained if I have hurt you. But—

QUENTIN: (*interrupting, angry*) All right! (*softer*) If you are truly sorry, why can't you let me go on paying you visits? Why am I to be shut out like a common robber? You need not even see me when I pay you a call. If I can only feast my eyes on your beautiful—

JULIA: Enough. (*pausing*) I see I have been selfish and wrong. I had no idea my house would have given you the happiness you say it has bestowed on you.

QUENTIN: Then you won't shut me out if I call again?

JULIA: Oh, I never meant to shut you out, Quentin. But the shock of seeing Dana! (*stops*) And the joy of seeing you, Quentin. (*another pause*) It was all too much for me.

QUENTIN: And then I had to get drunk and make a fool of myself.

JULIA: That part is all erased from my memory, dear Quentin. (*painfully*) You shall always be welcome. It's very little reward for all you'd done for Dana.

QUENTIN: (*cautiously taking her hand in his, but still fearful*) I'll not be shut out again?

(JULIA, *too moved to speak, nods and holds his own hands tightly in hers. Exit* QUENTIN. *Shortly afterwards,* SADIE *enters.* JULIA *is now seated, and in such a bemused state of mind she's hardly aware of* SADIE's *presence.*)

SADIE: (*in a hushed manner*) Julia, what on earth has been going on? I have been so anxious!

JULIA: (*looking up absently*) Oh, Sadie, I hardly know myself what has transpired.

SADIE: (*somewhat miffed*) I only thought I was carrying out your instructions, Julia. That you never wanted to see this young man again! I only—

JULIA: (*interrupting*) I know! I know. You'll have to forgive me. (*as if to herself*) We have a very remarkable young man on our hands.

SADIE: (*somewhat stiffly*) Then you wish to allow him to visit you?

JULIA: (*in a strange mood*) Allow? *Welcome* is the right word, I believe. . . . We must welcome someone who, as he says, we have given such happiness.

SADIE: (*troubled; in a low voice, as if to herself*) What has come over you, my dear friend?

JULIA: (*as if soliloquizing*) We can't deprive someone of the only happiness he has ever had, can we? (*She looks up fixedly at* SADIE.)

SADIE: (*somewhat heatedly*) But, Julia, you told me only today, in the most emphatic way possible, that we could never let in full-bodied life here—your very words! For, you went on, these young men have the sunlight about them, and we have only the tinsel and the soft lights. Julia, you went back on your own word to me! You are contradicting, even destroying, everything you ever stood for. Everything you always told me you stood for—you are discarding your own way of life, which I have shared with you from the very beginning! And after that glorious meeting the other evening with the young men, you drew me aside then and there and said in almost a prayerful way, *Sadie, we must never let what we are cast its shadow on Dana and Quentin.*

JULIA: You've cut me to the quick by using my own words against me. But, Sadie, let me say this. It's too late now for me to follow my own words or all that I have told you over the years. I can't give him up. I can't close my door on Quentin. No matter what happens, no matter how much as you say I contradict my own way of life—contradict even myself. For it's Quentin and his love that have contradicted everything I have stood for. I can no more forbid him to come here than I can shut the door of this house on myself. He has to be given the privilege he asks for. If I refuse him, I think I shall die. Don't cry now, Sadie, for God's sake! (*approaching now and taking her hand*) So I've gone back on my word, gone back on myself, have I? Then that's my destiny. Something stronger than me or our house here has obliterated the past—obliterated what I was or am. Sadie, Sadie, have no fear, our friendship will continue! I will always care for you—protect you. I don't know what will happen now. It's beyond my strength or will. All I know is my door must be open to him.

Scene 5

MEG BATTERSHELL *and* GWENDOLYN *are in conversation.* GWEN *is looking at some old photographs of herself and* MEG *taken many years ago. Both women are laughing, but at the same time near tears at the remembrance of old times.*

GWEN: To think we looked like that, Meg. Ready for the altar, both of us! How pretty you were, Meg.

MEG: How gorgeous you were, Gwen.

GWEN: I can't believe we were those girls, Meg. Time—how insidious a thing, so noiseless and imperceptible. What if we were to meet those girls who were, after all, us? What if they were to come into the room and meet us now! I'm afraid they would run away.

MEG: Nonsense, Gwen. I still see in your face that young girl in the photos.

GWEN: Oh let's put them away. They're too precious. (*hands the box of photos to* MEG)

MEG: You're not sorry I let you see them.

GWEN: Sorry? You know better.

MEG: What if time didn't change us, Gwen? What if we always stayed so young and pretty? What would our lives be?

GWEN: I have often thought of that. Well, I wouldn't be a grandmother today with all the problems that face me.

MEG: But when we were those young girls, Gwen, we didn't know what we know now. Those young girls, Gwen, knew nothing!

GWEN: That's why they looked the way they did, pretty—as they say, *pretty as pictures*—without a clue to what was in store for them— without a clue as to what life is about.

MEG: Gwen, have you heard from any of your grandsons?

GWEN: Not a word from Quentin after his visit. But Dana has called many times. He always seems to call when you're out.

MEG: And?

GWEN: I've never known a young man who's so changed. Remember how we always talked about his sunny disposition and carefree ways, his winning smile, and so on? That's all gone. He's sour and deep and oh so sad. He hates his mother. Hates Quents. (*looking at her wristwatch*) Oh my stars, he'll be here any minute. And I don't know what to say, what to tell him.

MEG: You always find the right words, Gwen. Always. You're better than that psychic medium we used to go to when we were girls. You could listen to anybody from kings and presidents down to young girls who got in trouble. You always have the right thing to say.

GWEN: But not to Dana. I don't know what to say to him. Oh, he should never have had to go see that woman. I was as wrong as anybody. *I* should have gone to see her. We should have pretended Dana had visited her and let Endors fume and fuss and pretend Dana had visited her also! Then everything would have gone on as it had been, and our dear Quentin would not have . . . (*doorbell rings*) Go, dear. (MEG *exits.*)

(*Enter* DANA. *He goes up to his grandmother and kisses her on the cheek.*)

GWEN: Sit here, Dana, where I can hear you perfectly well. You look a little less tired than when you paid me your last visit.

DANA: I don't know if I am tired or not. I don't know what I feel, ex-cept all I can think about is what has happened to Quentin.

GWEN: You said he spends all his time now with . . . Julia.

DANA: (*nods*) He puts it another way, Grandma. He says it's the house he visits. The music, the dancers, the joy. Those are his words. The joy.

GWEN: My own words, Dana, have come back to haunt me. For if you remember I always told Quentin he should have more fun out of life, more diversion. *You work too hard, too long hours. A young man should have some pleasure in life and not work, work, work.* . . . And now . . .

DANA: Now he never goes to work. Or almost never. And whereas before all we ever tasted was that mild mulled wine, now . . . he brings home enough hard liquor for a saloon.

GWEN: Dana, I am going to speak to your mother. I'm going to her house tomorrow. I will see that there is a stop to this.

DANA: If anybody can put a stop to it, Grandma, it would be you. But you forget the Quentin you and I knew no longer exists.

GWEN: That's a passing stage.

DANA: If that were only true. (*He takes her hand and kisses it fervently.*)

GWEN: Dana, Quentin is your whole life. That is not the best thing either, I am afraid.

DANA: (*coldly*) Why do you say that, Grandma?

GWEN: It's too late now not to speak frankly. Quentin's abstemiousness, his devotion to work, work, work was, I am afraid, his weakness. And from his sacrificing everything to work and duty . . . you see what has taken its place! There has to be a balance, Dana, in how we are and how we live.

DANA: And you mean in my case my lack of balance was caring only for Quentin?

GWEN: Don't put it so . . . cut and dried.

DANA: But isn't it too late now not to tell the truth? I see it now—my whole life was him. But now, (*standing up*) there is no Quentin. He's as different as storm and calm.

GWEN: But he will change back, Dana, mark my words. This is only a passing phase.

DANA: Maybe so, but he will never be Quentin to me again.

GWEN: He's your own brother, Dana. He will come back.

DANA: My half-brother. He will never be my whole brother. Not now. Tell me, Grandma, (*sitting down abruptly*) what will you tell that woman?

GWEN: I wish you wouldn't say *that woman*.

DANA: I hate her. I hated her the moment I saw her. Whereas Quentin said he saw joy and beauty and music and dancers, I saw only a woman painted like an Easter egg, and heard music for drunken dancers.

GWEN: But Julia was forced into this by the family of your father. She was from the wrong world, so they said. She was the one wronged in the first place. She has done what she could do.

DANA: And she's taken over Quentin as her revenge.

GWEN: You don't know that, dear. . . . Wait till I speak to her. Maybe I can put everything to right.

DANA: Maybe you can get him from her clutches by some miracle. But he will never be Quentin again. Not to me. I know what I have to do.

GWEN: (*frightened*) Dana!

DANA: (*calmer*) I am going away. I have my blood money. I will use it to go a long, long distance away.

Scene 6

LILY *has just entered* QUENTIN'S *house. She is wearing a heavy coat and scarf.*

QUENTIN: Lily come in—don't stand on ceremony. (*kisses her*) Here, let me help you off with that coat. Why it must weigh a ton!

LILY: Well, it's really bitter outside, and it's snowing ever so lightly.

QUENTIN: (*abashed, sad, even bitter*) Oh, Lily, come over here and sit down.

LILY: No, no, I can't stay. I've just been worried about you two boys. Haven't seen hide nor hair of either of you for I don't know how long.

QUENTIN: I know, I know. Lily, don't rub it in please. (*pausing*) Let me fix you something to drink. (LILY *acts unreceptively.*) Oh come on now. I could stand with a drink anyhow.

LILY: I'll have some of your homemade cider, if you have some.

QUENTIN: But you look half frozen. Let me give you a real drink.

LILY: (*She looks at* QUENTIN *closely and realizes that he's already been drinking.*) All right then, but only very little. After all, Quents, it's still morning.

QUENTIN: Morning, noon, evening, midnight, Lily, they're all the same now to me. (*goes to a little cabinet and retrieves a bottle of brandy and glasses*) Can you drink it neat, Lily, or shall I get some ice and water for you?

LILY: (*gloomily*) Whatever you're taking, Quentin, I'll be satisfied with.

QUENTIN: You're always so agreeable, Lily. You're a fine, yes, a wonderful girl.

LILY: (*taking the glass*) Oh, please. (*watches* QUENTIN *drink his down and pour himself another*) There have been so many changes, Quentin! (*hardly tasting the brandy*)

QUENTIN: Oh, we can both say that again. Changes, changes. (*He looks furious.*) Beginning with that damned will and Mr. Endors. Beginning, Lily, oh so far back. The past has caught up with us. Damn it all to hell, Endors should have arranged the will better. (*drinks*)

LILY: Quentin, excuse me, (*pausing*) but I've never seen you drink the way you do. What—?

QUENTIN: (*interrupting*) I've never seen myself do what I've been doing. And Dana and I are on the outs.

LILY: He's worried sick about you.

QUENTIN: (*bitterly*) I wonder why. . . . Well, what does he say, I wonder?

LILY: That you don't go to the forge anymore, when that was your lifeblood, as he put it.

QUENTIN: My lifeblood. (*laughs angrily*) Do you know something, Lily? Search me, I don't know what has happened either.

LILY: If I could do anything, you have only to call on me.

QUENTIN: The truth, Lily, is . . . (*pauses*)

LILY: Please don't stop.

QUENTIN: Don't stop. I can't even begin. (*pausing*) The truth then, Lily, is I've taken a bad fall. Oh, not just off the housetop. I've fallen from a bigger height. I've fallen all the way a man can fall and not knock his brains out.

LILY: You know, Quentin, I love you and—

QUENTIN: (*interrupting*) I was afraid you would say that.

LILY: I will always love you, no matter what comes to pass.

QUENTIN: (*rising, then pacing the room*) I don't know how a man can be one thing one day and the next day he's another totally different man, breaking with all he's been, all he's lived for. (*raises his voice*) Mr. Endors was right, the old devil! He warned me. I guess even poor Dana warned me in his way. I chose the place to fall from, the precipice.

LILY: Perhaps, Quentin, if you went away for a while. Maybe far away.

QUENTIN: I don't have the strength. Or the manhood, or the will!

LILY: It makes my heart ache to see you drink. I always looked up to you—

QUENTIN: And you don't anymore then.

LILY: I care for you now as much as I did then.

QUENTIN: *Then!* That's the word. I was what I should have been or thought I should have been *then*. And now, I'm not me. (*He throws down the empty glass and smashes it. After a while, he begins very slowly and angrily picking up the pieces. He throws them in a container, cursing softly.*) I have fallen in love with a woman I wouldn't have allowed in my house a short time ago. Don't cry, Lily, for Christ's sake. Listen, but don't cry. (*stands, head bowed before her*)

LILY: Oh Quents, it's you who is crying. Go on, I don't mind. Whatever you do, don't you see? I care so deeply. Let me do for you, Quentin.

QUENTIN: Don't say that again. You will kill me.

LILY: It will pass, Quentin. It will pass.

QUENTIN: God almighty, if it were only true. Lily, you've never fallen then have you. From a big height I mean. (*He slowly begins walking away from her.*) All at once I am cold sober. First time in a while. (*pacing*) Cold sober.

QUENTIN: You say it will pass, Lily. God in heaven I hope you're right. Tell me you are right.

LILY: But do you want it to pass, Quentin? Do you want not to love Dana's mother?

QUENTIN: Dana's mother, is it? You mean I'm in love with someone that old? Oh, I've thought of that. And do you know what . . . ?

(*LILY, rising, goes over to him; he takes her by both hands and brings her almost to him in an embrace.*)

QUENTIN: . . . I don't think she, Julia you know—yes, she has a name—Julia doesn't love me. She pities me, I think. For on the return to her house after the *great evening* we all had, she barred the door to me. But then to use her words, *like a housebreaker* I forced my way through to her. That's when she took pity on me. (*LILY, moved, breaks away from* QUENTIN.) Oh, Lily, don't leave me now.

LILY: I'm not leaving you, Quentin. Let me sit down though, please.

QUENTIN: Do anything you like, but don't leave. Tell me again, dear girl, it will pass. This feeling I have, it's thundering through my rib cage, cutting through to every vein and artery. (*Gets up, pours himself another drink, drinks it off, then pours another and drinks. Wipes his mouth furiously and laughs.*) I love the way you accept me, Lily. The way you don't judge me, like that little bastard Dana. You take me as I am, don't you, Lily? (*a long pause*) Tell me once again before you go, for I suppose you have to go—tell me, Lily, it will pass. Please, tell me I will go one day back to myself.

LILY: (*approaching him, smoothes his hair, but avoids his attempt to kiss her*) Quentin, I must be going. I have a thousand things I've got to do today.

QUENTIN: Tell me, though, you'll come back one day, Lily. Can't you? This isn't a farewell visit now, for cripes' sake.

LILY: Quentin, you asked me awhile ago if I had fallen from a great height.

QUENTIN: Lily, maybe you'd better not say it then.

LILY: I will, Quents. The great height, Quentin. I think today maybe I have fallen from it too. (*He moves closer.*) Please, Quentin, let's not say anymore.

QUENTIN: I wish you could stay awhile. . . . After saying what you just said.

LILY: I can't Quents, I just can't.

QUENTIN: You won't come again, then.

LILY: I told you, Quents—and I can say it again—I will always care for you.

QUENTIN: You mean you'll always care for the Quentin you used to care for.

LILY: (*moves toward the door*) Don't make me say more, Quents. Please, I implore you. (*She goes out, closing the door.*)

QUENTIN: (*Goes over to the closed door and presses his head hard against the wood, sobbing. Then angrily raising his head, he beats his fists against the door.*) You shouldn't have come here, then, in the first place, Lily. You shouldn't have let yourself see me if you had to come.

Scene 7

JULIA *and her lover,* NEALE ASTOR, *are in a fierce argument.*

NEALE: What do you mean, I'm to be quiet? No one tells me to be quiet, least of all someone like you.

JULIA: I won't be spoken to like this in my own house.

NEALE: Her own house! One word from me and you could be out in the street, where you started.

JULIA: I never started there. And for all the little you have given me I have given you a thousand fold more.

NEALE: I ought to slap you to sleep for talking like that. You owe me. . . . And I'm telling you something for the last time. You are going to marry me or I will close this house down on you and not leave one piece of lumber in place.

JULIA: Your threats! How sick I am of them! When you don't get your way, you try to frighten me. But I am one woman no one has ever truly frightened.

NEALE: Billing and cooing with someone who ain't dry behind the ears yet! Haven't you got any sense in your dizzy head? I suppose you're expecting him now all dolled up the way you are.

JULIA: I'm expecting his grandmother.

NEALE: His grandmother! I'll bet she's coming to read you the riot act also.

JULIA: A lot you know about anything! Gwen Ludworth is one of my dearest friends. She once even was my benefactor.

NEALE: Come over here, you. Come on. (JULIA *showing some fear, moves over to him.* NEALE *takes her in his arms and presses his kisses on her.*) You know who your benefactor is. (JULIA *wipes her mouth on a handkerchief, which he seizes and throws to the floor.*) You used to beg for my kisses.

JULIA: I won't be bullied by you or anybody! I owe you nothing.

NEALE: I want to tell you something. And I want you to listen and not waltz around the room as if you was hearing that syrupy music you have playing here all night. You promised to marry me, and you are going to keep that promise, do you hear?

JULIA: I will never marry you or anybody! There is only one person I will ever be beholden to, myself. Let go of me.

(NEALE *draws her closer to her, then kisses and embraces her violently.*)

JULIA: (*breaking away from him*) You make me ashamed, somehow— I guess of myself.

NEALE: Why should you be ashamed of wanting me, needing me?

JULIA: (*bitterly*) Yes, why should I?

NEALE: You can flirt and palaver with this little know-nothing all you like, but when you need a real man you will always come back to my arms.

(*The bell rings from the outside door.*)

NEALE: (*picking up his hat*) I'll be back tonight, do you hear? See that you are ready and waiting for me.

JULIA: Don't come back, Neale, don't come back. Not tonight. (NEALE *takes her in his arms. She appears to give in to his ardor—at least, she does not resist him.*) Go on, go, please. It's Gwen Ludworth.

(NEALE *exits and* JULIA *tries to compose herself, straightening her dress, and wiping her lips with a handkerchief.* GWEN *enters.*)

GWEN: Julia, Julia! (*They embrace.*) Was that Neale Astor, dear, leaving as I came in?

JULIA: I'm afraid it was, Gwen.

GWEN: Don't tell me you still see him, dear.

JULIA: I'm afraid I do, Gwen, when I have to. But sit down.

GWEN: (*seating herself*) But I thought he was in prison.

JULIA: (*not sitting down and looking gravely at her guest*) Yes, you're right. He was in prison, but I guess even the prison could not stomach him.

GWEN: Must you see him, Julia? Sit down, dear, you look so troubled. (*She takes* JULIA'*s hand in hers.*) Perhaps I can help you.

JULIA: You've helped more than I deserve. No, Gwen, nobody can help. May I offer you some refreshment while we talk?

GWEN: No, dear. I haven't really that much time, I'm afraid. I think you know why I've come. (*looking around her*) Julia, you've kept this house in beautiful repair and in such charming taste. You always did know how to turn the most ordinary room into something elegant, yet quieting to the nerves. Like you, Julia. Everyone responds to your rare and beautiful quality.

JULIA: Oh, Gwen, please, please, say no more about me. I know too why you have come. Let's begin with what you want to say.

GWEN: I haven't come to blame you, criticize you, or command you. You know better than that.

JULIA: You want me to give up Quentin. I know.

GWEN: But, Julia, you can't give up somebody you don't possess.

JULIA: I don't know what you mean. We all fall prey to infatuation, Gwen, when we are very young. And infatuation has never been a basis for anything but itself. (*dreamily*) Infatuation . . .

GWEN: Yes, now he is infatuated. Now he finds your house here and you what he has always dreamed about and thought did not exist anywhere. . . . But tomorrow he will find he has awakened from his dream. He will know he cannot live in ceaseless joy and watch endless throngs of dancers endlessly experiencing pleasure, endless . . .

JULIA: Don't go on, Gwen. It's enough. But how am I to shut the door on him now? After all, I never invited him that first time, nor have I invited him back since. He can't get enough of what is here.

GWEN: I told you I did not blame you, and I told you I had not come here to command you.

JULIA: What have you come to do then, dear friend?

GWEN: I only want to save Quentin. And I think you will want to save him also.

JULIA: But I love him. I love him more than I loved his own father. Gwen, listen to me, I am lost.

GWEN: And so is Quentin.

JULIA: You said you did not come here to advise or command me. Your presence though does both.

GWEN: Very well, then. If you love him—truly love him—you know you cannot have him.

JULIA: No, no. I cannot agree.

GWEN: You may not agree now. But if you continue with him, you will regret the very day you were born. I think I will take that refreshment now.

JULIA: (*Weeping, rings a bell. A servant,* TIM, *enters. Julia whispers something to him.*) The thing about you that makes you such a dear friend, for you are I believe my dearest friend: I always believe everything you say. But loving your grandson has done as terrible a thing to me as you and everybody else says it has done to him.

GWEN: (*tasting the drink and nodding with satisfaction*) You are the one, Julia, who will come to your own decision and your decision will be the right one.

JULIA: I hope I will have the strength to close all the doors (*She looks about her.*) and close all the joy there is here on both of us. But meanwhile, Gwen, I have lost my own boy, Dana. It was Dana who should have been my care and my love, but his brother came between that deeper love and parted us. If only . . . if only . . .

GWEN: Yes, if only what?

JULIA: . . . if only the world had been created in a different pattern. If there had never been men and women, only clouds and stars, rain trees and soft grass. It was a mistake from the first.

(GWEN *nods and drinks some more.*)

Scene 8

NEALE ASTOR *and* JULIA *are standing talking when* QUENTIN *enters* JULIA'*s house.*

NEALE: Come in. (NEALE *is obviously a little drunk.*) Don't stand on ceremony. I am just leaving.

QUENTIN: (*Looks nervously from* NEALE *to* JULIA. NEALE'*s presence has obviously upset him, for he expected to find* JULIA *in the room alone.*) Good evening to both of you. (*Advances toward* JULIA, *then stops.*)

JULIA: (*trying to rise to the occasion*) Sit down, all. Please sit down, gentlemen.

NEALE: (*almost bashfully*) No, I'm sorry, Julia, but I must run. I have a business appointment. I'm sorry too, Quentin, not to be able to talk with you. Julia has told me a lot about you.

QUENTIN: Thank you. (*He turns imploringly toward* JULIA.)

(JULIA *walks with* NEALE *to the door and says a calm, collected goodbye, but she is obviously very much upset and seems to send some message of great feeling to* NEALE.)

JULIA: (*turns back now, having closed the door on* NEALE) Neale is a good friend.

QUENTIN: (*as if not having heard*) I can't believe I am back here again. (*looking around*) And all of a sudden, the music is starting again! Just like the first time. May I call you *Julia* too?

JULIA: I see no reason why not, Quentin.

QUENTIN: You've known this Neale Astor, then, for some time. . . . Before he was . . . sent away, I presume.

JULIA: We have been friends since he was almost a child. I could never deny Neale's friendship.

QUENTIN: I always felt, somehow, you were always alone here in the midst of so many others who were dancing and happy and always hearing music. I never . . . thought of you with . . . anyone else— anyone, that is, like Neale.

JULIA: (*almost hysterically*) And where is Dana?

QUENTIN: (*as if annoyed, but also in anguish*) Ah, well, Dana. He is at home, I suppose.

JULIA: I do so want to see him again. I hardly got to know him at all that night.

QUENTIN: Yes, that night. I must have behaved very badly. Dana has scolded me so often about it. I felt Neale Astor too was scolding me with his eyes.

JULIA: Neale has no grounds for scolding you, Quentin. But as to Dana, oh how I wish he would come back!

QUENTIN: But I thought *I* was your favorite, Julia.

JULIA: You are both my favorites. Both! But Dana, Dana . . .

QUENTIN: (*irritated*) Yes, Dana, what?

JULIA: He is after all my son.

QUENTIN: (*bitterly*) And I am not!

JULIA: You are both dear to me, but you are dear to me in another way, Quentin. I thought you must have known that from our first meeting.

QUENTIN: I had hoped—I don't know how to say it, but still I will say it: I had hoped you would have room in your heart only for me. I hardly know what I am saying. But I see now . . .

JULIA: Please. Quentin, please.

QUENTIN: Please what, Julia? I was very disturbed too this evening at the way you looked at Neale Astor.

JULIA: But he is an old friend. How should I have looked at him, then?

QUENTIN: I don't know exactly. I don't think you ever looked at me quite that way.

JULIA: Let's have some refreshment then, Quentin.

QUENTIN: You want to change the subject. All right, some refreshment. But nothing strong.

(JULIA, *rising, goes to the next room to order some refreshment. On returning,* QUENTIN *rises and takes both her hands in his.*)

QUENTIN: I want to have the favorite place in your heart—that is all I ask!

JULIA: (*trying to be a bit offhand*) And that isn't asking a great deal of me.

QUENTIN: I thought you wanted me to ask a great deal of you. And now this talk of Dana, Dana, and the way you looked at Neale Astor. I see I am not high in your estimation, Julia.

JULIA: No one is higher, Quentin. No one. (TIM enters with a tray of hot coffee, puts the tray down, and proceeds to serve each of them. Having served them, he exits.) Coffee always makes one think a little clearer, doesn't it?

QUENTIN: (*his voice rising*) Does it? I thought I was thinking clearly from the time I entered this room. Julia, tell me, please. (*sips the coffee, then puts down his cup*)

JULIA: What is it, Quentin? Please go on.

QUENTIN: You do prefer me to Dana, don't you? It would break my heart I think if it was the other way.

JULIA: I thought we had settled that. Dana is my son.

QUENTIN: But he does not think he is.

JULIA: But how could he think otherwise, Quentin?

QUENTIN: He does not love you, for one thing; it's me who has that feeling. Dana does not want to come here again. I have asked and asked.

JULIA: Perhaps someone has prevailed on him not to want to come.

QUENTIN: You mean me. . . . No, Julia, no one needed to prevail on him, I am afraid. (*He picks up his coffee cup and takes a long swallow, then wipes his mouth in a kind of impetuous even course manner.*) I talked you up, but to no avail. He is a very emotional young man. I am his only . . . companion.

JULIA: He must come again. He must give me a chance. You could arrange it, being so close.

QUENTIN: Why should I?

JULIA: Quentin, what is it? (*He suddenly takes her in his arms, kissing and embracing her almost recklessly.*) Quentin, you are hurting me! (*She breaks away.*)

QUENTIN: Neale Astor, then my brother. I see I'm left out.

JULIA: Sit down, Quentin and drink your coffee. We must talk this thing out.

QUENTIN: Let me listen to the music, then I will go.

JULIA: I don't want you to go.

QUENTIN: You mean that? Cross your heart, and so on?

JULIA: Quentin, listen to me. I may have led you to believe . . . but . . .

QUENTIN: Don't say what you're getting ready to say. I know deep down, deep . . .

JULIA: Deep down *what*? (*She is becoming riled, almost fierce.*)

QUENTIN: I know you care for me the way I care for you.

JULIA: I care for you deeply, as Dana's brother.

QUENTIN: (*making a gesture of impatience and anger*) I don't want to hear about Dana or Neale Astor now.

JULIA: (*getting riled*) What do you want to hear about?

QUENTIN: I want to hear how you love me, for I know you do. I know you are playing a part now. Though I suppose you have loved Neale. But I can see that is over.

JULIA: Neale is long ago, Quentin. You are right on that score. But he has no one.

QUENTIN: And you mean I have everyone?

JULIA: (*caught in the argument*) You have Dana, certainly, and he has you.

QUENTIN: But Dana is not enough. Julia, I am begging you, can't you see? I want you. I don't want to share you with anybody else, Dana or Neale. You have got to tell me, Julia.

JULIA: Tell you what?

QUENTIN: You know what! That you love me. Only me.

JULIA: You don't know what you are doing to me.

QUENTIN: That is because you are changing—because you are planning to go back on your word.

JULIA: I never gave you my word, Quentin.

QUENTIN: Liar! With your eyes and your lips you told me, Julia, you wanted me. You know you did. Now all at once you have changed.

JULIA: Quentin, think what you are doing. Think what is against us loving.

QUENTIN: (*kneeling down before her*) Don't think. I won't think if you don't. All I want is you. I have never loved before, never. True, I have loved him, Dana, my half-brother. But you are not my half—you are my whole. I must love you, Julia, or I will die. Can't you see what I am offering you, my heart, not half my heart all of it? And you sit there unmoved.

JULIA: I am not unmoved. I am beside myself.

QUENTIN: Tell me you are beside yourself for love.

JULIA: I am! I am! That is the trouble, dear boy. We cannot, we cannot.

QUENTIN: Don't say any more. (*putting his hand on her lips*) You have told me what I waited to hear. You love me. You love only me.

214

Don't spoil what you finally said. What do we care about the rest? If you love me, and I know you do, there is no need to say more. (*He holds her and draws her to him.*)

JULIA: (*half-smothered by his embraces*) Oh Quentin, what is it we are doing. Quentin? Quentin! What is it that has befallen us, can you tell me?

Scene 9

JULIA and SADIE are in conversation.

JULIA: I always feel so down when it rains as hard as it is tonight. And you say Neale is outside waiting?

SADIE: I asked him if he wanted to come in. He said he would be in after a while.

JULIA: After a while? What a strange thing to say! Why doesn't he come in or go, especially since he always complains the damp weather bothers his chest?

SADIE: I've never seen him so . . . agitated.

JULIA: Ah well. One can't please everybody.

SADIE: Julia, listen to me. You mustn't turn him away.

JULIA: Turn him away! What are you talking about?

SADIE: That's what he feels. Since Quentin has been paying you all these visits, Neale feels left out.

JULIA: Left out? How absurd! After all he and I have been through together.

SADIE: He feels you've changed. He says . . . you're distant now . . . and cold.

JULIA: So you've been talking together?

SADIE: You know me better than that, Julia. Whenever he sees me he complains about the change.

JULIA: There is no change. Things are just what they were. As to Quentin, he is like my other son. While Neale . . . (*stops*)

SADIE: Go on, Julia.

JULIA: (*shaking her head*) You know me better than I know myself, Sadie. There has been a change of course. Can I help it? But I will always care for Neale and his devotion.

SADIE: He doesn't want to be cared for because of his devotion, Julia.

(*There is a knock at the door.*)

SADIE: Should I answer the door, Julia?

JULIA: It's him of course. Who else would knock at this hour of the night . . . ? Yes, dear, let him come in. (SADIE *exits.*) What a pallid word *change* is.

(*Enter* NEALE ASTOR, *wet from the rain.*)

JULIA: (*rising*) Come in, Neale. (*He goes up to her and kisses her gently on the cheek, but she turns her face away.*)

NEALE: You're mad I came, aren't you?

JULIA: Of course I'm not mad. . . . But look at you, you're dripping wet. Oh, Neale. Go in the small back room and put on some dry clothes there from the closet.

NEALE: Tell me you want me here tonight, Julia—that's all I ask. I don't need no dry clothes if you'll smile a welcome.

JULIA: How could you not be welcome, Neale? But please, go put on something dry. Remember what the doctor told you, dear.

NEALE: Thank God, for that *dear*. (*exits*)

(SADIE *enters.*)

SADIE: I'm going to go upstairs, Julia. It's so very late. If you need me just call, dear.

JULIA: I will darling. Sadie, I'm glad you let Neale in. He's so wretched, isn't he?, poor boy.

SADIE: Yes. And I don't need to tell you, Julia, you're all he has.

JULIA: I'm afraid you're right. It's hard isn't it, Sadie, when someone looks only to one other person in the world.

SADIE: (*nodding*) Goodnight, Julia.

JULIA: See you tomorrow. (*walking up and down nervously*) I don't want to hurt him. But he knows I have changed. Neale knows everything.

(*Enter* NEALE.)

JULIA: How nice you look, Neale. You've put on that nice jacket, too, I like so much.

NEALE: And don't you like the man under the jacket, Julia?

JULIA: More than ever, Neale.

NEALE: If that was only true!

JULIA: But it is true, and you know it.

NEALE: (*sitting down heavily*) Can I stay tonight? (*at a sign from her*) Oh I'll sleep in the little room, never fear.

JULIA: (*penitently*) Of course you can stay. Who else is there, after all, Neale but you?

NEALE: Julia, stop it, please. You maybe forget I come from gypsy stock. My mother, my grandmother, my great grandmother all had second sight. I was born with a caul on my head. So I know what you feel now, and I don't blame you.

JULIA: Neale, you do not know what I feel.

NEALE: Listen to me, Julia. You love that young man. Don't contradict. You maybe have never loved before.

JULIA: I loved you, and I have kept faith with you.

NEALE: No, that was not love. I loved you. You had no one else then in your trouble, and I was only a boy. I became your son, and then when I was older I became your lover. You loved me sort of like, well, let's say a favorite horse.

JULIA: Stop it, please.

217

NEALE: (*absentmindedly*) I want to stay the night because I am afraid of the rain.

JULIA: You shall stay. You can stay forever. But you are mistaken about the young man.

NEALE: He loves you. He's blind with love. I have watched him; I have studied him.

JULIA: (*beginning to weep*) Please, say no more. No more.

NEALE: Why fight it, Julia? It all comes by decree or fate or the cards. Call it anything—it is the way the world comes down on us. We do what we are propelled to do.

JULIA: I won't ever turn my back on you. Never.

NEALE: But you love him and not me. That is the biggest sorrow now for me.

JULIA: It will come to nothing, Neale. So don't be afraid—I have nothing Quentin can want.

NEALE: You have everything he wants.

JULIA: But it will pass and he will see me for what I am. It's the house and the music he likes more than me. He's as much as said that.

NEALE: But the other boy, Julia. Your own boy. What about him?

JULIA: Yes, what about him, Neale?

NEALE: Don't he love you too?

JULIA: No.

NEALE: Why don't he?

JULIA: Would you love someone if she'd deserted you and turned her back on you when she was the only one who could love and protect you?

NEALE: Julia, why don't we go away together and leave this house— (*he motions with his hands to the walls*) forget where we both came from and what life has done to us. I would protect you—never turn my back on you. I would be like the sun shining always for you. I am strong, the doc says, though I have a bad cough. Why can't we put all this behind us?

JULIA: My only son despises me. He will never love me.

NEALE: Because you deserted him.

JULIA: No, because I gave him away when I was all he had. How could he love me now? He cannot bear the sight of me. And as if what you call destiny or the cards, or fate were working, his brother, Quentin, has found in his heart all the love my own son can never have for me.

NEALE: But you love me, don't you, in your own way, Julia? I would die if you did not.

JULIA: Neale, I've loved you from the moment I first saw you. I love you now.

NEALE: But you love this Quentin. Don't answer. Don't say no more. Do you have a drink, Julia.

JULIA: Over there, dear. Fetch me one too.

(NEALE *goes to a small cabinet, opens it and retrieves a bottle and two glasses, which he puts on a tray, then pours them a drink.*)

NEALE: I bet you was saving this for your new love.

JULIA: I was saving it for you. (*They drink.*)

NEALE: As long as I can be near you, Julia, it don't matter if you have a hundred Quentins. Just to be near you, to catch a whiff of your pretty scent as it comes through your clothes. I want never to be far from you. Can't we go away, Julia, far away?

JULIA: In time, Neale, I think so. In time.

NEALE: (*rising and finishing his drink*) I will go upstairs to the little room.

JULIA: Neale, it's all right your being here. It's all right.

NEALE: I could no more leave you, Julia, than I could stop my own breath. I breathe only through you, my dearest. (*They embrace.*)

Scene 10

QUENTIN *has entered* JULIA's *room but* DANA *still stands at the threshold.*

JULIA: Don't just stand there, Dana, come in. This is your house. And Quentin's too. (*to Quentin*) I never thought I'd be this happy to see anyone.

QUENTIN: And you're not happy to see me?

JULIA: I'm always happy to see you, but I can call you a regular visitor while having Dana here is something special.

QUENTIN: All right, all right. Anyhow, you can never say I failed to keep my promise. But it didn't take as much coaxing as I thought. The little devil seemed to want to come tonight.

DANA: It's true. He didn't have to coax me. Not tonight.

JULIA: You don't ever need a reason for coming here.

DANA: Thank you for that. I'd forgotten what a spectacle of a house this is. Yes, I'd really forgotten how grand and great it is.

QUENTIN: I don't know what it is, but my little brother is changed. It's as though he's calling the shots.

DANA: Oh come on, Quents, you'll always call the shots.

QUENTIN: No Dana, you've changed. You're different. (*turns to Julia*) He's got something up his sleeve.

DANA: Well maybe I have, Quents. Maybe that's why I came tonight.

JULIA: Whatever the reason, thank fortune you're here. But why are we all standing up like we're waiting for a parade? Won't you please sit down?

QUENTIN: Maybe we should wait till he tells us what he has to say. Maybe we'll think different when he tells us.

DANA: Oh, I'll come to it by and by.

JULIA: The important thing, Dana, is that you are here.

QUENTIN: It's not like Dana to keep us guessing.

DANA: Maybe I never had anything to hide from you before, Quents.

QUENTIN: Deeper and deeper, are we?

DANA: It's hard for me to tell you, Quents. And hard to tell . . . Julia too.

JULIA: You make it sound like something to be alarmed about.

DANA: Not exactly. Well, once the inheritance had been handed over to me by Mr. Endors, I felt I had to do something. I couldn't live forever—

QUENTIN: (*surly*) With me, you mean.

DANA: I mean, I had to start my own life.

JULIA: I can understand that.

DANA: And now I guess I've made a beginning. I'm leaving for New York. And from there I've signed up to go on a cargo ship to the North Sea.

QUENTIN: And you kept such a thing a secret from me?

DANA: I was afraid you wouldn't let me go.

QUENTIN: Wouldn't let you go? Doesn't your brother have the right to know?

JULIA: (*in disbelief, almost talking to herself*) On a cargo ship? And all by yourself?

DANA: I'm afraid that's the way it is. Yes, after all, who could I go with now?

JULIA: (*stung by this reference to DANA's brother*) You've told your grandmother.

DANA: I have.

JULIA: And what did she say?

DANA: It wasn't so much what she said as the way she looked at me.

JULIA: She didn't want you to go?

DANA: I guess not. I told her it don't matter where I go—but go I must.

JULIA: I wish I could persuade you not to.

DANA: Nobody can persuade me to do anything ever again.

QUENTIN: So you came here to say goodbye?

DANA: Come to think of it, I don't know why I came. (*with a kind of bitter humor*) I guess to say goodbye to myself.

QUENTIN: So, after all I've been through with you, you're just going to say goodbye and light out?

DANA: Put it any way you like, Quentin. But I am leaving.

JULIA: We'll miss you so very much.

DANA: How can you miss someone you never knew—will you tell me?

QUENTIN: Careful. Careful, young man.

JULIA: Let Dana speak, Quentin.

QUENTIN: So let it all come out then, why don't you? Don't mind my presence.

DANA: Let me say this: I don't know how Julia could miss someone she had so little trouble giving away in the first place.

QUENTIN: I think you've said about enough.

DANA: Look, I don't take orders from you anymore.

QUENTIN: So none of us are good enough for you now? What an ungrateful little pup you've turned out to be.

JULIA: Will you sit down, Quentin? And mind your own tongue. Let Dana say whatever is in his heart. Dana, I know what you're feeling, believe me. I can't blame you for your bitterness.

DANA: Is that what I'm feeling—just bitterness?

JULIA: I know you're feeling many things. You may not acknowledge me, Dana, but I am your mother. I was your mother before you came into this world. I would like to be your mother always, if you would let me.

DANA: It's too late for speeches, Mother. And it's too late for anybody to give me a helping hand.

QUENTIN: Selfish little bastard. And after all that's been done for you! I should take you apart for that.

DANA: Go ahead and try! Then I'd be free of you forever. I wish the sea I am going to sail on is even deeper and stormier than sailors say it is.

JULIA: Dana, if we could turn back the past and make it over. But I read once in some book of wisdom that even God cannot alter the past.

DANA: (*bitterly*) Maybe God can't do anything about anything.

JULIA: We can learn perhaps to forgive each other, even if we are not able to love the person who has wronged us. I have learned over the years to forgive even your grandfather.

DANA: If I was you, I'd never forgive him.

JULIA: Oh, I felt that way about him for many years.

DANA: I hated him. I hate him now. And I hate you!

JULIA: That is what I felt from you the first night you came to the house.

DANA: I didn't come, ma'am. I was ordered to be present. Do you have any idea how you robbed me?

JULIA: Robbed you?

DANA: First you gave me away, so I had no family except my cold-hearted grandfather. Then my family became my brother, Quentin. I looked up to him more than to God. And then you, my alleged mother, pulled the final rug from under my feet. You deprived me of a family in the first place and now you deprived me of my half-brother who was my real and only family. But I don't want Quentin back. And why don't I? Because I'd be getting back only the husk of what he was. Do you hear me? The husk.

QUENTIN: Let me speak now, for Christ's sake. Have you any idea the long years of struggle, devotion, and sweat I've extended on you? Nurtured you? Watched over you? Educated you? And yes, loved you when no one else—except maybe your grandmother—gave a damn about you? My life has been mostly a slavery of bitter toil and caring for you. But when I came to Julia's house for the first time, I experienced relief from that pain. And also, for the first time I experienced a joy I never thought possible in this world. And you begrudge me that.

DANA: You call the life you've been leading *joy*! I call it drunkenness. Slobbering, insensible drunkenness! You're no more the man and brother I loved than the sun is a sputtering candle. Quentin is dead so far as I'm concerned! And now I wonder why we are standing here speaking to each other like people in a courtroom or movie actors in some stuffy theater.

QUENTIN: Will you tell your rotten little heathen of a son to shut his mouth?

JULIA: I'm afraid the fault is on all sides even though, Dana, you blame me as the principal cause of all your sorrow and pain.

DANA: Thank you for saying that! For it's what I feel. Well, we've had our say and I can leave now.

JULIA: No, Dana, we have not as a matter of fact even begun. You see everything in black and white, don't you? One is either innocent or guilty. Just the opposite is true in life. You don't understand what it is to be alone and friendless in a society of men who make all the rules. Men who forgive the wrongdoings of other men, but punish down to the last drop of her blood a woman when she makes one mistake. When I became pregnant with you, your father sent me back to America from France. To your grandfather! Your father's own mother and grandmother were dead or he would have sent me to them. And this would have made everything different for us both. Believe me, I was at the time scarcely more than a child, Dana. I was without family and without a country. I was younger than you are now by a year-and-a-half. Look at me, Dana. Don't look down at the carpet.

DANA: I'm listening then. Go ahead and speak.

JULIA: I was forced by your grandfather to give you up to him, or both you and I would have been reduced to beggary—to every kind of want. I could have perhaps endured being without a roof over my head and as an outcast, but I had no right to subject a young child to such suffering. When the world of men strikes down a woman, whatever she does will be wrong.

DANA: See here! I would have preferred to starve rather than not have you for my mother. That would have been a better life.

JULIA: No, Dana, you have never known hunger, cold, and disgrace. Maybe you'll understand this when you become a man. I know all the pain I've caused you, but you'll never know the pain life has visited on me. How could you? As to my love for your brother . . . (DANA *puts his hands over his ears.*) . . . perhaps I fell in love with Quentin because he looked like your own father to me. When Quentin and you visited me for the first time, I would have sworn it was your own father who had come back to me. You'll never understand, because you never knew your father so you can't understand my sorrow at losing him. People have accused Quentin of being too perfect, too sinless, and on too high a pedestal. Perhaps now this is a better description of you. No, Dana, it was your father's death and your grandfather's stern righteousness that have destroyed both our happiness.

DANA: Goodbye, Julia, we must be like we were before. Before Quentin brought me here to meet you, we were unknown to each other then. We'll be unknown to each other now forever. The sea will make everything right.

JULIA: Why can't you stay on so we can come to a better understanding?

DANA: Did you come to a better understanding when you gave me away?

QUENTIN: I should shoot you for saying that.

DANA: I would thank you if you did. Goodbye, ma'am. (*exits*)

JULIA: (*almost inaudibly, almost to herself*) That's the last we'll ever see of him.

QUENTIN: Julia, we have each other. I know all too well how much Dana has broken your heart, but let me say it again: we have each other. We'll always have each other.

JULIA: That's my fondest hope also.

QUENTIN: But it's got to be more than hope. (*They embrace.*) Oh Julia, I can feel a change in you. Tell me I am wrong. Tell me he hasn't changed our love for each other. (*She nods apathetically.*) Don't you see? If anything, perhaps, his leaving is the best thing after all.

JULIA: Yes, Quentin dear. Perhaps you are right.

QUENTIN: I have the feeling you need rest—rest even from me.

JULIA: (*mysteriously*) I think a new day is coming for both of us.

QUENTIN: Let me stay tonight. Let my love make up for all your other loss. Julia! Julia! (*She hesitates, then kisses him.*) Don't turn away, for God's sake. Don't go back on me. You're all I have.

Scene 11

JULIA, NEALE, *and* SADIE *are in earnest conversation.*

JULIA: If I didn't think I was doing the right thing by you both, I would be even more heartbroken. . . . Sadie, Neale—you are my dearest friends. You are my family. But hear me out: If I remain here, I will die. No, I am not being dramatic. I have felt for some months, even years now, that I must give up the house. Give up our way of life. You know I must close the house. You know that we three must leave together.

NEALE: When I came in this morning and saw the workmen dismantling everything, I felt as if I was having one of my dreams. But when I took one look at you, Julia, I knew the worst of what I feared had come true.

JULIA: We can all three at least be together. Once we are settled far away from this place, you see! We will find a kind of contentment and peace we never thought we could have.

SADIE: So the decision is made—everything is final.

JULIA: Mr. Endors will be here presently. Yes, Sadie, everything is final. I signed the last of the papers and Endors is bringing me the copies, duly notarized. The house is already sold.

SADIE: The house is already sold? (*JULIA nods.*) And who is the purchaser.

JULIA: I asked them not to tell me. Some large concern is the purchaser, I believe.

SADIE: Oh, Julia, are you sure you won't regret this? Neale, can't you speak out now?

NEALE: I have told Julia everything that can be told. But Sadie and I know the real reason for your decision, Julia. There should be no lack of frankness at this stage of the game.

JULIA: You want me to say I am leaving because of Dana and young Quentin. All right, Neale, I can say that. But they are only the last of the reasons—perhaps the deciding factor, the push over the abyss. For months—years, as I have said—I have not been able to bear the atmosphere where everyone rejoices but me. Why should everyone rejoice except the one who is the purveyor of happiness? It is too unfair. For years, I deceived myself that their happiness was one I shared. But I can no longer deceive myself. I can no longer pretend that I am such a person who is happy in other people's happiness, only content if others are for a few hours freed from the cares and sorrows of their lives. All I ask of you, Sadie and Neale, is that you never leave me. We can then begin our new life together. I know it is the only way we can go. (*They draw near each other and embrace. The front doorbell rings.*) That's Mr. Endors, would you please go into the next room while I speak with him? (*Exit NEALE and SADIE.*) I must compose myself—I mustn't break now. If he sees I am hesitant and unsure, he will force me to tear up the contract and go on here forever—go on as a dead woman.

(*Enter MR. ENDORS.*)

ENDORS: There she is! Julia, Julia! (*He embraces her warmly.*)

JULIA: Yes, here I am.

ENDORS: You have changed so little Julia over the years. And the house! I stood outside for a while in a kind of lost feeling of admiration. It is something that belongs in picture-books.

JULIA: I see you have brought the papers, Mr. Endors. Won't you sit down?

ENDORS: Thank you. (*sits and looks imploringly at her*) Julia, listen to me. If you have any qualms or last-minute indecision, let me say, as I said yesterday, that we could terminate the agreement with one word from you and another from me. Then you could live on for all time here in your mansion with your friends.

JULIA: I knew you would say that, Mr. Endors. Your words are as familiar as if I'd seen them in blazing letters before your coming here. But my decision is final; my mind is totally made up.

ENDORS: Let me plead with you one more time. Please. (*He says the next after a movement of impatience from Julia.*) Please, hear me. You are making an unwise decision. You need not operate the place for the purposes you have been conducting it. It can easily be made into your own private domicile. We can construct a kind of fence and barriers so that no one can enter.

JULIA: They would enter, though, and climb the highest fence if they knew I was still here, Mr. Endors.

ENDORS: You are leaving the house because of young Dana and Quentin, Julia. Don't tell me you have any other reason. But your knowing Quentin will come to an end all of its own, and soon, my friend. It will end, like the spring, and he will be out of your life. Don't you understand that? And you will one day regret that you've given up this magnificent property merely because you learned to care too deeply for Dana's brother.

JULIA: Let us say I am leaving, then, because I love Dana's brother. But the day you predict, when Quentin finally leaves me and I find myself again as when I lost Dana for the first time to his grandfather—don't you see then this house will be worse than a prison? Worse than a mausoleum or grave! No, no, Mr. Endors. And, besides, let me speak from the heart. I have grown to hate this house, because it bestows happiness on everyone but me. I am like the starving looking in at feasters at a banquet. My hunger has grown over the years until it is famine. The house is for me airless, without substance or nurture. Long before my Quentin came to me, I was wasting away from the misery of my hunger. (*rising*) Yes, I will miss it. I will pine for it—probably for the rest of my life. But I will no longer be the beggar at the feast. I will be quiet—at peace—finally still.

ENDORS: Julia, I accept your decision and I bless you for what you have just said. I will never forget your words, or you.

JULIA: Mr. Endors, I must ask you a favor. . . . Will you give this letter to Quentin? He should read it—tell him in your presence.

ENDORS: But, Julia, is a letter the right thing, my child?

JULIA: I don't know if it is the right thing. Is there any right thing I could do for him? But it is my only means of saying goodbye, for I could never say goodbye to him in person. I would die in his embrace! (*hands him the letter*) For pity's sake, Mr. Endors, give him the letter when you see him here tomorrow. For you are to see him here, are you not?

ENDORS: I am, my dear. And as the envelope is open, should I read it before I give it to him?

JULIA: You may—or wait until you see him.

ENDORS: And now, my dear, if you will be so good as to sign these papers . . . (*After he points out where* JULIA *should sign, she carefully and slowly signs the papers, then hands them back to* MR. ENDORS.) Good and proper! And now it is all over and done with. (*He blows on the fresh ink until it is dry, then rises.*) Julia, I want you keep in touch with me. There are some other affairs that have to be settled. Of course if you would rather someone else be in charge of your affairs . . .

JULIA: You know best. And you must know I will always be in touch with you.

ENDORS: Goodbye, then, Julia. A long goodbye.

(*He kisses her, then exits. Very distraught,* JULIA *leans against the great chair. She rings for* NEALE *and* SADIE, *who enter.*)

JULIA: (*affectedly calm*) So, it is all over, children. I have signed away my jurisdiction over here, and with it all the years! A strange and perhaps wonderful feeling of lightness is coming over me. That dream I have always had of a bird carrying me away—perhaps that is the feeling. I no longer command here, Sadie, Neale. I am free. And to be free may be the heaviest thing to bear, but it's the only thing I can bear now.

Scene 12

QUENTIN *enters the front room of* JULIA's *house. The room has been stripped of all furnishings except for two chairs.* QUENTIN *stops short for a moment, then begins looking around in dismay. He walks over to a door that formerly led to the dance hall and musicians, shaking his head in disbelief.* MR. ENDORS *enters and looks with concern at* QUENTIN.

ENDORS: Quentin!

QUENTIN: (*turning around*) Oh good morning, Mr. Endors. Thank you for your note.

ENDORS: I know it must seem odd for me to have invited you to Julia's house. But somehow I felt we would both be more at ease with each other here than in my stuffy old office, with its filing cabinets and harsh light.

QUENTIN: I'm not sure about that, Mr. Endors, to tell you the truth. They've left nothing, have they, the movers? I was just trying to find my way around in all the emptiness when you came in. Look at those bare walls, sir, and the bare floors. . . . No music now, is there? Or dancers.

ENDORS: Why don't we sit down? (QUENTIN *sits down heavily in one of the chairs.* MR. ENDORS *takes his time following suit.*) My boy, I hope you don't mind if I say something at this point. I think I understand what you are feeling.

QUENTIN: Thank you. I'm not quite sure *I* understand what I am feeling. (*looking around him*) I would never recognize this as the place where I met Julia that first time.

ENDORS: Let me say something, Quentin. Your whole life is before you.

QUENTIN: (*in bitter anger*) You mean, the long rolling years ahead, full of nothing—nothing without her.

ENDORS: Later, your grief will not be so painful, Quentin, and you will have good times, good days. Eventually you will find someone to make up for everything.

QUENTIN: I don't think my heart will ever have the strength to love anyone again. Losing her—losing all she gave me in her house in her arms.

ENDORS: Everything is change in this life, Quentin. Everything. And change is very painful. The more we try to hold onto love, the more it seems to elude our grasp. There is always something else waiting for us, Quentin, if we will only seek it. And knowing you as I do, Quentin, let me say, you will go on despite your terrible loss.

QUENTIN: You mean drag on, stumble, creep!

ENDORS: Quentin, I have brought you this letter. It's from Julia, of course. (*offers him the letter*)

QUENTIN: (*reluctantly accepting the envelope*) Must I read it, Mr. Endors?

ENDORS: Julia instructed me that you should read it in my presence. Indeed, that is why we are here.

QUENTIN: Don't the empty rooms and silence say it all?

ENDORS: Read it, my boy. (*sits down*)

QUENTIN: (*Trying to read, but, unable to see owing to his tears, he hands the letter back to* ENDORS.) Read it for me, Mr. Endors.

ENDORS: (*putting on his glasses deliberately*) I'm not sure I can read such a letter properly.

QUENTIN: The words will give out the meaning.

ENDORS: (*reading*) *My dear Quentin, One day you will understand why I have left you, and it is my belief and hope you will on that day thank me. I will always love you and cherish our few times of happiness together. You will be with me in my thoughts always. I will thank all the powers that be that I was able to share the precious hours with you. I hope you will remember me for those hours and not think I have left or abandoned you through any other reason than the very love I feel for you and for Dana. Had I remained here in this house, welcoming you and loving you endlessly, I would have finally taken away our love itself and left you with bitterness and regret. Leaving you now is not deserting you, dear Quentin, but keeping our love perfect forever. I will hold you in my heart forever. Your friend who will always cherish you through all time, Julia.*

ENDORS: (*folding the letter and trying to hand it back to* QUENTIN) Quentin, please accept the letter.

QUENTIN: No, Mr. Endors, no. Grant me the favor of your keeping the letter for me. I know you have many places where you can deposit precious documents. Perhaps even the day will come when I will come to you and ask you to read it again. But now I dare not trust myself to be its guardian. I think for one thing my tears would blot out all her words and I would be left with only stained paper, empty as this room and this house.

ENDORS: Very well, Quentin. I will keep it for you. Will you come out with me now?

QUENTIN: May I stay for a while until I am a bit more collected?

ENDORS: Yes, for a little while. But the new owners will be coming shortly, and they may not wish you to stay.

QUENTIN: I will be gone by then. (*rising*) And Mr. Endors, thank you for reading it, for I would not have been able to do so, aloud or silently.

ENDORS: Goodbye, then, my boy. Remember: call on me whenever you feel the need.

QUENTIN: Before you go, Mr. Endors, will you let me say something? If you will pardon me for speaking like this: When you read the letter, I heard her voice. I will hear that voice forever. Maybe Julia told me the truth in the letter, and maybe not. I know only one thing—I have been deserted. Had I never met Julia, had I never been so headstrong as to insist on accompanying my brother to her house, had all this not happened, I might have gone to my death never having known true happiness. But from true happiness to experience the fierce pain and endless loss that is mine now! To be shut out of happiness! (*He takes hold of* MR. ENDORS's *arm.*) No, sir, Julia couldn't understand what she has done. What need therefore is there ever to come to you to read her letter again, since I have lost her—lost Julia—and lost myself? Do you see, Mr. Endors: she gave me *life* . . . then she snatched it away from me!

(ENDORS embraces QUENTIN. They remain embracing as the scene ends and the curtain falls.)

RUTHANNA ELDER

CHARACTERS and their ages

TED SCANLON, 40
DR. ULRIC, 80/40
JACK PALMER, 25
JESS FERENCE, 18
JUDD FARNHAM, 15
RUTHANNA ELDER, 18

A small town in the hill country of Ohio, 1950 and 1910.

ACT I

Scene 1

DR. ULRIC, 80, *is seated in a huge armchair, looking through an album of old photographs. He does not hear his attendant of some ten years,* TED SCANLON, *calling him.*

TED: Dr. Ulric! Are you asleep?

ULRIC: What time is it, Ted?

TED: Well, Doctor, if you look out the east window there you'll see Old Sol is only halfway up the heavens.

ULRIC: The days are so long. The afternoons seem to be interminable.

TED: That's because you miss your practice. Doc, you should never have given up . . . doctoring.

ULRIC: I never gave up doctoring, you simpleton. I outlived all my patients. And people today go to the city for treatment. Don't let me hear you say that again, I *gave up my practice.*

TED: I mean, Doc, you could bestir yourself a little and find new patients.

ULRIC: Bestir myself, the devil.

TED: Doc, that gent from the Historical Research Society is here again. Says he must see you. Says it's urgent.

ULRIC: Is he here as a patient?

TED: No, no I told you on the last call he made, he wants to ask you about old times here. And so I wrote down the specific question he wants help with. You scolded me so the last time he came because I didn't inquire the exact story he was after.

ULRIC: And he doesn't want my professional diagnosis?

TED: (*reading slowly from the paper*) He's writing something about, yes I think I have the name right—

ULRIC: Well, spit it out, Ted.

TED: Ruthanna Elder.

ULRIC: (*spoken almost with horror*) Ruthanna Elder? You can't be serious.

TED: What is it Doc? Are you all right? You look like you'd seen . . .

ULRIC: Yes, finish your phrase.

TED: A ghost. Doc, it's upset you so much. I'll tell him to be on his way.

ULRIC: What sort of a chap is he?

TED: Nice-looking fellow, young, smooth-shaven, not like the ones today. Soft-spoken.

ULRIC: Ruthanna Elder! Ted, I'd rather see a ghost than be reminded.

TED: Shall I send him away, Doc?

ULRIC: (*pausing*) Let him come in. Let him . . . speak . . .

TED: You're feeling good enough for visitors?

ULRIC: I said, let him come in. (*tries to reach for a pillbox and a glass of water*)

TED: Let me help you. (*TED opens the pillbox and extends a pill to DR. ULRIC, and when he puts it in his mouth TED hands him a glass of water from a pitcher nearby.*)

TED: You're sure, Doc, you're up to it.

ULRIC: Why wouldn't I be up to it?

TED: The name of the woman upset you so.

ULRIC: Woman! She was the most beautiful . . . girl I ever saw, but she was more than beautiful. She was my "spring beauty."

TED: And it was . . . long ago?

ULRIC: Yes, but didn't you see how even I at my age had no trouble recalling.

TED: I'll let him come in then, Doc. (*exits*)

ULRIC: Ruthanna . . . Ruthanna Elder. The name . . . sort of restores me. Yes, that's the word. Restores! (*smiles*)

(*Enter the young* JACK PALMER. *He is about 25, light brown hair and blue eyes, about six foot tall, and awkwardly carrying a large Record Book. Breaking away from* TED SCANLON *he extends his hand toward* ULRIC.)

JACK: Jack Palmer, Dr. Ulric. Do you remember me?

ULRIC: Excuse me not rising. Of course I remember you. You're Agnes' son!

JACK: (*correcting amusedly*) Grandson!

ULRIC: Of course of course. Sit down. Do you want something to drink?

JACK: Oh no, not really . . . (*at seeing the look of disappointment on* ULRIC's *face*) Maybe later if you are having something.

ULRIC: (*musing*) Later, later, yes. You're a breath of fresh air, Jack. As I was saying to Ted here, my patients have all gone and deserted me. And there's so few visitors. In the old days, my waiting room was crowded. All hustle and bustle, talk, singing even, laughter. The sick all got well they used to say when they paid a visit to me . . . but now . . . today . . . but you have business. The Historical Society. You're in that line?

JACK: Only in my spare time. I'm bookkeeper at the Refinery.

ULRIC: And you like that?

JACK: Well, it's something, as my mother says, better than twiddling one's thumbs.

ULRIC: You're not married.

JACK: Not on my salary.

ULRIC: (*somewhat darkly*) The name Ted brought in. The name you mentioned to him.

JACK: (*anxious*) Yes?

ULRIC: Did he have the name right? Well. Tell me.

JACK: Yes, he had it right, (*looks over at* TED) Ruthanna Elder.

ULRIC: But, Jack, shouldn't it all be forgotten, except of course in our heart of hearts. But see here you're too young to have known her.

JACK: That's not entirely true, Doctor. I used to see her, well, when on fine days she sat on her front porch. The first time going past when it was growing a bit dark, I thought she was a young woman.

ULRIC: (*urging him on*) No wonder!

JACK: Why do you say that?

ULRIC: Because Ruthanna kept her youthful look till the end. Long after . . . what happened had happened why, she would sit there looking no older than when she was prom queen . . . the townfolk called her Sleepy-Time Gal!

JACK: Exactly! Exactly. Oh I wish I had been alive then.

ULRIC: Then? Do you know what you are saying, Jack.

JACK: Maybe, maybe not. But things seemed so much more real in those days.

ULRIC: I'm not sure, though, why you want to, I mean I don't see why the Historical Society would want the story of Ruthanna Elder. For those of us who really knew her keep her memory here. (*points to his heart*)

JACK: I must confess something, Dr. Ulric on that score. . . . I'm afraid it's me and not the Historical Society who is so interested in her.

ULRIC: I thought as much when you came through the door, Jack. You don't look like any dry-bones archivist. And her story is more, well, like a poem than something for a historical archive.

JACK: If you would tell it to me I would keep it as safe as I believe you've kept it. If I wrote it I would write it only for your eyes and mine to see.

ULRIC: Ted, do step into the kitchen and bring us all a cup of that fresh chocolate you made a while ago. You will have a cup, Jack. (JACK *nods.*)

JACK: (*almost to himself, almost like singing a solo in church*) I sort of fell in love with Ruthanna Elder when I was looking through the old high school annuals of so many years ago. There she was the prom queen, and in other photos she was with Jess Ference, I believe.

ULRIC: Oh, yes Jess. The boy she was to marry.

JACK: Exactly. And do you know I thought they looked more glorious than any movie star! I wonder they did not become stars.

(*Enter* TED, *bearing a tray of the chocolate. He serves each of them, until—*)

ULRIC: Sit down, please Ted, and join us if you feel like it.

TED: I hope this all won't upset you, Doc, for you started so when I pronounced the name Ruthanna Elder.

ULRIC: Now, now, Ted. (*to* JACK) Ted may not be too partial to stories like that of Ruthanna and Jess, and of course the other boy.

JACK: Ah yes, the other boy. I was going to ask you about him in particular.

TED: I believe, Doc, I will tend to some chores outside if you will both excuse me.

ULRIC: Ted does not relish these old and nearly forgotten histories. Well, if Jack will excuse you, Ted, you may leave our company.

JACK: I'll be sorry to see you go, Ted. I was hoping you might add to the Doctor's reminiscences.

TED: I'm afraid I don't have a very good memory for stories like this. I'm sorry if I seem brusque or unpolite, but I do have a lot to tend to outside. I've been cutting the wood for winter for one thing.

ULRIC: Go along now, Ted, and if we need you we'll call. (*a long pause in which* ULRIC *and* JACK *sip their drinks*)

JACK: And what was *his* name, Doctor?

ULRIC: (*who has been lost in reverie*) Whose, my boy?

JACK: Why, the rival, you know, the young very young uncle.

ULRIC: Ah, yes, imagine having an uncle who is younger than you. It does occur. It's not too uncommon. The other boy, the uncle—his name was Judd. Judd. I can't remember his last name.

JACK: Wasn't it Farnham.

ULRIC: Judd Farnham—it was! What a memory you have.

JACK: I'm afraid it's not my memory which is so good, Doctor, I read his name in some old newspapers I found in the basement of the library building.

ULRIC: So you *are* an archivist after all.

JACK: Please, please, no. Not in this case. Not at all. I don't know why the story haunts me so.

ULRIC: That's the word. It doesn't let go of you, her story. In all these years, and they are many, she stays with me. And Jess and poor Judd Farnham too. They're realer than any of the living. Oh how I remember the first time she came to me. It was just before the prom ball. Despite her distress she had never looked so young or so winning-fair. I should have known then, Ruthanna did not come merely to chat about the youth of her uncle. . . . I knew something was amiss. . . . But being busy and let me say, I was for all my medical training, not always too perceptive. Not intuitive enough. Or say when intuition warned me, I sometimes shut intuition out and chose science and medicine. But it's intuition which is always right. Always always. Ruthanna had a secret.

(*The lights begin to dim.*)

Scene 2

The lights come up again in DR. ULRIC's *house but in his consulting room this time of long ago.* ULRIC, *standing, gazing at* RUTHANNA EL-DER, *who has just entered.*

RUTHANNA: Doctor! You are staring at me like you'd never seen me before!

ULRIC: Oh, overlook it, my dear. . . . I'm staring at you because I've never seen you look so . . .

RUTHANNA: (*a bit worried*) Look so what, Doctor Ulric?

ULRIC: Ruthanna, you look like some princess in a story book.

RUTHANNA: (*flushed, embarrassed*) Oh, aren't you the flatterer.

ULRIC: And you're so composed, so easy, and you walk like you're barely touching the ground. Like Juno would walk, hardly touching earth.

RUTHANNA: May I sit down a moment?

ULRIC: Sit, stand, do anything you like. But what is it, dear? You're excited I'm sure, on account of you're the senior prom queen and of course there's your graduation. And your engagement to be married to the one young man who's probably worthy of you, Jess Ference.

RUTHANNA: (*brightening up a bit*) Perhaps that's it, then, Doctor. So much excitement has made me a little . . . unsteady!

ULRIC: (*comes over and takes her hand in order to examine her pulse*) I'm sure you're right, my dear. But you're the picture of health.

RUTHANNA: The moment you touch me, Doctor, I feel better already. Am I all right though?

ULRIC: Your pulse is a little rapid, that's all. Nothing to worry about.

RUTHANNA: There is though another matter. But I know you're very busy. I don't want to take up your time.

ULRIC: You can take up all my time, my dear. You don't know how much the very sight of you does for me! Like all the spring flowers in the world had suddenly opened in this gloomy old consulting room. Just think, Ruthanna. The whole world is before you! No wonder you're a little excited. Who wouldn't be? You're all right. You're fine. (*pauses*) And Jess? How is he?

RUTHANNA: (*starts*) I think he is more nervous than I am, Doctor. . . . He is very . . . irritable lately. He sort of . . . picks on me, you might say.

ULRIC: Oh, Jess, that's the way he is.

RUTHANNA: Do you know he's jealous!

ULRIC: (*passing this off*) And who wouldn't be?

RUTHANNA: But let me tell you who it is, and you'll be as surprised as I am.

ULRIC: Can I guess?

RUTHANNA: I don't think anybody could guess. . . . It's little Judd Farnham.

ULRIC: Judd!

RUTHANNA: I know what you're going to say. . . . He's . . .

ULRIC: (*finishing for her*) A mere child.

RUTHANNA: (*musing*) But the other day I noticed, and I laughed but it made Judd cross. . . . He's beginning to show ever so little a light-corn silk fuzz on his cheeks.

ULRIC: (*laughs*) Well, then you tell Jess to go find somebody else to be jealous of.

RUTHANNA: And Judd is such good company. He's my closest companion, next to Jess of course.

ULRIC: (*meditative*) Of course.

RUTHANNA: And Mother is so pleased Judd can be depended on when he's needed. But to think, Doctor, Judd is my uncle! And he is at least three years younger than me. Imagine a 14- or 15-year-old uncle. Isn't it delicious? (*rises*) But I'm keeping you from your important patients.

ULRIC: No, Ruthanna wait a moment. (*goes to back of stage and picks up something from a cabinet, brings it back*) These are something for you to take, my dear, when you feel upset or nervous. Go on take them. (*hands her a small box of pills*) They're not strong, my dear. Just something to quiet you. (RUTHANNA *takes the box and looks at it wonderingly, then thanks* ULRIC.) Come back whenever you like, dear girl. You won't need an appointment. Not at all. Never.

(*lights down*)

Scene 3

Light comes back on to show RUTHANNA *in her front parlor, standing.*

RUTHANNA: I could not get it out. The thing that is worrying me! Yet Dr. Ulric is so understanding. His brow has been described as benevolent. But his eyes can flash fire with anger, too. Oh, what if I told him the truth, or what I think is the truth. It's been more than two months now. . . . And I am different. And Jess knows I am different. I have told him it's the excitement and the thought we are to be married a month after the senior prom. A month after I am Queen. A month. Months ruled by the Moon! Men are not ruled by her as she steals across the sky or sets in the west, the Moon. . . . I can't forget what happened. My uncle. More like *my* child, he always seemed. How could we forget ourselves when so much was pending, so much was and is at stake. Oh oh . . . (*she buries her face in her hands*) Mother is almost always gone. Since Papa died as she so often reminds me, she has had to be mother and father, guardian and breadwinner for me and so on. How glad I am, she often has said, you have someone as loving and steady as your uncle Judd. Oh, my God, if she only knew, if she only (*almost inaudible*) only . . . (*she remembers now how it occurred*)

(*Enter* JUDD, *a dark complexioned boy with coppery skin.*)

JUDD: Oh, look what has happened, Ruthanna. Would you ever think? (*He laughs.*)

RUTHANNA: What's wrong with your shirt?

JUDD: (*continues to laugh*) That's it! Well, it's pretty plain, it's ripped. I fell in the hedge from my bike, and got tangled up all over. There are thorns growing in the hedge or something sharp as spikes.

RUTHANNA: (*laughs also*) Ah, well there is a thorn tree near the hedge.

JUDD: So what shall I do, Ruthanna? Look at me!

RUTHANNA: You know my dad left behind a number of shirts . . .

JUDD: But it wouldn't be right to wear one of his now would it?

RUTHANNA: I don't know why not. You can't go around in that tangle of rags.

JUDD: Well, if you think it's all right.

RUTHANNA: Mother is so fond of you I'm sure she wouldn't care. We won't even need to tell her. Well, take off your shirt, why can't you, and I'll see if one of my father's work sheets won't fit you.

JUDD: But, Ruthanna . . .

RUTHANNA: Judd, don't be so bashful. After all (*laughs*) you are my uncle.

JUDD: (*speaking thickly*) Am I now? I wish then I wasn't.

RUTHANNA: You shouldn't speak to me that way. (*she shows she is pleased he has*)

JUDD: Why not, Ruthanna?

RUTHANNA: Because I am promised.

JUDD: Oh that.

RUTHANNA: (*flaring up*) Yes, that!

JUDD: Ah, yes, Jess Ference!

RUTHANNA: We were betrothed by both our parents when we were . . . about your age. In a special church service, Judd.

JUDD: But, Ruthanna, that is not binding, is it, church or no church?

RUTHANNA: But it is in Jess' mind at least.

JUDD: And in yours?

RUTHANNA: Now stop it! (*They suddenly engage in a little romp, running around the room like children playing tag.*)

JUDD: Oh well . . . (*kisses her stealthily*)

RUTHANNA: Judd, Judd. Well, take off your shirt since it's falling off of you and I'll go upstairs and fetch a new shirt for you. (*suddenly seeing his chest now as he has taken off his shirt*) Why, Judd, you have a wonderful . . .

JUDD: (*aroused*) What, Ruthanna?

RUTHANNA: A sculptor would want to sculpt your chest, I bet. . . . And your skin there is so white. Almost like a girl's.

JUDD: Oh not like a girl's I hope.

RUTHANNA: How handsome you look. I'll go upstairs and get the shirt.

JUDD: Oh don't bother. (*He suddenly touches her and then presses her to him.*)

RUTHANNA: Judd, Judd! (*She breaks away from him and leaves.*)

JUDD: (*sitting down and rubbing his right hand over his eyes*) Oh my God. She smells like what? Some wild flower I don't know the name of. And my arms smell strong. (*He puts his nose to one armpit after another.*) Promised to Jess Ference! We'll see about that.

(*RUTHANNA reenters with one of her dead father's shirts. She is obviously very much changed by what has happened between herself and JUDD. She coldly extends the shirt.*)

RUTHANNA: Here, Judd, put this on and then I think you had better go home, shouldn't you?

JUDD: Oh, should I? Why, Ruthanna? Why?

RUTHANNA: Because.

JUDD: Ruthanna have you ever noticed how wonderful it is when we feel the pure air against ourselves, without our clothes on I mean. Because we're all clothes, and then when the air reaches our skin, like it is reaching mine now, you feel so free, so real, Ruthanna. Like coming out from a prison. One's body feels so fresh not being tied down and hampered.

RUTHANNA: Stop it.

JUDD: No, no, it's the truth. Look at me.

RUTHANNA: I have looked at you. Now stop it. Put on this shirt and go home.

JUDD: Ruthanna, listen. I want to see your chest too. It's not fair that you can look at my chest and I can't see yours.

RUTHANNA: Judd. Stop it. Stop it at once, put on the shirt and go home.

JUDD: I dare you to touch my chest, now that the air has cooled it. Aha, you're a fraidy cat, aren't you. You pretend to be so ahead of all the other girls but you are as prissy as an old maid.

RUTHANNA: I am not. Only I want you to go home.

JUDD: No, you don't. You want me to stay. And you want to touch my bare chest but you're scared to.

RUTHANNA: I'm not, but I don't want to.

JUDD: (*going closer to her*) Touch it and see.

RUTHANNA: (*moving as if sleepwalking she touches his chest*) Ah!

JUDD: I thought you would say Ah. (*They both laugh.*) Ruthanna, if you put your ear to my chest you can hear my heart beating.

RUTHANNA: I bet.

JUDD: Go ahead. I dare you, fraidy cat.

RUTHANNA: All right. I want to hear your heart beat. (*She listens and she shows great excitement.*)

JUDD: Now it's only fair I get to hear yours beat also. And I hope it beats for me. Ruthanna, take off your blouse.

RUTHANNA: No, no. You can listen to my heart through my blouse. I won't take it off.

JUDD: All right, let me listen through your clothes then, but it's cheating.

RUTHANNA: Cheating? How so?

JUDD: I can't hear your heartbeat properly through clothes. Let me listen, let me hear your heart. (*he begins to remove her clothing*) Oh, Ruthanna.

RUTHANNA: I hope you're satisfied. (*She weeps a little. JUDD has removed all her upper clothing. He puts his ear to her heart and then places his mouth there and begins to kiss her rapturously.*)

JUDD: Oh, Ruthanna. Be good to me, be good. Here, kiss my breast too. Go ahead, it's not poison. It's my heart beating for you, Ruthanna, beating beating with love. I love you. You are my girl. My heart is telling you that.

RUTHANNA: (*overcome with feeling*) Oh, Judd, Judd. Take me then to your heart, Judd. Take me to your beating heart. Yes, yes. (*They hold each other in rapture.*)

(*lights down*)

Scene 4

Lights up. RUTHANNA *alone in the center of the stage. She is dressed in a beautiful muslin gown, suitable for the dance she is to attend.*

RUTHANNA: How can I tell anyone what I felt that day! How can I express my happiness—and my terror. I had never felt anything that swept me so far away. The message from his parted lips stayed with me all through that day and the night and the day that followed. I could hear his beating heart everywhere. His heartbeat within me. His breath seemed to come out of my own breath. That is when I went to the Doctor. I felt I had to share my happiness and my terror with someone. And as I spoke with him I realized he, yes, Dr. Ulric would understand if I ever had to come to him again. And I knew I would! Yes, the day would come when I would have to go to him again. And he would understand. He must understand. I had no one else. My terror was Jess. My terror was Jess Ference. He stood over me in my sleep like some all-knowing unblinking presence. For you must remember oh I cannot say it enough times, we were betrothed. That is the custom in our town from far far back. The leading families have the tradition. And so we were betrothed from childhood. We were in the eyes of our church and our families already man and wife, in the eyes of God, we were one flesh. And yet what had I done! I had committed some act that was enormous. And yet I could not be sorry because I had known bliss. Dr. Ulric must understand that. For I have no one else to whom I can go. But my terror was Jess. Jess is terror. His strength, his nobility, yes his handsomeness. No one is more handsome than Jess. His arms are like steel fibers when he touches me. And we have hardly kissed. But he will know. He will read my heart. He will know. He is my terror. I hear him coming. Oh God pity me and defend me, for I have known bliss. He will read it on my lips, he will hear my heart beating with my love for Judd!

(*Enter* JESS. *He is over six feet tall, and with a crown of fair curly hair, piercing blue eyes with large black pupils, and a mouth which though beautifully formed, is a bit too large and has a kind of fierce almost brutal turn to it.*)

JESS: (*coming forward*) Where have you been, Ruthanna? I have been looking everywhere for you. (*He takes her gently in his arms and kisses her on the forehead.* RUTHANNA *almost cowers in his arms.*) What is it?

RUTHANNA: What is what, Jess?

JESS: Your eyes look full of some kind of, well, what would you say. Not sorrow exactly. Worry? Care?

RUTHANNA: (*puts her head on his shoulder*) So much is about to happen, Jess. Isn't that it?

JESS: Do you love me, Ruthanna?

RUTHANNA: Why, Jess, what a queer question. Yet you always ask that, sweetheart.

JESS: I saw you coming out of the doctor's office the other day. I could not get that out of my mind.

RUTHANNA: Then you'll be glad to know there was nothing wrong with me, dear. . . . How fine you look today, Jess, in your new jacket and tie.

JESS: We're going to the dance then of course.

RUTHANNA: Of course, of course.

JESS: But the doctor . . . I mean, why?

RUTHANNA: I thought, Jess, that my heart seemed to flutter at times like it would skip a beat.

JESS: Your heart?

RUTHANNA: But the doctor assured me—it was nothing at all. My heart was . . . beating as it should.

JESS: Thank the Lord.

RUTHANNA: He said it was a bit rapid because of the wonderful happiness I feel is in store for me.

JESS: The wonderful . . . Ah, well . . . But that does not sound like a doctor, does it? The wonderful . . . Hmmm.

RUTHANNA: He knows how much I look forward to my . . . our wedding.

JESS: Oh, Ruthanna, I hope you love me as much as I do you. That is what I keep coming back to, I know. You have told me before I should not say it, let alone think it. But I can't—

RUTHANNA: (*closing his mouth with her hand*) I love only you.

JESS: (*repeating worriedly*) Only me. I don't want you to see the doctor! Please. Please, don't go there again!

RUTHANNA: But I won't have to now, Jess. He said . . .my heart was strong and beat . . . like a young girl's heart should.

JESS: (*kissing her*) And how is that?

RUTHANNA: A little rapid when she thinks of her bridegroom.

JESS: Oh, Ruthanna, let's dance the whole evening through, till the last star goes out.

(*lights down*)

Scene 5

Lights up on the porch of the Green Mill Dance Hall. JESS and RUTH-ANNA have just closed the glass doors behind them.

RUTHANNA: It was so stuffy in there and everyone was pressing so close to us.

JESS: They already call you the Queen of the Prom, Ruthanna. And that's what you are to me, you rule my heart. (*spoken with a queer anguish*) Ruthanna, I'll never let you go. I hope you feel the same way about me, that without me, nothing would have any meaning or . . . savor.

RUTHANNA: (*frightened*) Oh, Jess, you know how I feel. You know I love you . . . let's dance here, dance like we always do. And let's not talk.

JESS: (*anguished still*) But I want to talk too. . . . All right, let's dance then. After all we came to do that. (*They dance in the shadows of the huge revolving globe of illumination coming from inside.*) You're different tonight, Ruthanna. You're more beautiful, you *are* the Queen, but something's changed in you.

RUTHANNA: No, nothing has changed. You're cross.

JESS: Cross, me? No, no. I love you more than ever. Why can't we be married at once? Ruthanna, sometimes I think I can't wait. . . . Look I brought something tonight. My mother's wedding ring. Had she lived she would have blessed our marriage. Here, let me put it on you.

RUTHANNA: (*frightened*) But Jess, isn't that bad luck to put on a wedding ring before the ceremony.

JESS: Our love won't know bad luck. Let me put on the ring. (*He puts the ring on her finger and kisses her hand and then her face.*) You do love me, Ruthanna. Look how I am. . . . Oh why do we have to wait.

RUTHANNA: Jess, this is so unlike you. You always spoke to me of Christ, your church, the elders of your church. Now what are you asking me to do? Can't we just hold one another and dance, like we used to.

JESS: (*impassioned*) I want you. Now now now. (*He shivers, swallows spasmodically, then calming down, they dance slowly, almost dazed.*)

RUTHANNA: (*suddenly*) Can't we sit down. Jess, I feel just a little bit faint. It's so good to catch some of the first spring air. (*They sit in the garden.*) Oh, I have disappointed you, dear. But I do need to rest.

JESS: Ruthanna, what is it? You don't act like yourself. You act like you don't care! You don't hold me as you used to hold me. You seem . . . distant, far away.

RUTHANNA: No, no, dearest boy! Distant to you . . . never! I told you I feel a bit faint.

JESS: Are you sure you told me the truth about your visit to the doctor?

RUTHANNA: I always tell you the truth. Don't fuss and fret. Let's sit here and you can hold me. I'll feel better then.

JESS: (*mollified*) Hold you! I could hold you forever. I could dance with you under that big globe of a light till kingdom come. Oh, Ruthanna, why do we have to wait . . . for a ceremony. (*He kisses her hair deliriously. They are quiet then.*) She's fallen asleep, I do believe. Asleep—she's more lovely than ever. Oh, why do we have to wait. What's a ceremony when we've been betrothed for so long, when we are already yes as the church says one flesh. Oh my darling. How I adore you. I could rise up and fly, fly with you in my arms.

RUTHANNA: (*in her sleep*) Oh Judd, Judd. You are as beautiful as a young girl.

JESS: (*horrified*) Ruthanna. Ruthanna.

RUTHANNA: (*in sleep*) Your chest is white as a girl's.

JESS: (*shaking her violently*) Ruthanna, wake up wake up!

RUTHANNA: (*coming to with a start*) What is it?

JESS: (*enraged*) Yes, what is it? You should be able to tell me what is it. I should hit you. What is it indeed? (*stands up*)

RUTHANNA: Oh, Jess, my beloved, what have I done wrong. Look at you!

JESS: You said something in your sleep. . . . And then, why *are* you so sleepy after all? Why when your real bridegroom is here are you sleepy. What have you done? Whose name did you call on just then in your cursed slumber, will you answer me? Or shall I strike you.

RUTHANNA: The doctor gave me a strong medicine.

JESS: No, the doctor be damned. Somebody else has given you strong medicine.

RUTHANNA: (*alarmed*) Who, precious boy?

JESS: Don't call me precious boy. The one you called on in your sleep. . . . Judd! *Judd* you called, and spoke of his white breast like a girl's!

RUTHANNA: Oh, no, no. Why, Jess, what in heaven's name.

JESS: Heaven's name no. You love somebody else. I knew it. I have known it. Your love for me has cooled. You called on another man's name.

RUTHANNA: If I said Judd, think a while. He is only a child. How could I love a child.

JESS: (*maniacal*) Yes, how could you love anybody but me. Have you forgotten our betrothal. Have you forgotten we are promised to one another. Look here, you never spoke my name with such earnest feeling, such swooning tenderness. Oh, Ruthanna, look out. Look out. I will get to the bottom of this, don't you ever think I won't. Ruthanna, Judd is no child. I saw him only yesterday. Judd is a young man. And as you said in your sleep, Judd has a fair fair chest.

RUTHANNA: God in heaven, what are you accusing me of?

JESS: You have lied to me. I'll get to the bottom of this. (*He moves away.*)

RUTHANNA: Oh, Jess, where are you rushing to? You can't leave me here. I have no way to go home! Oh, Jess, Jess. (*he goes*) God alive oh my God! What have I done? What has happened? Could I have spoken all that in my sleep? Oh I was so tired. God in heaven what is to become of me, of us, yes of us, all three of us. He is like that. He has a savage temper. And he stands so tall over me, like a fierce guardian angel who will never forgive or forget!

(*lights down*)

Scene 6

JESS: (*alone*) *Look at me!* I said that to myself, coming awake after I walked, ran, sauntered, and slept in the forest. My hair was full of the bark and leaves of trees. But do you think it was where I had fallen and cut myself brought me to the Doctor. Do you think it was the blood from my cut arms and legs. Think again! No, I went to the Doctor to tell him what I had lost. And what was that? Everything. From the day I was betrothed to Ruthanna until the night in the Green Mill Dance Hall when I heard her call the name of her true love. (*He enters* DR. ULRIC's *consulting room.*)

ULRIC: (*stands up from his chair, alarmed*) What on earth has happened to you? Let me see your arm. For pity's sake. Sit over here. You'll have to roll up your sleeve or, better, remove your shirt. (*JESS takes off his shirt.*) How did you cut your arms, wait a minute till I get the bandages and the rest . . . (*goes out*)

JESS: How would I know how I cut my arms. I wish I had cut them off. . . . Had I been carrying my gun I would have put a bullet through my heart, and if enough strength remained another through my brain.

ULRIC: (*reentering*) What are you muttering about?

JESS: What kind of medicine did you give my fiancée?

ULRIC: (*almost forgetting now who he means*) Your fiancée.

JESS: Have you forgotten too she is betrothed to me.

ULRIC: Ah, Ruthanna.

JESS: Ruthanna! Ruthanna! You gave her a strong medicine.

ULRIC: Not so, my boy, (*working to clean his wounds and putting the bloodstained rags one after another into a little basin on the floor*) I gave her the mildest kind of sedative.

JESS: I hope you won't give me medicine of the same kind. It makes the tongue wag. It makes the breast give up its secrets.

ULRIC: My boy . . . you're light-headed.

JESS: I won't take your medicine.

ULRIC: Listen to me, Jess. Pay close mind.

JESS: How can I listen to anybody after what she has said to me.

ULRIC: What has happened to you? What has set you on like this? Jess, I want you to lie down over here.

JESS: Don't give me any medicine.

ULRIC: I am going to put this coverlet over you, and take off your shoes.

JESS: No medicine. I don't want to speak or hear the truth. (DR. UL-RIC *takes out the hypodermic needle and first daubs* JESS' *arm with alcohol, then gives him an injection.*)

JESS: Ow ow ow . . . Oh oh oh.

ULRIC: A big strapping fellow like you, crying out!

JESS: No medicine.

ULRIC: What happened, Jess? (*taking his pulse*) Racing like the wind. It will get slower now.

JESS: Our engagement will be broken.

ULRIC: Nonsense. Why should it be?

JESS: She loves somebody else. She told me. In the dance hall. Your medicine made the truth come out.

ULRIC: Who could Ruthanna love but you?

JESS: Aha, you are you see as big a fool as me. I'll tell you who. (*rises up*)

ULRIC: (*pushing him gently down*) You must lie quiet. You've lost quite a bit of blood. Lie quiet. Be still.

JESS: She was sleeping on my shoulder looking oh looking yes . . . like the snow on the cherry blossoms. Then she talked through the medicine you gave her.

ULRIC: No medicine I gave her would make her talk that way. What she said came from her own heart.

JESS: That's the worst thing you could say! (*rises up and* DR. ULRIC *pushes him down again*) Worse than the worst! She loves somebody else.

ULRIC: But who could she love, after all. Only you, Jess.

JESS: Judd Farnham. She pronounced his name.

ULRIC: Why, Judd is a child.

JESS: Her words. You both lie!

ULRIC: I've never seen you riled like this. Who has put this nonsense into your head, Jess. Ruthanna loves only you.

JESS: Lies! Lies. I have known for some time she loved another. Then when she had taken your pills the truth came out. (*He talks more and more sleepily, his eyes close, he moves somewhat spasmodically, and then is quiet.*)

ULRIC: I wish I knew more than I know. That's Jess lying there of course but it's a Jess I never knew till now. He's in some fearsome struggle with himself. Imagine him saying Ruthanna no longer loves him. Imagine him running wild in the forest all night. He'll be over the cuts and bruises but his fear of losing Ruthanna will take longer to mend. (*suddenly* JESS *cries out in his sleep and interrupts* DR. ULRIC) Oh Jess, if you could only listen to me. Why can't you beautiful young people be satisfied just in being young. Why can't you rejoice only in your youth and good looks and perfect health. Why do you have to afflict one another. Why isn't your youth enough? I'm afraid Jess you'd be the last man on earth to know the answer to my questions. Ah, well. But just think, not to be satisfied with youth! (*suddenly,* JESS *rises up in a start and cries* NO!*) Jess, lie down, you must remain quiet!

JESS: No, no. . . . You can't tell me he is a child. (*rises up and then puts his feet on the floor and stares at the* DOCTOR) I know he is more than a boy. (*rises and then almost falls down*)

ULRIC: Jess, you must lie down and remain quiet. You must remain here tonight.

JESS: No, no. Don't hold me, let me alone. (*begins to go toward the door*)

ULRIC: But, Jess, where are you going in this condition?

JESS: What condition! The condition of a man who has been robbed. And you say by a child. No, no, by a man. And I'm going to his house. Or his grandpa's house for the child who has robbed me lives with his grandpa. I will have it out with him. (*moves dizzily and acts as if to fall, the* DOCTOR *goes over to him and tries to steady him*) No, keep your hands off me. You're in league with them. Giving me a hype. Trying to make me forget. I will go to his house, his grandpa's house and have it out with him. Just you wait and see. (*rushes out*)

(*lights down*)

Scene 7

Lights up, a small bedroom in JUDD's *grandfather's house.* JUDD *has on only a thin pair of pajamas.*

JESS: (*speaking to* JUDD *who is lying asleep in bed*) Judd, wake up, Judd, it's me. Do you hear? Jess here. You once said I was closer than your own dad to you, didn't you. All right then see how close I can be, do you hear.

JUDD: (*yawning*) Jess, what are you doing here? Jess! What is this?

JESS: I've come to ask you something.

JUDD: Then be quiet. I don't want Grandpa to hear. Quiet, hear? (*frightened*) But, Jess, you've been hurt! Jess, you're bleeding. There's blood coming through your shirt.

JESS: (*hardly aware of what* JUDD *has said*) So you are the one has stole my girl.

JUDD: Stole who?

JESS: Don't act dumb. (*He strikes him hard.*)

JUDD: (*hurt*) Why, Jess. That hurt.

JESS: (*sitting down, and then looking at the blood coming from his shirt*) What, so it's true, I am . . . cut. Cut up. To the quick! I knew that before I seen the blood though.

JUDD: Have you been drinking?

JESS: Old Doc Ulric gave me a hypo.

JUDD: A hype for what?

JESS: I've had some bad news. . . . Ruthanna don't love me, that's what.

JUDD: She worships you, that's what. Look here, Jess, you've got to get that shirt off, and I will get a basin and some water and washcloths. Here, let me help you out of all that bloodstained stuff. Here!

JESS: Don't touch me. You are the cause. I'll take my own shirt off. Then you can compare my chest with yours!

(JUDD *rushes off to the back of the room to get the basin and the water and cloths.*)

JESS: (*He has removed his shirt and glares at* JUDD, *who begins to bathe and then wipe him dry—all done with a kind of awe and reverence which begins to quiet* JESS.) No, I'm beginning to see. You can't be the one. You can't have cheated and betrayed me.

JUDD: (*still drying and wiping off any stray bloodstains*) You know I am your friend. Remember when we used to go swimming at the Stone Quarry. You taught me to swim, Jess. You said then I was like your own boy. I would never harm or betray you. And here is a secret, like Ruthanna, Jess, I sort of worship you too.

JESS: (*strangely mollified*) I like to hear that. Say it again, Judd.

JUDD: I sort of, well, it makes me blush to say so, but I worship you too. You're my idol in a way, not having father nor mother. You're my . . .

JESS: (*puts his hand over* JUDD's *mouth*) Enough! Enough. I must be crazy. I must be . . . Judd, take off your shirt, why don't you.

JUDD: But why, Jess? I mean—

JESS: Just do as I say.

JUDD: But you've seen my chest before, what are you looking for. You used to see my mother naked in the Stone Quarry a few seasons past. But if you say so—

JESS: I do say so. Here let me help you. (*he takes off* JUDD's *top paja-mas*) Take off your pajama trousers too.

JUDD: Jess, I'm shamed to.

JESS: You said I was like your dad, cause you don't have none, so . . . (JESS *removes* JUDD's *trousers*) I could see you better if you walked around.

JUDD: In my birthday clothes? Well, Jess, if you say so, I will. I'd do anything for you. (JUDD *moves around the room acting foolish in his nudity, giggling and finally laughing*) Got an eyeful, have you?

JESS: (*goes over to* JUDD *and bear hugs him*) I think it was all a bad dream, Judd. That you would steal Ruthanna. I can see you're after all yes, hardly more than a child. Put your clothes on again. I must be crazy. (*half laughing*) And your chest is as white as a young girl's.

JUDD: (*anxious*) You're my friend then, Jess?

(JESS *nods drunkenly.*)

JUDD: I would never want to lose you. You're my idol, Jess. You're my family. I always looked up to you.

JESS: Stop it, god damn you. (*He grasps him almost painfully with both his hands, then in some kind of blind fury.*) I don't want you to love me.

JUDD: (*frightened*) Love you? But you're like my father.

JESS: Your father be damned. You be damned! Somebody has stolen Ruthanna. That's all I know.

JUDD: But aren't you betrothed. Aren't you as good as married. How can anybody steal her then. She worships you too.

JESS: Ah, that again. Then I'd best be going.

JUDD: You can stay the night, Jess, until you feel better.

JESS: I don't need to feel better.

JUDD: Don't leave mad. Please.

JESS: All right. I'll hug you goodnight, then, and pleasant dreams. (*He takes* JUDD *in his arms.*)

JUDD: You're my family, Jess. I couldn't hurt you.

JESS: (*goes out toward the door, mutters jocularly*) Yes, you with your clean pure body. (*then suddenly brooding as if to himself*) But who stole Ruthanna then. Who stole her from me!

(*lights down*)

Scene 8

Lights up, RUTHANNA *and* JUDD *are in the front parlor of* RUTHANNA'*s house.*

RUTHANNA: I knew he would get to you! I knew it from the start. God knows what you told him!

JUDD: Ruthanna. Please. (*He tries to take her hand.*)

RUTHANNA: Don't you dare to touch me. Don't you ever touch me again. You've ruined me. Do you hear, ruined me. Oh I could throw myself in the river. I haven't slept a night since it happened. (*furious*) Well, what did he tell you, what did he get out of you is more like it. Don't stand there like a slobbering idiot.

JUDD: How you've changed, how you've changed.

RUTHANNA: How you've changed me! And people call you a child. A devil is more like it. You've made me throw my life away. There's nothing ahead . . . but grief. Grief!

JUDD: Oh calm down, calm down. He let me go didn't he?

RUTHANNA: (*almost with maniacal insight*) Yes, this time he let you go.

JUDD: What do you mean by that?

RUTHANNA: Do you think you fooled him with your child-boy face. And do you think I will be able to hide the truth from him. Never, never. Oh, you don't know Jess.

JUDD: He was my closest friend.

RUTHANNA: You can say that and not have the heavens fall on you?

JUDD: But what we did was so simple and peaceful, Ruthanna, so natural.

RUTHANNA: Only a man could say that. Or a man-child. You know nothing about anything. You took me! You took me. (*sobs*) You took all I had for *him*. You took . . . his jewel.

JUDD: I don't follow you.

RUTHANNA: Don't, then.

JUDD: Where is your mother?

RUTHANNA: Where she always is. Traveling. Earning a living as a traveling saleswoman. Always away. And my dad dead before I knew him. Nobody to protect me, to make me feel close, and guided.

JUDD: See, Ruthanna, nobody need know. How can anybody know. But if you go on carrying on like this everybody will know. The whole town will hear of it. We must be quiet, silent, never opening our mouths. I tell you he does not suspect me.

RUTHANNA: But you said he put you through a third degree, didn't you. That he grilled you with questions.

JUDD: And I stood the test. (*comes over and tries to touch her*)

RUTHANNA: Stay where you are. Keep your distance. You are as full of guile as the Serpent himself. Oh, God, God.

JUDD: Then I'd best be going. How cold you are. How different from the girl I loved.

RUTHANNA: You never loved me. Never. You stole Jess' jewel. You are a common sneak thief.

JUDD: You are breaking my heart now.

RUTHANNA: Since you've come this far with your storytelling, what then did he get out of you?

JUDD: We talked about the times when he was my teacher, and like my dad.

RUTHANNA: Leading up to what!

JUDD: Ruthanna, calm down, please. I'm trying to lay your fears to rest.

RUTHANNA: Then kill me and be done with it. Let me tell you something. We have been betrothed from the beginning, Jess and me.

JUDD: How many times must I hear that!

RUTHANNA: As many times as it will take to blot out what you did to me.

JUDD: And you didn't want it? Why, you took *me* if the truth be known. You swallowed me up in your burning caresses. Don't stand there like some plaster saint that ice runs in your veins. And why if he loved you so didn't he take you in the first place.

RUTHANNA: You have killed everything. Killed me.

(*JUDD starts to go.*)

RUTHANNA: All right, go on, go ahead with your story. Tell me what he said.

JUDD: Then quit screaming and interrupting. I'm trying to give you hope. (*quiet, musing as if alone*) He was comforting and kind.

RUTHANNA: Yes, waiting to trap you into confession. I know him. Let me tell you something. He can read our minds. He has some sense of delving into all we think and are. He will never stop until he knows everything.

JUDD: (*still musing*) He comforted me like a father. He even kissed me. He was all cut up and bleeding you know.

RUTHANNA: (*contemptuous*) So you said. So you said.

JUDD: I had him take off his shirt because it was all bloodstains.

RUTHANNA: I was all bloodstains too after you got through with me also!

JUDD: (*still as if far away*) I began to feel so at ease with him. I knew I loved him like my own dad had he not been killed. He put on the shirt my dad wore. And then, (*JUDD speaks as if praying in church all alone*) he asked me if I would mind taking off my clothes. I want to find out something, he said. I didn't think anything . . .

RUTHANNA: Stop, stop . . . (*sobs*) No, go on. Don't spare me. Why should you spare me when you've ruined me. Go on. Speak! Get it all out!

JUDD: (*acting as if he had not heard her wild speech*) At first I said I was shamed to. But after all when he gave me my swimming lessons in the Stone Quarry, I had nothing on either. But I was younger then. Now I was growing up. So I stood there in my birthday clothes for him. Walk around the room a little, Judd, he said to me. I see you're hardly more than a child. Yes, you have a beautiful fair chest, he said.

RUTHANNA: He said that to you? Or are you lying to me?

JUDD: That is what he said. Your chest is as white as a young girl's.

RUTHANNA: Oh Christ in heaven, I cannot believe it. Then he knows everything already!

JUDD: No, no, Ruthanna. Be calm. Be quiet. He loves both of us. He is our friend.

RUTHANNA: You have not eased my pain. You have not quieted my worry. You have not taken away my sorrow . . . so go, and when you're gone don't come back.

JUDD: Ruthanna, I love you and I think you love me too. That is why you are so angry. You love me, not him.

RUTHANNA: You lie like the little fiend you are. I belong to him. I am his! From the beginning.

JUDD: You belong to him but you love me.

(*RUTHANNA strikes him.*)

JUDD: I take pleasure in feeling your flesh against mine.

RUTHANNA: (*strikes him harder*) Get out. And don't ever let me see you here again, do you hear. Out that door and forever.

JUDD: Hit me all you like. Kill me if you like, but you know I know the truth, and your heart knows it also. So goodbye then. (*goes*)

RUTHANNA: I have no heart. The dogs have eaten it. I have thrown away the jewel that belonged to him, my bridegroom. I have thrown it away for nothing, and can never retrieve it.

(*lights down*)

ACT II

Scene 1

DR. ULRIC, *a bit tired from his speaking with* JACK PALMER *has dozed off in his easy chair.* TED SCANLON *watches the* DOCTOR *a bit concernedly, then places his fingers to his lips and whispers.*

TED: Shhh! He often dozes off like this.

JACK: I had no idea the story of Ruthanna Elder was of such crucial meaning to Doc. It seemed to give him back something of his own youth.

TED: I am very happy, even relieved you've come by. You've restored something in Doc. Do you understand. Don't worry.

ULRIC: (*coming to with a start*) Can you beat that? I must have dropped off. Excuse me, Jack, and Ted! But let me explain to Jack here, for Ted has heard me talk about my dreams for too many years and too many times, I suspect. Jack, it was as if Ruthanna herself had entered this room. I thought I was speaking to her as I so often did—in private, in the consulting room. (*He hesitates then speaks emphatically, almost as if testifying in court to something which may prove incredible.*) I said to her, don't let your crown fall, Ruthanna! For she was wearing her prom queen crown and long shimmering dress. You took my breath away, Ruthanna, I went on, when I saw you in the procession today! It was all—yes, *beyond* anything beautiful. Ruthanna, I told her, you should not harbor anything but happy thoughts. Youth *is* happy thoughts, and it don't come again! . . . But, Jack, and Ted, I can't explain it, but I can't get over the sight of her crown. When I opened my eyes just now

I expected to see if not Ruthanna, at least her crown placed some-where in the room—waiting for her! And yet her real crown, what was it, only gold foil! Paper!

TED: (*a bit embarrassed by the* DOCTOR's *speech in front of a stranger*) Well, the store kept, Doc, while you were dozing. And while you sneezed, Jack and I have got acquainted in the meantime. . . . He's a fine chap. (*looking at* JACK *contentedly*) We're lucky, if you ask me, he dropped by. (TED *slaps* JACK *good-heartedly on his shoulder.*)

ULRIC: (*to* JACK) I knew Jack was the fine sort the minute he stepped foot in the house. Maybe life is after all, Jack, just what we remem-ber in our dreams. When you came in today I felt I had known you from the very beginning. . . . But I have a confession for both of you. Much as I stand in awe of dreams I don't very often remember mine. But today I did, and it must be thanks to you, Jack. No, no, I mean it. It's thanks to our young visitor, Ted. Shall I tell you the whole dream? I'm not sure the Historical Society will buy it! But Jack Palmer, listen. I saw the whole thing as if it was happening now before my eyes. The day Ruthanna was crowned prom queen. She rode in some old-fashioned glittering open carriage, the horses lifting and lowering their sweaty necks as if they understood the whole pageant better than the onlookers. Ruthanna would from time to time throw out stems of yellow, red, and white roses to her friends and admirers. But again it was her crown that caught my eye. It seemed so perfectly right for her to have on. I saw in my dream what I saw when it happened so long ago, but more vividly in dreaming: that she *was* our queen. She was the only queen this small town ever had or will have. And to think then, Jack, she went on being queen so long after what happened did happen. Sitting before the pillars of her house unchanged, unchanging. As I say, some people called her the Sleepy-Time Gal. But no, the word (*almost inaudibly*) is *queen.*

TED: (*worried*) Doc, you mustn't get too excited now. . . . Remember . . .

ULRIC: Oh, Ted! I know what Ted is thinking, Jack. He is so afraid I will overdo! He's afraid I am going to die on him, Jack. . . . But Ted, listen, we all are going to . . .

TED: (*defensive, almost indignant*) No, no Doc, I was thinking no such thing. (*to* JACK) See how he puts words in my mouth!

ULRIC: (*hardly having heard what* TED *has said*) You know, Ted, when you get to be my age—and I have to remind myself how much younger you are than me, though even you, my boy, are no longer so young. But I still see you, Ted, as on the day you came here to be my friend and attendant. I see you young as I see Ruthanna still our queen. Ted, Jack, listen. Will you both let me go on with my story. Look, how Jack Palmer is getting out his pencil and pad!

TED: All right, Doc, all right. You win. (*turning to* JACK) Doctor always wins. Always. All right now, go on with the story, Doc, but I fear maybe it upsets you.

ULRIC: Well, but if it upsets me it also gives me all, and everything I require. And I mean *all*. (*He looks intently at* JACK PALMER.)

(*lights down*)

Scene 2

Lights up on the DOCTOR's *consulting room so many years past. Enter* RUTHANNA. *The* DOCTOR *gets up.*

ULRIC: I won't soon forget the vision of you, Ruthanna, as you rode with your crown on during the ceremony. . . . I couldn't believe I even knew you, you looked as the song says like you had come down from the stars. Did you know you threw some roses in my direction.

RUTHANNA: Oh, did I, Doctor?

ULRIC: What is it? (*She throws herself into the* DOCTOR's *arms*) You should be happy, my dear. You should not be weeping unless it is for joy.

RUTHANNA: Joy is the farthest thing in the world now from me.

ULRIC: Ruthanna, you should always wear your crown.

RUTHANNA: Please, please, no. Let's forget crowns and processions and dances.

ULRIC: I think I know, Ruthanna, what troubles you.

RUTHANNA: I believe you do. All I want to know is—

ULRIC: Go ahead, don't be afraid to ask anything or tell me anything. You may give me your complete trust.

RUTHANNA: Trust, yes. If there only were such trust with others.

ULRIC: Go on! I'm listenin' up Ruthanna.

RUTHANNA: May be going to happen could never happen. I would be queen then for real. Forever. When I put on the crown yesterday, somebody should have snatched it off of me. Crown such a person as me, no, no.

ULRIC: Then who is he, (*said with a kind of outrage*) this other?

RUTHANNA: I see you are judging me after all.

ULRIC: I am the last man on earth to judge you.

RUTHANNA: I wonder. Yes, I wonder. Then listen, Doctor, and take my hand. Forgive my snapping at you. Forgive everything. I have nobody else to go to. My mother is a hard cold ambitious woman. She thinks only of . . . Who knows . . . accumulation of funds, bank ledgers, mortgages. . . . She never thinks of me at any rate. She's as remote as the stars. I despise her.

ULRIC: Ruthanna.

RUTHANNA: Go ahead, chide me, lecture me, turn me out. Do you know what I feel like doing with my crown? . . . I wanted to throw it in the river. I will not be queen.

(*ULRIC bows his head.*)

RUTHANNA: Then here it is! It was not Jess who took me, who made me give myself up. It was Judd.

ULRIC: Judd Farnham?

RUTHANNA: Oh I know, I know what is coming. You are going to tell me he is a child. Well, he was a child, let us say. A child Cupid who possesses after all what any man would be satisfied to have. He came to me when, oh who knows how or what I was that day.

He came to me. He came as Cupid. He was Cupid. A dozen, no a hundred arrows he loosed on me. I could no more resist him that drowsy afternoon than I could have bathed in the river and kept dry. He carried me away with him as if he had come down for me in an air-borne chariot. . . . Don't ask me to explain it, I can't explain it to myself.

ULRIC: But you are not going to have a baby. You are not pregnant! You will be all right for Jess. He need never know!

RUTHANNA: What are you saying? How can I be, how can I look him in the eyes. All right for Jess! He lives for what his church believes. For what he thinks Christ holds him to.

ULRIC: My advice, at any rate, is you keep your secret. If it seems wrong to do so still it is my advice. You can marry Jess. He need never know. And you will be happy.

RUTHANNA: Happy!

ULRIC: Go to the dance tonight, dance with your real betrothed. Forget this episode with a young boy who does not know night from day.

RUTHANNA: No, no, it's me doesn't know night from day. And then (as if in a trance) I love Judd, too. I don't know what kind of a love it is, but there it is, in my heart. My lost heart.

ULRIC: Then tell Jess now. Tell him you cannot marry him.

RUTHANNA: Do you know what that will do to him? Do you? Oh you men of medicine! Don't you know no one can test the heart. Oh, God in heaven. Listen, please, give me some medicine. But not the kind you gave me before which makes the tongue speak what the heart knows. Give me something that will seal up all that is inside me, and make me light as eiderdown and quiet as the sleeping dead. Then I will be grateful to you forever. Will you Doctor?

(ULRIC *nods again and again and takes* RUTHANNA *in his arms.*)

RUTHANNA: Something to quiet the throbbing and seal the lips from speaking.

(*lights down*)

Scene 3

JESS *and* RUTHANNA *are in the garden behind the dance hall.* RUTH-ANNA *wears her prom queen crown. The sound of the prom music can be heard as well as the occasional sound of exploding fireworks.* RUTH-ANNA *holds on to* JESS *as if she might fall if he did not let her grasp him tightly.*

JESS: What is it, dearest, you're trembling so?

RUTHANNA: The excitement. Everything seems to be coming upon us too close. And then all that noise from the fireworks!

JESS: You're not wearing your ring!

RUTHANNA: I am so afraid I will lose it, Jess. It's so very precious to you, coming from so far back in your family.

JESS: And precious also to you I hope.

RUTHANNA: To me, to me of course, dearest Jess.

JESS: Shall we dance just as if we were all alone in the dance hall? It seems so long since I held you to me. Oh Ruthanna, how can we wait until our wedding. Why can I not hold you to me the livelong night! I love you so deeply.

RUTHANNA: Dearest Jess. (*They begin to dance, indeed as if they were back inside the dance hall.*)

JESS: I sometimes wonder, Ruthanna, if you love me as much as I love you. I wonder and wonder at night when I cannot sleep.

RUTHANNA: You should never wonder about such a thing, Jess. We've been betrothed after all since childhood.

JESS: Maybe that is what is wrong.

RUTHANNA: (*frightened*) But what is wrong, my dearest? What?

JESS: I can't say. No, of course, nothing is wrong.

RUTHANNA: Hold me tighter, don't let go of me, Jess.

JESS: I feel sometimes, Ruthanna, you only love me because we are betrothed. That you take me for granted as if we were already long married. Yes, that's it, long taken for granted. And that you take me for granted whilst I long for you day and night and all the while as if I saw you for the first time. I long for your love.

RUTHANNA: But Jess, I love only you.

JESS: But my love seems the stronger. (*begins to break down*) Oh Ruthanna, let's stay here for a while. The moon's coming up.

RUTHANNA: But won't it look odd if we don't get back when it's in our honor.

JESS: In your honor, dear heart. Everything, Ruthanna, is yours. I feel lately I am nothing. It's because my love for you has made me weak, as if I had lost all the blood in my body wanting you so. Why do we have to wait! (*He bends down slowly and kisses the hem of her dress.*)

RUTHANNA: Come, we'll take our seat here. We'll watch the moon come up, and maybe we'll both feel better. (*They sit down—the faint appearance of the moon through dark scudding clouds in the background.*)

JESS: Yes, this is better. My forehead is so hot and wet with cold drops of perspiration.

RUTHANNA: (*almost to herself*) It was so fearfully close inside.

JESS: No, it's close here. (*He motions to his heart.*)

RUTHANNA: I am concerned about you, dear Jess.

JESS: Ruthanna, you do not love me. No, don't interrupt. You don't love me as I love you. You love me as your betrothed, as your dutiful betrothed. As your husband to be, as the promised one. Duty! Obedience! Respect! Admiration! But not love. Whilst I love you body and soul, heart and mind I am aching for you, Ruthanna. Oh why do we have to wait, when my veins are on fire for you. You ask why my forehead is hot! Well, the sweat pours down from my scalp, and an icy flow of seeping liquid comes from my armpits day and night. It is because I am sick for you, Ruthanna, sick for your lips and your breast, for all of you. Whilst I know you do not long for me the way I do. That is what has broken my own heart in two.

RUTHANNA: Oh, then Jess, I am ready and willing to give myself to you body and soul. You will see then how much I love you.

JESS: Oh, if it could only be. But I know you. I know the people of this town. It would spoil our betrothal, I know I know. Yes, we must wait and I must die from waiting. You should not have said what you just said, Ruthanna. It is not like you. About willing to . . . give yourself now!

RUTHANNA: (*angered*) But Jess, you brought it out of me. Saying how much you needed me . . . now. That to wait makes you suffer, makes you tormented and on a bed of hot coals.

JESS: Did I say that? . . . Ruthanna I have had a terrible dream again and again . . . and I see the dream even when awake!

RUTHANNA: Do you want to tell me?

JESS: No. No, it would disturb you too.

RUTHANNA: But maybe it would calm you, my dear. Make you feel less . . . miserable.

JESS: Oh, do I look that too. Ruthanna, I dream you love somebody else. I see him in my dreams, this other, only he is so young. He looks like he still had the fuzz on his upper lip and yet in the dream you love him more than me!

RUTHANNA: (*standing up*) What are you accusing me of?

JESS: (*shocked, almost horrified*) Ruthanna, Ruthanna!

RUTHANNA: Yes, Ruthanna. What are you trying to do to me. Do you realize how you are tormenting me. First you tell me you cannot stand not being with me before we are joined together as man and wife. Then you tell me how you suffer and that I do not love you as much as you love me. Then you accuse me of loving somebody else.

JESS: (*terrified*) Ruthanna!

RUTHANNA: Accusing me of loving Judd. That's what you mean. That I love him and not you.

JESS: (*suddenly beginning to understand his dreams, and his fate*) And do you?

RUTHANNA: My God, you should see your face when you say that. Jess, I am afraid, afraid when you are like this!

JESS: But answer my question. Is the boy in the dream Judd?

RUTHANNA: I do not know your dreams, Jess. I am not the dreamer.

JESS: No, perhaps you don't need to dream if in actuality, he —

RUTHANNA: Be careful, watch your tongue.

JESS: And do you love little Judd?

RUTHANNA: Of course I love him.

JESS: Be careful, Ruthanna. (*He suddenly seizes her throat.*)

RUTHANNA: Take your hand away from me. (*She strikes him.*)

JESS: Ruthanna!

RUTHANNA: Do you realize how strong your fingers were against my throat. (*She begins to cough and weep.*)

JESS: Oh, Ruthanna, forgive me.

RUTHANNA: You are abusing me.

JESS: How could I abuse you?

RUTHANNA: You were almost choking me. Accusing me of loving little Judd. A mere child.

JESS: (*dreamily*) A young man, yes, already at manhood's threshold.

RUTHANNA: What do you mean by that?

JESS: Perhaps you should know.

RUTHANNA: Know what? What are you accusing me of. . . . You are a terrible man.

JESS: Yes, my love is terrible because it is all-consuming. Whilst your love for me is only partial, like that waning moon out there. Your love for me, never too strong, is waning.

RUTHANNA: Lies, lies, I love only you.

JESS: I don't believe you. You love another. My dream is true.

RUTHANNA: But what other could I love when I see only you.

JESS: You see Judd, don't you.

RUTHANNA: As a child, in the presence of my mother. What are you accusing me of? Jess, I will not stay here to be treated like this. (*She takes off her crown.*)

JESS: Put back your crown. Do you hear me.

RUTHANNA: Jess, (*sobbing she puts back her crown*) you have made me afraid, and you have humiliated me.

JESS: Perhaps you should be afraid. If you do not love me wholeheartedly, perhaps you should fear, for you have broken my heart. The waiting, the constant longing for you, the terrible postponement. While I have wanted you for years and more years. And my dreams seem to me true, so true.

(*Suddenly there is the sound and the sight of fireworks. A band strikes up.*)

RUTHANNA: We must return and let our friends from the school and the town see us. . . . Jess, come to your senses. Dearest!

JESS: I am not your dearest. I can read your eyes and lips. I can read your heart.

RUTHANNA: I have told you with my whole heart I love only you.

JESS: Then why cannot I believe you.

VOICES: (*crying out*) Jess and Ruthanna, please come forward! Jess, Ruthanna.

RUTHANNA: Let me tell you then, Jess, for the last time, I am yours. (*She kneels.*) We are betrothed. We are like one. The day will come when you will have all of me, heart body soul. Until then, believe me!

JESS: (*moodily*) Here, let me straighten your crown.

RUTHANNA: Tell me you believe me, dearest Jess. Tell me you know I am true.

JESS: (*strangely*) Your crown is straight now. We can go out and meet everyone. Come, Ruthanna, get up.

RUTHANNA: Oh my God, Jess, my God in heaven. (*rises and they go out together arm in arm*)

(*lights down*)

Scene 4

Lights up on JUDD's *bedroom. It is past midnight.* JUDD *cannot sleep and tosses about wildly in the bedclothes. He hears a noise like footsteps, but outside one also hears the tree toads and the nightjars calling, and he is not sure somebody has entered.*

JUDD: Who is it? Is there somebody standing there? Please! (*He falls back when there is no response and tries to sleep, mumbling in his half-slumber*) I wish I could sleep like I used to.

JESS: (*coming out of the shadows and into the room, and standing at the edge of* JUDD's *bed*) Judd.

JUDD: Yes, who is it? It's not Dad, is it?

JESS: No, Judd, you must be still asleep. Your dad has been gone a long time. (*He sits down on the bed.*)

JUDD: All at once when I hear you talking to me I feel as if my dad were back and helping me go to sleep like he used to. . . . Jess! How long have you been here? Oh, Jess! (*said with strong feeling*)

JESS: Lie back and get comfortable. I won't stay long. I know I shouldn't have sneaked in again like this. But you see I couldn't sleep either. I felt like talking to somebody.

JUDD: Why couldn't you sleep, Jess?

JESS: Oh, I don't know. . . . The excitement of the prom dance and the ball and Ruthanna's being queen, and then . . . the thing that's ahead for us? Our wedding.

JUDD: (*strangely mournful in tone*) Oh, yes the wedding.

JESS: I have . . . things that worry me. . . . And why can't you sleep, Judd? (*He touches his hair and lets his hand rest on the boy's pajama tops.*)

JUDD: My dad used to touch me that way, just as you are touching me now when I couldn't sleep.

JESS: Yes? And how did he get you to sleep then?

JUDD: Let me see. So long ago. Yes, I told him what bothered me I guess. How I missed Mama. And how I wished he stayed home more often. You know he was a dam inspector and was gone . . . well all the time. Like now he's gone forever. . . . That's why your visit cheers me.

JESS: But why can't you sleep now, Judd. Come on, put your head in my arms, I'll hold you. (*embraces* JUDD *in his arms*) There, does that feel better?

JUDD: It does. I think I could go to sleep in your arms.

JESS: (*looking at* JUDD's *chest which has come out from his pajama tops*) You are a handsome young man. You are coming into your first youth, do you know that?

JUDD: My worries seem gone now.

JESS: Judd, when you are worried you can tell me what those worries are, understand? Look here, I will be your father now. I will stand in for him if you want me to. And you can tell me anything, like an older brother. I love you too, Judd. I have always cared. (*He hugs him.*) But I am . . . for you. I don't know what it is. Very stricken these days.

JUDD: (*alarmed*) Stricken? What on earth is that?

JESS: Hurt, deeply hurt, wounded even. I have been . . . torn apart by sorrow lately.

JUDD: And who has done it, Jess?

JESS: Who? Oh, myself I guess. I have hurt myself. . . . But the fact is I love her *too* dearly! Ruthanna! I have always loved her too dearly.

And I don't think she loves me as much in return. She loves some-body else.

JUDD: But she has always told me she loves only you.

JESS: (*taking the bait*) But how would she tell *you* that?

JUDD: Oh, all the time. She always tells me there is only you in her heart.

JESS: Ah, if that was only true.

JUDD: But why isn't it true if she says it.

JESS: (*impassioned*) Because there is somebody else! Somebody has come between us just as the time is growing near for our marriage. Another love has come between us.

JUDD: (*breaking loose from* JESS's *embrace*) But who on earth would come between you?

JESS: Look at you, Judd. God what a handsome boy you are. I can see how . . . a girl would be smitten with you.

JUDD: But I don't know no girl, Jess. Nobody's smitten . . . on me!

JESS: Judd, Ruthanna loves you. Don't say anything. Let me speak my piece. That is my worry. That is why I don't sleep. And that is why you don't neither. We are both sleepless because she loves you more than me and you are fearful of her love and fearful of me. Tell me if that is not true. (*He suddenly kisses* JUDD *on the mouth.*)

JUDD: (*dreamy*) You kiss me just like my dad used to do when he put me to sleep.

JESS: Well, since I have kissed you just like your dad, let me tell you also whatever you say to me I won't hold against you. (*He kisses him again, and* JUDD *kisses him in return.*) It's your good looks have driven her to love you. My chest is not so handsome or white. My chest is that of a soldier or wrestler, whilst you, Judd, look like a young angel. That's it. It's your angel good looks has driven her over the edge.

JUDD: Hold me again when you tell me these things.

JESS: I'll hold you all you like. And you'll tell me then what transpired.

JUDD: If you swear you love me, Jess, and won't harm me, if you'll swear on the Good Book you won't hurt me I will tell you then why I can't sleep.

JESS: Where is the Good Book? I'll swear on anything. I'll swear by my own heart, which is clove in two. (*He takes* JUDD's *hand and holds it.*)

JUDD: Oh, what a weight has been taken off my chest, Jess. I feel I can go on living now. . . . You see, I thought for a while I would die after what happened. I have . . . been in such pain and turmoil.

JESS: Then speak out to me as if your dad was here now listening, your dad who loves you and will never harm you. Speak your heart out, dear Judd.

JUDD: I think the truth is, Jess, I loved you more than I love Ruthanna. For I have missed my own dad so pitifully. So hopelessly did I grieve when he went away.

JESS: Just consider then he is back with you and is listening to what troubles you.

JUDD: It happened you see when I tore my shirt. I had fallen in the hedge, and Ruthanna saw that I could not go about in a shirt torn to ribbons.

JESS: Right.

JUDD: (*troubled*) You are not angry, Jess. You look so strange.

JESS: How could I be angry with a young man who looks like an angel. (*he presses himself to* JUDD) Tell me what occurred.

JUDD: And then I asked her. . . . No, first she touched my chest.

JESS: Ah, yes.

JUDD: And I said for her to touch me again. And then, I said she should listen to my beating heart.

JESS: But why, Judd? (*He touches his lips as if he was touching* RUTH-ANNA's *lips.*)

JUDD: Because (*as if in slumber*) I said my heart was beating for her.

JESS: And was it beating . . . for her.

JUDD: Jess, at that moment, yes, it beat for her.

JESS: And who is your heart beating for now, Judd? For I can hear it beating in the stillness of the dark here.

JUDD: I think . . . it beats for you and me now.

JESS: What does that mean?

JUDD: Jess, your face . . . You look like . . . white anger has stole over your whole face and body.

JESS: Your heart then beats for love for her.

JUDD: And then I said, Ruthanna it's not fair I let you see my chest and you are permitted to hear my heart beat, and I cannot do the same for you.

JESS: (*cries out*) Christ in Heaven. . . . No, no, continue. Pay me no mind. Tell me all, everything.

JUDD: (*taking* JESS's *hand which at first* JESS *pulls away from him, and then limply lets* JUDD *hold his hand*) And then she removed her blouse and let me hear her own beating heart.

JESS: And did it beat fast like a trip-hammer? And did it beat for you?

JUDD: It beat like a racing horse I thought.

JESS: (*almost hysterical*) For you?

JUDD: I don't know.

JESS: You don't know? How can you not know?

JUDD: I think her heart just beat for love. Probably in memory of her love for you. I think love made her heart beat, and it did not exactly beat for me.

JESS: But who else was there to make her heart beat like a race horse running? Who but you, don't you see. She loved you!

JUDD: I don't know what happened to make it all carry us away like on wings of some kind, we soared away like white doves with one another. Our hearts beat together there with our bare chests uncovered, and all by chance, the chance of me having fallen in the hedge and the thorns had torn my new shirt.

JESS: But then, you were not content were you merely to listen to your hearts beating. Love must have carried you further than *that* that day, Judd? . . . Remember, I am your dad now, and I love you. (*He embraces him.*) So no matter how it pains one of us or both of us—we must hear it all, mustn't we, handsome young Judd.

JUDD: (*nearly prostrate*) I suppose. I suppose. I need a drink of water. It rests over there, the glass and pitcher.

JESS: (*leaps up and gets glass and pours water from pitcher and brings it to* JUDD *who drinks some of it*) Let me drink after you now. From the same cup. (*he drinks deliriously*)

JUDD: (*as if in delirium*) And then, then . . . Our bodies freed from our clothes and our hearts beating like in unison, yes, that was it, our bodies slipped into one another like we were in the river together and the river washed into the both of us, the river . . .

JESS: No, no! Jesus! I think I will pass out. (*He falls back on the bed on his back, gasping.*)

JUDD: (*hardly aware of the state his story has produced in* JESS) And that is all that happened. . . . But I know one thing. Jess, Jess, what is it? Jess, why are your eyes closed?

JESS: Judd, you should kill me now, or I should kill myself.

JUDD: Listen, dear Jess, you have nothing to worry about.

JESS: That is so, Judd, because I am dead. You have killed me. I am no longer a man even. Your story of hearts and white chests and river water blending your bodies together have dealt me my death.

JUDD: Hear me out, there is more!

JESS: More? I can't take more. Judd, if you have a knife cut my throat. Don't spare me. Let me die . . . now. I want death now.

JUDD: If you would listen, after we had . . .

JESS: Yes, after the water of the river had passed over and through you both.

JUDD: She loves only you. She loves you and you alone. Ruthanna loves your manhood and your soul. She does not love me, Jess. Cross my heart, only you!

JESS: I haven't heard a word. Because I am dead. I died when you obeyed me and told. (*He gets up.*) Where did I come in? (*He looks for the door.*)

JUDD: Jess, you must listen to me. She loves only you.

JESS: Judd, hear me now. I will come back when I have rested, are you listening? I will come back about daybreak to say something to you. When I am made myself again. Hear? When I'm made myself.

JUDD: (*leaps out of bed and throws himself at* JESS's *feet, embracing him*) Jess, I love you so dearly. Don't leave me now I have confessed to my sorrow. Don't go away like my dad did. Don't you see what you have done to me?

JESS: I done to you, you crazy boy. I to you? (*He pushes* JUDD *away.*)

JUDD: I love only you, Jess. You are my all, my family, my only hope. Stay the night with me for I will never sleep now. I will never sleep again, if you desert me.

JESS: I must prepare for the day, Judd. We will meet again. And I will set everything aright. Do you hear. I will put everything to rights.

JUDD: (*stands up*) Kiss me then before you go, dear Jess. Hold me to you like my dad did, won't you.

JESS: Oh well, Judd. Put on your pajama tops though. (*JUDD rushes to the bed and puts on his pajama tops.*)

JESS: (*hugs and kisses* JUDD *dispassionately but* JUDD *holds him in fierce embrace*) And don't forget, be here about dawn and I will set everything to rights. You hear me? So long then. (*He goes out.*)

JUDD: I hate the sound of the nightjars. They are calling someone said this time of year for their mates. But they don't sound like lovers to me. They sound like souls in pain! Not like birds calling to their mates.

(*lights down*)

Scene 5

JESS's *bedroom. He enters with head hanging down, shuffling as if an imponderable weight was falling upon him, heavier with each step he takes.*

JESS: (*looking at his bed*) I will never sleep tonight. Maybe I will never sleep in that bed again. Even if I lay in it I would only see him, hear him. You see I could not take it all in as he spoke. (*sits down in chair facing audience*) I wonder if he knew what he was telling me, angel face. How I loved him at the same time that he drove the blade again and again through my heart. When he robbed me, (*he puts his face in his hands for a while, then looks up again*) when he took my own life and ended it. My life is ended. Did angel face know that? If he did not know then why should I blame him. No one could know but me what betrothal signifies. My betrothal was me, was all of me, my life in this life and the life to come. . . . Now I have nothing, not even a shred of myself. (*cries*) He does not know he has robbed me of everything. But is that the work of a child? . . . (*He stands up.*)

    Now I remember, it is coming back to me, my own dad's words. For like Judd Farnham I once had a dad too who comforted me, who held me to him and kissed me and put me to sleep, to the softest slumber. But he left me something. (*looks toward a chest of drawers*) He could not only hold me in his arms until I slept but he gave me a gift. A gift to defend myself against enemies. . . . I can hear his voice, *Only to be used in dire necessity.* Well, hasn't it come then, Father? (*said with terrible rage*) Hasn't dire necessity overtaken me! Then where is it? (*rushes toward the chest of drawers and begins frantically going through the drawers, throwing out articles of clothing and handkerchiefs*) Here, here it is, the gift from my father. (*He produces a revolver of the finest and most expensive craftsmanship.*) *When the day comes,* my father said, *But son, may that day never come.* Amen, amen. But the day has come, and it is almost daybreak. And then, why should he live since he has brought my life to nothing. Since he has ended my life, for my life was betrothal, was Ruthanna. Was the promise of her love for this life and the life to come, and who knows perhaps we were angels before this life here below. That is all ended. (*He puts down the revolver on a table.*) I must think it through though. But I cannot live. As I told the angel last night I am a dead man. And shall he live and be her love whilst I am cold in death! No, Judd must follow me into the nothingness he has bestowed on me. Yes, damn him, angel or no angel, child or no child with his beautiful chest and his sweet lips. He must follow me to death. He shall not live and enjoy Ruthanna's love when life has deserted me and left me cold as dead ashes. But then (*He looks at the revolver and then touches it.*) Of course, of course (*spoken with a kind of wild glee, he presses the revolver to his mouth*) I am in death's kingdom already. Do you hear me, Ruthanna. I am already in death's kingdom because the angel has touched you before your bridegroom. Christ alive. (*looks at the gun closely*) Jesus Lord, Christ above . . . And neither of us has fathers! Judd, did you understand that last night, that I too have no father. I have nobody. (*picks up the gun and walks toward the door*) I have nothing, less than nothing.

(*lights down*)

Scene 6

Lights up on JUDD's *breakfast room. He is reading the comic section and eating his cereal. He smiles, almost laughs occasionally. Puts down the paper and spills some of his cereal when he sees* JESS *enter, the revolver bulging in his back pocket.*

JUDD: Jess. (*begins to rise*) I am so happy—

JESS: Keep your seat, Judd. No occasion to stand up. We only just parted, it seems to me. (*looks around*) But see, it's daybreak. I've kept my promise. Did you sleep?

JUDD: I did—at last—thanks to you.

JESS: Judd (*going close to him*) you slept because you do not know what you have taken from me. I could not tell you last night because your words had taken from me all I have or ever had, or ever will have. You took my breath last night.

JUDD: That cannot be true, Jess.

JESS: You see, you understand nothing. You are like the thief in the night, unexpected, and all destroying. You are the destroying angel, Judd. You have killed me. I am speaking to you not as a man but someone passed over in death. The death you gave me. Do you understand?

JUDD: I am trying. But listen, Jess, what I did, I was carried away in doing. I never chose to . . . betray you.

JESS: Betray, yes that is so. But you also have slain me. Don't you see. No man of flesh and blood is talking to you.

JUDD: Jess, your terrible face, do you realize how you look at me. I cannot bear the way you look.

JESS: I cannot bear that you have destroyed my betrothal. You have taken away the structure, the very edifice of my life and existence. I have lived all these years only to be the husband, the spouse of Ruthanna, who was to wait for me until we were joined by Christ in . . . (*almost inaudible*) marriage. Forever and ever. As we were husband and wife before we were born, before there was time itself. Ah, I know this to be true.

JUDD: Oh, Jess, you must forgive me, you must not look at me like you do. Like some terrible avenger in the Bible.

JESS: I am, I am. I am him.

JUDD: You told me you loved me last night.

JESS: I spoke the truth. I love you. And through my love for you I have the right to chastise you. You called me Father, didn't you. The father can chastise his disobedient son.

JUDD: But you would not harm me.

JESS: I have no father. Don't you understand how bereft I am. Don't you understand now that I have no father and no betrothed. All through your hands.

JUDD: But you must know forgiveness, pity. . . . I am asking to be forgiven by the love I feel for you. I am not a bad man.

JESS: You have spoken your death. You said *man*. You are a man, for you gave my betrothed a man's love. (*pulls out the gun*)

JUDD: No, Jess, think of Ruthanna now! You must not kill me for her sake! Think of, oh think . . .

JESS: I will think no more, do you hear. Thinking has also killed me. Judd, you have destroyed the scaffolding and the soul of my life. Open your shirt so I can see your white chest, the white chest you gave to Ruthanna with your beating heart. Do it. Quick!

JUDD: (*takes off his shirt and touches the place over his heart*) Then, shoot, Jess for I don't want to live without your love. I don't long to live. Here, here it is. (*He points to his heart.*)

JESS: (*Shoots* JUDD *three times. He suddenly topples down on his knees.*) I have killed the angel. Jesus, look from wherever you are look down. (*goes over to* JUDD, *and puts his fingers over his eyes, closing them*) How easy it is to slip from life to sleep. He won't have that trouble again, will he, falling asleep. Oh, Judd, I loved you too. I loved . . . and the shirt, look how thick the blood has bathed it, it's now all covered with the red of death. (*He brings the bloodstained shirt to his mouth and kisses it.*) And look how white his chest is now, whiter than when Ruthanna loved him. But hear how quiet that chest is. Listen! Not a beat, not a beat. His blood is still warm but his heart is cold, and his chest is whiter than death itself. I will take this shirt and give it to Ruthanna. And then presently, (*beginning to go out, and putting the revolver back in his pocket*) and presently I will know the same kind of sleep. (*turns back*) Goodbye . . . I said goodbye, (*goes out*) Judd.

(*lights down*)

Scene 7

Lights up on RUTHANNA's *house, with the white pillars and severe Greek Revival lines to its structure.* RUTHANNA *is seated in a huge wooden chair on the porch. Her eyes are vacant. Presently* JESS *comes into view. He carries the bloodstained shirt that belonged to* JUDD *over his arm.*

JESS: I didn't think you would be up so early, Ruthanna. Good morning!

RUTHANNA: Don't you think it's early to pay a visit?

JESS: But you're awake, and—I've brought you something.

RUTHANNA: I've been awake all night. I couldn't close my eyes for an instant. Perhaps it is the unusual heat.

JESS: No, it's going around. Sleeplessness. I hear it on all sides.

RUTHANNA: (*bitterly*) You speak as though it was catching.

JESS: I think we'll all sleep better from now on. Ruthanna, here, rise up now to receive my gift.

RUTHANNA: You know Mama would not approve of your coming here at this odd hour.

JESS: Then rise up will you please, for I don't have forever.

RUTHANNA: Well, wait until I put on my sweater. All at once there seems to be a cold breeze from the west.

JESS: (*to himself*) Breeze. I don't feel any. I feel . . . nothing. Yet it must be done. (*He puts his hand on his revolver in his jacket pocket.*)

RUTHANNA: (*buttoning her sweater, looking straight at him very worried*) Jess, what is it? You look . . . very careworn and troubled.

JESS: I was . . . yes careworn. And I am troubled. (*He extends the blood-soaked shirt.*) Here.

RUTHANNA: (*alarmed*) But what is it?

JESS: It is the shirt that belonged to Judd. Yes, Judd, that was his name. Your lover. Your child lover. The one you gave your jewel to. The one who deprived me of my betrothal . . . I have killed him. This is his shirt soaked with his blood. Take it.

RUTHANNA: (*cringing, drawing back*) Jess, for sweet mercy's sake. For God's own sake. You cannot be telling the truth.

JESS: You must take it. For you caused his death. And you let him rob me of my betrothal. So he had to die. (*He forces the shirt into her hands.*)

RUTHANNA: I feel my brain has turned. Tell me you are not telling me the truth.

JESS: (*taking out the revolver*) I want you though to live, Ruthanna.

RUTHANNA: (*fearful he will kill her*) No, no, please, Jess, don't.

JESS: Have no fear, Ruthanna. (*He points the revolver away from her toward the ground.*) I want you to live. I want you to live to remember both of us, Judd whom you also betrayed, and Jess, who will presently be with Judd in the underground kingdom, Jess whose betrothal you took away to bestow on a child.

(RUTHANNA, *holding the shirt, cries out.*)

JESS: Kiss that shirt with his blood stains on it, or I will kill you too. Do you hear me, kiss the blood stains of your lover.

(RUTHANNA *deliriously kisses the shirt and holds it against her face shutting out the light of her eyes.*)

(JESS *shoots himself in the breast, falls down, writhing.*)

RUTHANNA: (*taking the shirt away from her eyes and letting it fall*) Merciful Jesus, no! Oh I will go mad, insane. I am insane. I cannot believe believe believe. (*She kneels down beside* JESS.) Oh my beloved. Can you hear me, Jess? Can you hear my voice. Jess, listen to me, if you can hear. I never truly loved little Judd. True, I betrayed you, but not willingly. Jess, can you hear, I loved only you. Jess, Jess. . . . No, I see, I understand, he can hear nothing. What did he say about the underground kingdom. Oh, Jess, let me, don't forbid me now. Jess, Jess, let me kiss you. His lips are still warm, but his heart is still. His heart is still. . . . I feel—what do I feel? As if a thousand years had passed over me. Two thousand! I see everything as if time itself was no more. (*she raises* JESS *up into her arms against her breast, holding him, even rocking him*) There is no more time, time has come to an end.

(*lights down*)

Scene 8

ULRIC: (*coming out of his shell of storytelling, with a kind of start*) And that is the story, so far as I can bring it all back. (*observing that* JACK PALMER *is acting a bit odd*) What is it Jack?

JACK: (*beginning to come out of his own reverie*) You've put me under a kind of spell, I guess you could call it, Doctor. Why, as you have been speaking, believe me, Ruthanna all at once has become more real to me than any of the people I see and know! You've brought her alive, Dr. Ulric!

ULRIC: Only because you are so receptive a listener. Why, I could talk to you far into the night.

JACK: But Dr. Ulric, there has to be more! More of her story! For Ruthanna—remember I saw her too at the end—she went on living!

ULRIC: (*sadly*) Living, Jack? Dreaming is the word. Yes, dreaming! I guess you know, I have always been a great walker. The *evening-walker* the townspeople used to call me. *There goes our evening-walker* they'd cry! At any rate, after the events I've chronicled for you, every late afternoon when the last of my patients had gone home, I would take a stroll past Ruthanna's house. She was always, unless the weather was too threatening, seated in her front porch chair under the pillars of the pre-Civil War mansion. And always, Jack, with her crown on!

JACK: Ah of course, the prom queen's crown. (*He jots something down in his notebook.*)

ULRIC: Exactly. And as I would walk past, I would pause and tip my hat and say, *good evening, Ruthanna. A very good evening. You are looking very well tonight, my dear.* . . . Here, I'd say, *may I do something. Let me straighten your crown. Ah, Ruthanna,* I would go on. *Ruthanna, I know you know what I am thinking too, though you no longer care to speak.*

JACK: She never spoke again, then, after the events you've chronicled.

ULRIC: (*as if not having heard* JACK, *he rises as if he were speaking directly to* RUTHANNA) I say, *Ruthanna,* I would tell her again, *you and I know the same things, my dear. So there is no occasion for words, is there? . . . No occasion for speech.* And she would smile ever so faintly, and then I would take my hat off and bow, and then put my hat back on. *I will look in on you again tomorrow, my dear. Meanwhile, be well. But before I go, may I straighten your crown again just a bit.* There, I would say, straightening it, *now it's perfect!* I was tempted to give her a kiss. *Yes, you look like your old sweet self now, Ruthanna.* (DR. ULRIC *slowly is seated again.*)

JACK: And she understood what you said, Doctor?

ULRIC: (*silent for a while*) I hoped, I hope she did, Jack. I think deep down perhaps she did, our Sleepy-Time Gal. I think she was deep in thought, and what could words mean when one is that deep in thought, you see. Goodnight, Ruthanna. (*speaking now as is she were present*)

(As DR. ULRIC *himself seems lost in thought,* JACK *finally gets up awkwardly and tries to take his leave of the* DOCTOR.)

ULRIC: You're not leaving me, Jack.

JACK: I must be going, Doctor. . . . I'm afraid I've tired you too.

ULRIC: Tired? Fiddlesticks! Not a bit of it. No, renewed is the word, Jack. Renewed. You brought me from back there refreshed and rekindled to *now.* Not tired. Not tired at all.

JACK: It's a miracle of a story to me, Dr. Ulric. I can't tell you how much it means to me, how much it has carried me back and renewed and refreshed my spirit also. Rekindled was your word also. Yes, rekindled . . . I don't know what the Historical Society will make of it. . . . I don't care a great deal in fact. You see, Doctor, the story of Ruthanna Elder is beyond history, isn't it?

ULRIC: (*sadly, somberly*) I'd say you must be right, Jack. And isn't it splendid we can share it together. (*He rises now again and goes over to* JACK, *and they embrace.*) You've brought it all out from where it was lying sleeping, Jack. You've done it. So goodnight, my boy. . . . We'll talk again someday. Goodnight.

(*Exit* JACK. DR. ULRIC *gazes after him.*)

(*lights down*)

ABOUT THE PLAYWRIGHT

James Purdy (1914–2009) was born in western Ohio, later moved to Chicago, and lived most of his life in New York. He attended the University of Puebla, the University of Chicago, and the University of Madrid, after serving in the army. He published more than fifty works of fiction, poetry, and plays, including *Malcolm, The Nephew, Eustace Chisholm and the Works, Jeremy's Version, The House of the Solitary Maggot, Gertrude of Stony Island Avenue,* and *Moe's Villa and Other Stories.* He has been translated into over thirty languages. Mr. Purdy received numerous awards for his work, including the Morten Dauwen Zabel Fiction award from the Academy of Arts and Letters and the Fadiman Award from the Mercantile Library.